SAGGISTICA 12

Bordighera Press

Italian version
© Copyright 2012 Eurlink
Eurlink Edizioni srl
Via Nomentana 335, 00162 Roma
First Edition May 2012
ISBN 978-88-95151-571
Graphic Design: Eurilink s.r.l.
Printed by: Rubbettino, Soveria Mannelli (CZ)

English version
© Copyright 2014: Bordighera Press - Eurlink Edizioni srl

First Edition April 2014
ISBN 978-1-59954-074-0
ISBN 978-88-97931-36-2

No portion of this publication may be reproduced, copied, or transmitted electronically or otherwise.

Vincenzo Scotti

PAX MAFIOSA OR WAR?

Twenty years after the Palermo massacres

Translation by Lila Di Caprio

eurilink　　　　　　Bordighera Press

Contents

Introduction
Twenty years ago… to "be you have to
have been" (Braudel)   13
Not easy to recount   18
The Mafia is not a criminal organization:
it is an anti-state   19
The Mafia and Americans in Sicily   21
Was the anti-Mafia investigation also lost in'68?   22
Pulling out of coexistence   25
The anti-state is not invincible   27
Why the indifference?   29

Chapter 1
1.1 From pax Mafiosa to war   31
1.2 Others saw things differently   34
1.3 They acted in good faith: but they were wrong   35
1.4 The realism of the "war" supporters   37
1.5 The forerunners of change   38
1.6 Falcone's dream…and today   40
1.7 There is no alternative to war   42

Chapter 2
2.1 The political storm of the 90's   45
2.2 Change is possible: weakening the Mafia   47
2.3 Putting and end to emergency and extraordinary
reasoning   48

2.4 In harmony with Gerardo Chiaromonte	50
2.5 Giovanni Falcone and Paolo Borsellino	51
2.6 It was not just an Italian problem	53
2.7 The forgotten documents	55

Capitolo 3

3.1 The first explicit signs of a war strategy	59
3.2 The Mafia – Institutions complicity	61
3.3 The mutation of the Mafia	63
3.4 How to perceive the anti-state	64
3.5 The gray area	65
3.6 Consciousness raising	67
3.7 The "treasure" of the Mezzogiorno and the Mafia	68
3.8 Caution serves no purpose	70

Chapter 4

4.1 Attacking the Mafia	75
4.2 The fear after every massacre	77

Chapter 5

5.1 Servants of the state	79
5.2 The weight of political circumstances	81
5.3 A necessary parenthesis	83
5.4 A majority without a common political strategy	87
5.5 They didn't see the hurricane coming	89

Chapter 6

6.1 Getting back to the Mafia	93
6.2 The conditions of the "war"	95
6.3 Signs of a turning point	96

Chapter 7

7.1 A surprise nomination to Palazzo Viminale	99
7.2 The rapport with the left	104
7.3 Looking for a broad consensus	106

Chapter 8
    8.1 Security and freedom   111
    8.2 Falcone at the Ministry of Justice   115
    8.3 The first laws   117

Chapter 9
    9.1   Probing deep into the Mafia   121
    9.2   Speech at the Anti-Mafia Commission in
           March 1992   126

Chapter 10
    10.1   The Mafia in the era of globalization   133
    10.2   International cooperation against the Mafia   134

Chapter 11
    11.1   The Mafiosa society?   139
    11.2   Not yielding under any circumstances   142

Chapter 12
    12.1   The Mafia – political parties   145
    12.2   The Mafia – businessmen   147
    12.3   The Mafia – the Catholic Church and religious
            communities   147

Chapter 13
    13.1   Putting bosses back in jail: an act of war   151

Chapter 14
    14.1   The six "pillars"   157
    14.1.1 The first pillar – The problem of the Mafiosi in
            prison (art. 41bis)   158
    14.1.2 The second pillar - Collaborators in justice
            and "informers"   165
    14.1.3 The third pillar: DIA and DNA, a tough choice   167
    14.1.4 The fourth pillar: follow the money…   186
    14.1.5 The fifth pillar: changes to the code of criminal
            procedure   191

14.1.6 The sixth pillar: control over the territory and
the rapport between the Mafia, institutions and
politics   196

Chapter 15
15.1 The alarm of 1992   205
15.2 The political institutional crisis worsens   206
15.3 The period of the alert   210
15.4 Called to respond in Parliament   213
15.5 Beyond the "fake" alarm   216
15.6 My denouncement, consigned to oblivion   218
15.7 The conflict builds up   220
15.8 The approaching storm and election for
Head of State   221
15.9 The Capaci massacre   223
15.10 Falcone's deathshakes the "palace"   228
15.11 In the storm with Martelli   229
15.12 The days of reflection   232

Chapter 16
16.1 Towards a new government   235
16.2 Change at the Viminale?   237
16.3 The night of change   240
16.4 My pairing with Martelli comes to an end   243
16.5 As expected, I resign   246
16.6 The silence of friends   247
16.7 They keep asking me…and I keep asking myself   249

Chapter 17
17.1 From Falcone to Borsellino   251
17.2 Why in Rome?   255
17.3 The Via D'Amelio massacre   258
17.4 Remembering Giulio Pastore   259
17.5 My last speech as Ministero of Internal Affairs   260

Chapter 18
    18.1 The judiciary takes another look   263
    18.2 "Sit finis libris non finis quaerendi". (This may be the end of the book but not the end of the matter) 264
    18.3 And today?...   266

Post Scriptum   *273*

Appendix 1   277
Appendix 2   285
Appendix 3   291
Appendix 4   295
Appendix 5   301
Appendix 6   307

Index of the names   315

*Man does what he must –
in spite of personal consequences,
in spite of obstacles and dangers,
and pressures – and that is the
basis of all human morality.*

(John Fitzgerald Kennedy)

Introduction

Twenty years ago…..to "be is to have been" (Braudel)

Twenty years have passed since the Capaci and Via D'Amelio massacres[1]. This is approximately the same amount of time the Fascist regime lasted and the time it took for a historian such as Renzo De Felice to write his great biography of Benito Mussolini. Many books have been written in these years about Mafia organizations in general, and the massacres in particular. But after reading these works, we are undoubtedly left with more questions than answers.

The presence of the Mafia continues to be strong, its influence on civil and political life increasingly more evident, and many areas of the Mezzogiorno[2] remain under the grip of Mafia clans.

---
[1] Where the Sicilian judges Falcone and Borsellino were brutally assassinated.
[2] Southern Italy.

In the new world order, this form of organized crime has even succeeded in establishing links with other Mafia-type organizations, which have modified their means of operating to more closely resemble the Sicilian Mafia. These Mafia operations are interwoven with terrorist activities, and arms and narco-trafficking. The money laundering of proceeds from criminal activities has created an expanding "gray area", where the line between legality and criminality is blurred and interference has become increasingly violent. Public prosecutors, and not only Italian ones, must disentangle themselves from this criminal jungle, which finds fertile ground, above all, in politically weakened States.

Advancements in computer technology are opening up new virtual avenues for terrorism and criminal organizations, making way for new territories of criminal activity; the world has yet to realize the many risks that cyberspace holds. I have asked my friend Gerardo Iovane, a physics and mathematics expert, to provide an explanation illustrating the scope and gravity of this phenomenon in the appendix to this book. (see Appendix 6)

Over the past few years, the investigations of some prosecutors, and not only Sicilian ones, have focused on the events surrounding the terrible massacres that took place in the early '90's. Newspaper accounts report on the developments in these investigative proceedings which attempt to shed light on the alleged contacts between criminal clan members and government officials, whose aim was to contain, to some degree, the Mafia's violent reaction to the measures and acts of war which Falcone had championed. Indeed, this was the period in which a radical change took place in the way the Mafia was fought, notwithstanding the weakness of the political framework, the fragility of the government alliance, the consequences of the collapse of the Berlin wall on the national political situation, and above all, the loss of political credibility in the eyes of Italian citizens.

I have neither the knowledge nor the tools to provide an exhaustive contribution to the work of prosecutors, apart from what I was able to relate directly to the investigators involved in the inquiries and trials in Caltanisetta and Palermo. The contents of my testimony were amply covered in the legal chronicles of the time.

These pages, based on my memories and documents from the years in which I served as Minister of Internal Affairs[3] under two administrations from 1990 to 1992, have the modest pretension of offering a political perspective on the period of terrible massacres, the nature and contents of the turning point in the war against the Mafia, and its dynamics over time, both before and after the massacres.

Underthe current legislature, the Anti-Mafia Parliamentary Commission has initiated an investigation, one most certainly not parallel to the judiciary's. From the introductory report of its Chairman, Senator Giuseppe Pisanu, we can perceive the Commission's intent to provide a political response to the many questions that have been left unanswered for so many years. Are examination of these events, linked to the war strategies against the Mafia, may also provide insight into the "political" reasoning behind the changes that brought about an attenuation of repressive actions. These included the failed renewal of the prison regimes provided for by Decree 41bis, affecting a significant number

---

[3] Similar to the Secretary of Homeland Security in the U.S.

of convicted Mafia criminals, introduced by the Law Decree dated 8 June 1992. The 41bis prison (high security) regime had been introduced to prevent Mafia bosses from continuing to run criminal activities from within prisons.

For complex reasons, which I will shed light on later, much has been forgotten about the radical changes in the war against the Mafia adopted just on the cusp of the fall of the first Republic[4]. The patriots of those years were savagely murdered because they were determined to carry out an unyielding battle: not only because their continued presence would have made it impossible to concede the slightest degree of tolerance, but also because they were involved in the implementation of various new measures. In all aspects of the war against the Mafia, scarce attention was paid to the warnings of an institutional destabilization sounded in March 1991. Was it a form of refusal to acknowledge the risk the Mafia represented to democracy? Was it a deep-rooted under-estimation of the Mafia on the part of institutions? What did this alarm consist of, if not a warning to the State that a sick democracy is always a democracy at risk, as Giovanni Spadolini[5] said in August 1992? *"The aim of Mafia criminal organizations would appear to be identical to that of terrorism during the peak period of the Years of Lead[6]: overturning the State. Opposing the State – in a word - creating the anti-state. And if we glimpse - and we rightly do so – some international links between the Mafia challenge and terrorism, we justly ask ourselves: are we seeing a return to the scenario of eleven or twelve years ago? And that's*

---

[4] Post-war Italy from 1947-1992.
[5] Leader of the Italian Republican Party and Prime Minister from 1981 to 1982
[6] A period of socio-political turmoil marked by terrorism in which over 2,000 political murders took place, including the kidnapping and assassination of Prime Minister Aldo Moro. It lasted from the late 1960's to the early 1980's.)

all there is to say about it".

A democracy condemned to coexist forever with the Mafia was, and is, a sick democracy with destabilized institutions. And this is the reason why the alarm has not ceased with the end of the massacres.

In this book, I would like to make my contribution to developing an analysis of the events that took place during that extraordinary and painful period, free from preconceptions and motivated only by the need for an unbiased political debate. It is not a question of finger - pointing or demonizing any political party. It is, rather, incumbent on me to recount to younger generations, not only italian, who did not experience these events firsthand, the reasons for a war that cost the lives of exceptional men, symbols of loyalty to the dream of a world free from the Mafia. And not only!

It is not easy to understand the reasons why the massacres came to an end, while the Mafia did not, to explain the motivations for an alternative strategy which, while standing firm in its determination to strike the Mafia, weakened the intensity of its blow. This political clarification does not only serve to shed light on the past. It also affects our future, the possibility of answering the question asked of Falcone on one of his trips abroad: For how long will Italy have to live with the Mafia?

This is the most difficult challenge our democracy and the modern State subject to the rule of law faces today!

Not easy to recount

I am neither a judge nor a historian, and perhaps, not even a professional politician in the strict sense of the word, as defined by Max Weber. A good professional politician has to see only that truth which serves his political purposes: I don't think I have yet reached that level of perfection.

The CISL[7], launched me many years ago from the university into politics. Giulio Pastore, the great union leader who had begun working as a labourer when he was practically still a child, taught me and many other young bourgeois intellectuals how to experience the value of solidarity and the joy of committing oneself to the cause of justice.

For almost two years, from October 1990 to July 1992, I served the Republic as Minister of Internal Affairs. This coincided precisely with the period in which the political map was being radically altered and re-written; the USSR was wiped off the atlas - the Union of Soviet Socialist Republics, the greatest empire every known, covering over twenty-two million square kilometres, seventy-four times the size of Italy. Its disappearance represented an enormous upheaval, because it put the seal on the dissolution of the last totalitarian regime of the 20th century and overturned the global system of balances. I'm convinced that the Mafia also had a hand in the collapse of this system.

From my conversations with Giovanni Falcone, I realized straight away that the Sicilian judge had understood more clearly than anyone else - investigators, writers and politicians - the immediate repercussions of these global changes, and not only the political and technological ones, on the activities and power of the global "Mafia".

---

[7] Confederation of Italian Workers Unions.

In 1989, after the victory of the Catholics of Solidarnosc in Poland (in the first "almost free" elections since 1947), the Berlin wall collapsed and on November 24th, the central committee of the PCI[8] approved the motion of its political secretary, Achille Occhetto, to change the name of the party. One month later, in Malta, the historic meeting took place between George Bush and Michail Gorbaciov, which put a definitive end to the "cold war". The mist which had shrouded the obscure apparatus of the cold war had finally dissolved.

In the meantime, on June 22nd, on the coast of Italy near Palermo, Falcone had escaped a Mafia attempt on his life. It was an attempt aimed against a man who, by investigating and reasoning, had homed in on the true nature of the Mafia, identifying it as a "cosa nostra" entity, an anti-state. This made it totally different and more dangerous than any other criminal organization.

La mafia is not a criminal organization: it is an anti-state

The politician and economist Leopoldo Franchetti, while travelling in the Mezzogiorno, and above all in Sicily, in the first years after the Unity of Italy, stressed how, *"the a-sociality and individualism, which in the continental Mezzogiorno generated a tendency to resist change, was heightened in Sicily to a real and true from of government, or better, a social and political control, which paradoxically rejected the legitimate government, and succeeded in maintaining order and equilibrium among the most disparate of social classes"*. It was as if the Public Administration of the Mezzogiorno: *"is planted in the middle of a society*

---

[8] Italian Communist Party.

where all of its rules are founded on the presumption that the public authority doesn't exist".

Franchetti's trip led him to see the Mafia phenomenon as some thing more than a *"real and proper criminal organization".*
Diego Antonio Tajani, the King's ex-prosecutor in the Sicilian capital, in the 1870, speaking at a session of the Italian parliament, underlined the fact that the Mafia was an instrument of local government, *"almost a form of anti-state that could not be fought by special laws".* During the course of his investigation, Franchetti confirmed the truth of Tajani's statements, especially with regards to the anti-state nature of the Mafia. *"The existing historiography on the Mafia places its official birth in the Sicilian cultural fabric even before the middle of the 19th century. The General Prosecutor of Trapani, Pietro Ulloa, in a report sent to the Minister of Justice in Naples in 1838, warned against the existence of secret organizations, even though at the time they were not groups of mafiosi but unions or brotherhoods, types of sects*[9]*".*

The origins of the Mafia, however, are lost in history and even though it possesses an extraordinary capacity to adapt to change, its fundamental nature as an anti-state has remained constant. It has generated and given shape to all modern Mafia organizations, starting from those that have developed, under various names, in the Italian Mezzogiorno[10].

---

[9] From: "L'Altro diritto, Centro di documentazione su carcere, devianza e marginalità".

[10] In this book, the word Mafia is used to refer to the entire galaxy of organized crime, which in all of its "local" variants has inherited the nature and culture of the Sicilian Mafia.

The Mafia and Americans in Sicily

The Americans enrolled the services of the Mafia when they landed in Sicily during the second World War. This undisputed fact dates to 1943, when the allied secret services used the Mafia to build up a network of informers prior to the invasion of Sicily that took place between July 9th and 10th. The Italo–American boss Lucky Luciano, who was transferred to the island directly from a U.S. penitentiary, set up an extensive organization that contributed to the success of the invasion and that was subsequently used to ensure the necessary baggage trains and transport of twelve Anglo-American divisions. It should be remembered that the CIA had not yet been created and that information and strategic analysis services were entrusted to Armed Forces officers who often lacked experience. *"The gratitude of the Americans, according to Hesse, took the form of assigning most of the government positions within local administrations to the Mafia, granting them financial benefits and wiping police files clean of all criminal records, in acknowledgement of their special anti-Fascist commitment*[11]*"*.

Some sectors of the high command looked upon the creation of the MIS, (Movimento Indipendentista Siciliano) with sympathy, while others were more in favour of re-organizing the old Partito Liberale, believing that it would suffice in restoring the bourgeois democratic order that Fascism had destroyed in 1922. Under those circumstances, it was easy to assume that the party backed by the Allies would win, but surprisingly, the winner of the Sicilian administrative elections held in 1947 was the

---

[11] From: *L'Altro diritto, Centro di documentazione su carcere, devianza e marginalità.*

"people's block", a cartel that unified all the parties of the left. The post-war tension between the State and the anti-state reached its peak with the "Portella della Ginestra" massacre, in which the bandit Giuliano fired on the crowd, killing eleven people and wounding a further sixty-five.

Some years later, the young Captain Carlo Alberto Dalla Chiesa, an officer of the Carabinieri Corps[12], wrote a report for his unit in which he asserted that the Corleonesi were not only a branch of the old Mafia, but were a proper agency of criminal and/or illegal services that operated within the undergrowth of politics, arising after the advent of the cold war.

Was the Anti-Mafia investigation also lost in '68?

I crossed the doorstep to Palazzo Viminale as Minister of Internal Affairs in 1990, when the first cell phones were being sold in Italy and the Internet was about to become the worldwide web. A phase of Italian history had truly ended.

I had been elected as Deputy of Parliament in 1968, a crucial year of world history, right in the midst of the university student revolts that rocked the great industrial nations, the harbinger of a historic transition, of a change in habits and culture. The administration of that time was marked by the centre-left's growing

---

[12] A separate branch of the Armed Forces together with the Army, Navy and Air Force that acts as a military corps with police duties.

unease and Moro's[13] interpretation of a world steeped in innovative ment, a world we still find ourselves in today. Moro thus warned his Christian Democrat friends at the Congress of '69: *"Power will become increasing more irritating and off-putting and only a vision communicated in a discrete and respectful way will have value."*

If only we had heeded his warning, the lack of trust in politics and institutions would not have reached the point where the entire party system exploded!

Unbeknownst to many, in the midst of the political fervour of the V Republican legislature, an investigation was initiated by the II Commission of inquiry into the Sicilian Mafia, summarized in an exhaustive report signed by the then presiding chairman, Francesco Cattanei, a young and astute parliamentarian from the school of Paolo Emilio Taviani, one of the founders - together with Alcide De Gasperi - of the Christian Democratic Party. I have always been an attentive reader of parliamentary inquiries, both before and after Fascism. This was particularly true of the enormous quantity of reports and recorded debates from the Cattanei Commission, which revealed themselves to be a precious source of information for my work at Palazzo Viminale. It might seem strange, but the results of those investigations and the documents relating to the work of the pool of Palermo judges, the investigating judges in the first maxi-trial against the Mafia, have remained on my desk in Palazzo Viminale, the very desk, I was told, which belonged to, Giovanni Giolitti and Alcide De

---

[13] Prime Minister serving two terms - 1963-68 and 1974-76. Leader of the Christian Democrats, he was considered an intellectual and political mediator. He was kidnapped in 1978 by the Red Brigades Marxist Leninist terrorist group and assassinated after 55 days of captivity.

Gasperi[14]. They were a fundamental resource for me during that terrible, but at the same time, extraordinary "adventure" which I lived through for twenty months.

With this information and these resolutions at hand, I took on my responsibilities as minister, in the belief that the struggle against the Mafia required a radical change, to the point where it would acquire the characteristics of a "war". Without ever violating the fundamental rights guaranteed to all citizens by the Constitution, it would have the force necessary to root out and destroy one of the greatest enemies of democratic institutions: the ancient anti-state.

A State under the rule of law and a democracy could not continue to coexist with the Mafia without living under the constant threat of its own destabilization. It seemed to me that the time was ripe to attack that conduct which, for various reasons, during the course of the life of the State – as we will see – had resulted in a form of acceptance and acquiescence of the Mafia, in a climate of widespread surrender, in the mistaken belief that it was impossible to achieve the dream of a world without the Mafia.

In addition to reading the documents of the parliamentary investigations of the V Legislature, I read the documents of the anti-Mafia Commission presided over by Gerardo Chiaromonte with whom, during that period, I formed a close friendship. Thus, all together, I am indebted to the "teachings" of the three sources I have cited. To the pool in Palermo, however, made up of a select group of judges led by Antonino Caponnetto, I owe the greatest debt. This is also, but not only, because two members of that

---

[14] Two of Italy's most famous Prime Ministers.

pool, Giovanni Falcone and Paolo Borsellino, became symbols of the battle against the Mafia, paying with their lives for their dedication to the cause.

With the first maxi-trial of the Mafia, we had not only devised an innovative approach to Mafia criminal investigations, but had also realized the clear necessity of implementing a radical change in our "war" strategy against the Mafia. It was imperative to pull out of coexistence, and almost always, that sense of complicity founded on the Prince of Salina's[15] famous saying: *"Everything must change so that everything can stay the same"*.

And thus it is that the Mafia passed unscathed through national unification and the construction of a State ruled by law, Fascism, and republican democracy itself.

Pulling out of coexistence

The word "war", which I have used several times, is not meant strictly in the traditional sense taught at military academies, as has been applied mainly by some countries such as Mexico and Colombia in the fight against narco-trafficking and guerrilla groups. The word war is used to describe an overall holistic approach to the battle undertaken not to contain, but to completely destroy a criminal organization, rooted in the territory and with international links: "the Mafia". The term war has been used in the meaning which derives from the noun "werra" in ancient German, with the connotation of a scuffle, a word that in turn

---

[15] Character from the novel "Gattopardo" that chronicles the changes in Sicilian life during the time of Italian unification in 1860.

comes from the high German word "(fir) werran", whose meaning is to envelope or encompass. Etymologically, therefore, it refers to the necessity to encompass, to take on the organization in all of its ramifications and pull it out by its roots. Finally, the Latin noun, (but also the adjective) "bellum" incorporates all of the traditional dualisms: black and white, good and bad, light and dark, virility and femininity, night and day, earth and sky, Yin and Yang. Therefore, when we use the Latin word "bellum", we convey even more explicitly the contrast between the State and the anti–state. Whichever root of the word we choose to indicate a transition from a virtual acceptance of the unavoidability of co-existing with the Mafia to its opposite, that is the strategy of destroying it, the political message in those years was clear. The State apparatus aimed to extricate itself definitively from the quicksand of impotence and end, once and for all, the compromise of *pax mafiosa*.

Therefore, the goal of the war strategy aimed at destroying the Mafia was that of fighting the phenomenon in all of its manifestations - in the first place by undermining its cultural roots, to weaken and destroy the criminal organization's capacity to control the territory and condition the functioning of political institutions and public apparatus. And secondly, to make it impossible for it to money launder its considerable criminal activity revenues through legal financial markets. With the intention of attacking the Mafia with a 360° strategy, specific repressive and preventive measures had to be adopted hand-in-hand with projects to establish local economic and social systems. These were aimed, above all, at educating younger generations in order to favour a change in social behaviour. The education of young people, the development of a legal economy, and, at the same time, a transformation of society, were not identified as an alternative approach so much as a complementary and synergic repressive intervention.

"The holistic approach must never seek refuge", noted Falcone in his book "Cose di cosa nostra[164]" *"in the simplistic popular fallacy whereby the Mafia, being first and foremost a socio-economic phenomenon, - which is in part true – cannot be successfully repressed without a radical change in society, people's mentality, and the conditions of development"*. And he added: *"I assert to the contrary that without repression, we cannot reconstitute the conditions for orderly development"... "And, I repeat, we need to, once and for all, get rid of all the misleading theories about the Mafia being the offspring of underdevelopment, when in reality, it represents the synthesis of all forms of illicit exploitation of wealth". "... Let us not dally, then, in resignation, waiting for a far-off cultural, economic, and social evolution which should create the conditions for a battle against the Mafia. This would be a handy excuse offered to all those who would persuade us that there is nothing we can do"*.

The anti-state is invincible

The strong conviction that inspired the men who led the way, and the one which I think should inspire us all, is that the Mafia is not invincible. Every anti-Mafia operation aims to deprive the Mafia of its aura of impunity and invincibility and dismantle the insolence and arrogance of Mafioso who refuse to accept the authority of the State. A war cannot be undertaken without the firm belief that the Mafia was not, and is not, eternal and that it was

---

[16] 4 Cose di cosa nostra, by Giovanni Falcone and Marcelle Padovani, 1991.

impossible, and is impossible, to adapt to coexistence with the Mafia, even if it is kept under some form of control.
The enemy was, and still is, a real and true form of anti-state.

It was the second investigative commission on the Mafia in Sicily which, in an official parliamentary document, referred to the Mafia as a form of anti-state for the first time, recalling the same expression used by Tajani in the early 1870's, *"With its extraordinary mutability, the Mafia has always known how to survive and prosper even in environments very different from its place of origin: first of all, it has been able to do so because it continuously presents itself in the form of an autonomous extra-legal power and has searched out close ties with all forms of power, in particular public ones, to flank them and then use them for its own purposes or to infiltrate the structures themselves".*
... *"This search for ties represents an aspect specific to the Mafia compared to other forms of extra-legal power which can naturally be seen also in current manifestations of the phenomenon... Rather, in more recent times, the increased and often turbulent rapidity of social transformations and institutional changes has heightened the need for the Mafia to find and create new forms of relationships with social and public structures".*

This document contained, therefore, all of the information needed to create a strategy identifiable with the one that, at a distance of eighteen years, was proposed as an all out war. The Cattanei Commission, in all of its documents, including its sector monographs, had warned against the risks of under-evaluating the phenomenon and accepting any form of coexistence. In the absence of a clear-cut strategy and continuous repressive action, we would have reverted to a form of coexistence, having perhaps succeeded in cutting off just a few branches instead of pulling the tree out by its roots.

At a distance of twenty years, the State and Italian society, in remembering those who were brutally assassinated to guarantee the existence of a democracy and a State ruled by law, must face up to their undeniable duty to destroy this form of criminal organization, which we call the Mafia.

Cattanei wrote in 1972 that it was the duty of the State and the responsibility of politics to eradicate the organization from those power centers where it exerted *"all the impositions, and parasitical and violent forms of the exploitation of power."*

Why the indifference?

The considerations I put forth in this book have their roots, therefore, in the analysis, reflections and propositions of 1972 which, in my opinion, constituted an alarm that was unheeded not only in political spheres, but by the many power centers of Italian society. After March 1992, it has occurred to me many times that the Cattanei Commission documents also constituted an unheeded warning of the risks of political and institutional destabilization. If we read the chronicles of the time, Cattanei, the young deputy from Genoa, was deemed excessively impressionable even back then!

Analyzing the strong reactions following the massacres of the '90's, I have asked myself many times over where we politicians were when the Cattanei Commission launched its alarm, and also where we were in March '92 when it spoke of destabilization by the Mafia.

In March 1992, when it warned of a specific attempt at destabilization, attention was focused on some marginal details and on the reliability of sources; no one wanted to reflect on the danger of institutional destabilization taking place in many regions of the Mezzogiorno. What were the brutal murders of Piersanti Mattarella, Carlo Alberto Dalla Chiesa, and Pio La Torre, as well as the killings of many other judges and men belonging to security forces, if not an attack on the State's very core? And what about the forms of destabilization described by the Cattanei Commission in reference to the control of the territory, infiltration into local administrations, and the conduct of certain judges?

I have read over and over again, during the past twenty years, the chronicles and comments written the day after the Capaci and Via D'Amelio massacres, asking myself whether they were indeed describing and analyzing a destabilization process in action, an illness of democracy.

Chapter 1

1.1 From pax mafiosa to war

In describing the process by which, over the course of years, a strategy of all out war against the ant-State was defined, I will attempt to analyze also the political and institutional events of the early '90's to explain, - with sufficient clarity and reliability – the scope of the policies and measures which the Mafia tried to block in every imaginable way, resorting to massacres and blackmail against the faint-hearted. Those terrible years, which I intend to recall, coincide with a period in which, at the international level, there was rising awareness of the dangers that organized crime represented and of the need for close collaboration among nations to favour more aligned legislation, policies, and systems to fight the battle.

The resemblances between international organized crime and the Mafia drove many countries to consider a war strategy such as the one being adopted in Italy. Italian investigative findings and proposals began to appear in diplomatic papers, in international talks dealing with security issues, and in the texts of bilateral and multilateral cooperation agreements to fight Mafia crime: examples were the Convention in Palermo on organized crime, strongly supported by Falcone, security agreements for cooperation in Central America under the umbrella of the Sistema de la Integration Centro Americana (SICA), and cooperation documents concerning the fight against organized crime signed between European countries, the United States, Canada and many Latin–American nations.

Even countries and communities which had hitherto believed themselves immune from infiltration began to feel concerned about the transformation of Mafia organizations into *"international agencies of crime"*, capable not only of contaminating the legal economy by means of their enormous illegal revenues, but also of corrupting and manipulating public institutions and democratic systems themselves.

It was as a result of these very investigations into the danger that organized crime represented for States and communities that a seminar was organized in Washington D.C. in 2010, at the Supreme Court of the United States, dedicated to the findings of Italian authorities and to the memory of Falcone and Borsellino. I participated in this seminar together with Claudio Martelli[17]. In attendance were all of the members of the United States Supreme Court, together with the Secretary of Homeland Security, the

---

[17] The Italian Minister of Justice at that time.

Deputy Attorney General, and the heads of security and federal police forces. This initiative of the Italian Embassy, headed by Giulio Terzi, who would later become a Minister of Foreign Affairs, was organized by the Italian judge, Giannicola Sinisi, who had collaborated with Falcone at the Ministry of Justice. This reserved and scrupulous servant of the State, who was involved for a time in Italian politics, was later appointed as a legal attaché to the Italian embassy in Washington D.C., becoming a point of reference for U.S. security policies.

The various Mafia clans around the globe are like celestial bodies, distant and different from one another, but which move according to the same laws of violence and oppression. Working in the same spheres, dealing in activities ranging from drugs to arms, money laundering to gambling, trafficking in humans to prostitution, supplying criminal services of every kind and nature, they rely not so much on the protection, as on the indifference, of politics.

1.2 Others saw things differently

Others saw things differently; they thought the Mafia was an extremely dangerous criminal organization and nothing more, which had to be fought by prosecuting the specific crimes committed by each clan. At times, we also had to contend with the views of a particular legal culture, one of great dignity and tradition, but one which, with all due respect, we had to override. It would be unjust and absurd, however, to confuse their position with the policy which became, in practice, external support for *pax mafiosa* and the exchange of political favours for reciprocal gain.

The advocates, let us call them noble ones, of traditional strategies, have in practice always justified a policy limited to the mere containment of criminal activities. Given the impenetrability of the Mafia, traditional methods and investigative tools, in the great majority of cases, had not been effective in achieving concrete trial results. It is not by chance that most of the Mafia trials ended with acquittals due to a lack of evidence. The so-called "realism" of the noble advocates of the traditional way of fighting the Mafia, motivated them, even twenty years ago, to oppose a war strategy and the investigative changes proposed by the Palermo pool. Subsequently, it drove them to oppose the innovation of the establishment of the Direzione Nazionale Antimafia (DNA) and the Direzione Investigativa Antimafia (DIA), legislation for collaborators of justice, regulations on money laundering and the dissolving of municipal councils infiltrated by the Mafia. Even though it was never openly stated, there was always an underlying fear of aggravating the conflict and a desire to attenuate the violent reactions of the Mafia in the hopes of establishing a sort of social peace necessary for maintaining public order, which has been difficult to guarantee from the very onset of Italian national unity.

This conduct, backed also by rational and informed argumentation, was contrasted by forms of anti-Mafia rhetoric that led to ungenerous misunderstandings regarding Falcone, even by minent cultural figures, such as Leonardo Sciascia[18].

1.3 They acted in good faith: but they were wrong

In January 1992, in an interview granted just a few months before

---
18 The great Italian writer.

Capaci, Falcone recalled with particular vehemence: *"Until 1978, when I began my investigations, there were High Court of Appeals rulings against applying criminal conspiracy charges to the Mafia. Faced with the evidence of reality, they have come to the conclusion that there is an old Mafia and a new Mafia, which, for who knows what reason, or by what metastasis, or form of degeneration, has become a criminal conspiracy: the old Mafia was good, the new one is bad. None of this is true. There has been no change, the Mafia has always been the same, it has only changed its methods. The Mafia has always been a criminal organization and it has remained one".*

Can we say that the noble advocates of traditional methods were unable to discern the true nature of the Mafia? The nature of a galaxy that – from Palermo – had dealings with South America, and Central America, and had penetrated Russia after the collapse of the USSR. Furthermore, it had for some time been linked to organized crime in the Far East and was planting its roots in Africa with new drug routes. This agglomeration of organizations, at times distant and diverse, is united, however, by membership to "black capitalism", that illegal economy that generates enormous profits and which aims to create a gray area in which distinguishing between legal and illegal activities becomes increasingly difficult.

Falcone often used to say *"follow the money"*. This is how he had discovered the flow of Italian Mafia capital towards the prosperous and dynamic German economy. Falcone had become convinced that, in those years, a substantial part of the capital available for international speculation on currency exchanges, treasury bonds and commodities, was coming from illegal criminal activities, and not only Mafia ones. A "high Mafia" had set up "money-laundries" in order to launder dirty money and acted, also in this case, as a service agency at the disposal of the new allied Mafias with origins in the Balkan States, Russia, and China.

An attentive journalist at the financial newspaper "Il Sole 24 Ore" wrote in June 1992: *"The danger of a Mafia integrated with the State is no longer just a problem for Italy, but also one for East Germany. The warning comes from statements made yesterday in Berlin by Holger Bernesee. ... The operative center is naturally in Berlin, where, immediately following the collapse of the Wall, the Mafia started acquiring mass amounts of real estate, taking advantage of the chaotic situation created by the sudden re-unification of Germany. Billions of narco-dollars were used by the Mafia to purchase mostly companies in financial distress, probably also from the Treuhandanstalt, and property holdings. ... All of this, according to the Berlin State Prosecutor, Hans Jurgen Faetkinhauer, would allow the Italian Mafia to immediately exercise a certain amount of influence on the economy and on the policies of the five new Laender"*.

That is why the right thing to do was not to prosecute just each single crime, but above all, the whole Mafia organization – the associative network – to render it incapable of moving and acting unhindered, facilitated by an economic and financial situation which was deregulated and by institutions too weak to destroy these criminal networks because they were heavily infiltrated by the Mafia and because their political leadership was compromised.

It is only when we compare past acquittals due to lack of evidence and several High Court of Appeals rulings on the inexistence of the Mafia, to the sentences given at the maxi-trial, that we can fully appreciate the value of the changes instituted by the Palermo pool of judges.

1.4 The realism of the "war" supporters

I am convinced, today more than ever, that realism was on the side of those in Palermo and in Rome who believed in making a change to enable the investigation of the Mafia, the implementation of effective repression, and achieve the professional capacity necessary to put Mafia bosses behind bars and dismantle their organizations. This realism, which went beyond co-existence with the Mafia, required abandoning the adoption of emergency strategies, emotionalism, and hedging, in favour of consistent policies and adequate ordinary instruments at the service of the State and institutions, in a medium - to long-term perspective.

Falcone gave a good description of the realism of the ordinary, capable of destroying the Mafia, in recalling two incidents that actually happened to him: *"Many years ago in Palermo, one of those assassinations which had become commonplace occurred. While I was immersed in bitter thoughts, the telephone rang. It was the Anti-Mafia High Commissioner at that time. Now, what can we possibly come up with to allay the fears of the public? He asked me. Another time, after a series of crimes took place on the same day, once again in Palermo, the Minister of Internal Affairs called me, practically blaming me for the explosion of criminal violence".*

Together with other incidents, those recounted by Falcone highlighted the realism of those who were used to everyday dealings with the Mafia and who asked themselves what they should do, in each single circumstance, *"motivated only by the impression created by a specific crime or the effect that a specific government initiative could have on public opinion"*, as I heard Falcone say many times.

1.5 The forerunners of change

Taking this strategic assessment as his starting point, Falcone opened the way in Palermo to "true" realism and a rational strategy for the medium-term, provoking a reaction which over time resulted in his isolation, the impossibility of his becoming the head of the Court of Palermo Prosecutor's Office, having to "abandon" his city, not becoming the National Anti-Mafia Prosecutor, and finding himself in contrast with his colleagues in Palermo when he proposed the establishment of the Direzione Nazionale Antimafia.

No one could have imagined better than Borsellino the reaction that would be unleashed by his investigations. A few days before his death, in the entrance hall to the Palermo municipal library, Borsellino recalled precisely those events related to the Investigative Office, confirming Italian anti-Mafia judge Caponnetto's opinion that Falcone had started dying as of January 1988: *"What Antonino Caponnetto said is true, because now that everyone acknowledges the stature of that man, retracing the events of his professional life, we realize how, in effect, the country, the State, the Judiciary, which is perhaps guiltier than others, allowed him to start dying on January 1, 1988, if not the year before, as Orlando has just recalled, that is with Leonardo Sciascia's article published in the Corriere della Sera newspaper that branded me as an anti-Mafia professional"*.

The list is indeed long of servants of the State, judges, union leaders, politicians and members of security forces who had the strength to put an end to resignation and coexistence and who were, for this very reason, savagely killed by the Mafia. Each one of them has the right to be remembered as a "patriot" for carrying out a battle, almost always single-handedly, amid the indifference of their fellow citizens when, on the contrary, they were fighting against the anti-state for the very purpose of ensuring conditions of freedom and legality. We will speak here of Falcone and Borsellino, of a particular moment in the fight against the Mafia, and the sacrifice of all those men who succeeded in making a breach and bringing about a radical change. I believe, however, that it is only fair to list all the brave servants of the State fallen at the hands of the Mafia from 1940 to the present. (see. Appendix n.6)

At the end of the '90's, there were some members of the government and parliament in Rome who, with humility, took up the challenge that Falcone and some of his colleagues had launched in Palermo. With him, in Rome, they proposed that Italy adopt an "ordinary" strategy of war against the Mafia, with a medium-term perspective and strong internal unity. This strategy would need to be updated and developed over the years, given the speed with which the Mafia, absorbing the blows it received, reinvented itself and changed tactics. Indeed, the Mafia, taking advantage of the possibilities offered by technological evolutions, the free flow of capital at a global level, and the weakness of cooperation between States on these matters, created new challenges that would require further innovations in legislature and the organizational response of the State. The fact that this did not happen explains why we need to heed the alarm repeated today, twenty years after March 1992, on the risks that nations and civil society are taking.

1.6 Falcone's dream and… today

In 1992, the most important "players" in Palermo sacrificed their lives while some institutional leaders became the object of a process of de-legitimization originating from within these very institutions. Not one of them gave in, to the very end, even when their isolation increased and all was lost in the routine twists and turns of politics. Everything hinged on the dream which, together with Falcone, many attempted to pursue: an Italy without the Mafia!
What is the Mafia today? Undoubtedly, some progress has been made over the past twenty years on the path then taken. Both the judiciary and security forces have carried out successful operations and have dealt heavy blows to many Mafia organizations, spread throughout not only Southern Italy, but also in other parts of Italy, and outside our national borders. And yet, books on the Mafia continue to document, unequivocally, how many areas of our country are still under the control of various clans, that public institutions see growing infiltration and that local politics is strongly contaminated. Bookshelves are filled with new books on the Mafia and there is growing interest on the part of potential readers. Many of these books have inspired popular movies, such as Roberto Saviano's "Gomorra". In areas where the Mafia reigns supreme, even those who want to engage in politics in a totally legal way often don't know where to turn, crushed between the legendary sea monsters Scilla and Cariddi!
I don't think that most of the country, above all southern Italy, has disenfranchised itself from the description provided by the

Anti-Mafia High Commissioner, Domenico Sica in 1988: *"The situation of the State in the provinces of Sicily, Calabria, and Naples, is really dire. In some parts of these regions, it should also be said that the control of the territory by criminal organizations is total. I think this is common knowledge, even though it's not usually stated so openly. If someone believes that my statements are too negative, well then – to give a concrete example – they should also believe that the ever present systems of bodyguards, armoured cars, and security services are entirely unjustified. Instead, it is the State itself which, by every means and with great effort, has to work hard to infiltrate the territory"*.

The most significant changes, which existing instruments are ineffective in contrasting adequately, consist in the global expansion of organized crime, in the great international network which has become consolidated, in the great potential for crime that cyberspace has created, in the expansion of the gray area between legal and illegal activities, in the quantitative and qualitative dimension of the involvement of white collar workers, and in the new challenges of computer crime.

We should look reality in the face, exactly what not all politicians and the government wanted to do in 1993!

Current newspapers and publications describe certain situations which require us to reflect responsibly, to understand what else should be done, developing the strategic war policies implemented at the end of the 80's. These reflections belong today, first and foremost, to politics! These are the reflections which the following pages aim to stimulate.

1.7 There is no alternative to war

We must ask ourselves an urgent question: what is the most important thing we should do, what further strategic changes should be made, what new instruments, perhaps, do we need to devise? At a distance of twenty years, these questions are not only legitimate, but due. We should begin with a careful monitoring of the application of regulations and the effectiveness of investigative and judiciary tools, assessing also the inadequacies that have accompanied their implementation in the war strategy. It is in this context that we should also place all of the discourse on "bargaining", not so much the explicit type which takes place in the courts and may involve personal liability, as the kind that manifests itself in the behaviour more closely linked to ancient traditions, not in line with the strategy adopted twenty years ago. It would almost seem as if the underestimation of the March 1992 warning persists, even after the great surge of fear that occurred in the aftermath of the two massacres in Capaci and Via D'Amelio. In those days, it seemed as if the country, politics, and society had all discovered the destabilizing force of the Mafia.

Perhaps what is needed is to make these different opinions surface and contrast them with an unbiased approach, without attempting to demonize, *a priori*, the adversary. We should reinforce what has been done, exposing also any limits and inadequacies, and work together to take a further step on the path of war, facing each new challenge within a defined timeframe, no matter how long that timeframe may be. Indeed, we have the duty to ask ourselves how much longer we should have to put up with the Mafia: is it utopian to think we can live in a society without this type of organized crime, so deeply-rooted and dangerous for our democracy? We need the same type of courage that the great servants of the State showed, such a long time ago, in fighting for a radical change in the struggle against the Mafia.

We should not be afraid to expose, if they exist, any errors or decisions made to change strategies. If the alarm on destabilization and the need to uproot the Mafia from our national society, perceived in the face of the apocalyptic wake of Capaci and Via D'Amelio lasted only a short time, if in 1993, the application of article 41bis underwent some attenuation for reasons yet unclear, let us engage in a political analysis and debate on these events. Let the judiciary do its job in searching for those responsible, if indeed they do exist. I refuse to believe, however, that Giovanni Conso, the astute jurist and gallant gentleman, as were many of his esteemed colleagues, ministers, and prime ministers, who made perhaps disputable decisions on the prison regimes of Mafiosi, were motivated by anything other than the will to serve the State and fight the Mafia! There are, thus, other constraints which impeded us from implementing the changes that would last over time and prevent us from returning to the acquiescence of the past.

The important thing is to understand the reasons why it was considered proper to behave in certain ways and make decisions which, certainly, did not have any relation to contacts, not to mention, bargaining with Mafia members. It would be extremely useful to understand whether an alternative strategy to war was ever really considered.

To my knowledge, and according to my experience of the workings of Government and those of the forces responsible for guaranteeing our security, I think the hypothesis highly unlikely that the Government would choose to bargain with bosses in order to induce them to behave less violently. I also think it improbable that investigative strategies were adopted by security forces or that intelligence services used infiltrators or indirect forms of contact to obtain useful information and pass on messages to deter the expansion of Mafia killings. These paths are always mined and require extraordinary professional skill, and, in addition, investigators and judges now have at their disposal so-called "reward" legislation for collaborators in justice; the purpose of that legislation being, precisely, to avoid such dangerous association.

Chapter 2

2.1 The political storm of the '90's

A form of anti-state such as the Mafia, which aims not to destroy the State but worm itself into its institutions and bend them to the interests of criminal profit, operates in tune with political circumstances, taking into account its moments of strength and its moments of weakness. It is for this reason that I have always been convinced that the war against the Mafia is deeply influenced by the general political climate and the capacity of its political leadership to exert authority in applying repressive systems. In those years, I was able to see the truth of this, apparently banal, statement.
At the beginning of the '90's, the destruction of the so-called first Republic[19] was almost complete: the Capaci massacre in which

---

[19] Lasting from 1948 to 1994.

Judge Falcone, his wife Francesca Morvillo, and his entire police escort were killed, took place in May 1992; two months later, a bomb killed Falcone's successor Judge Borsellino, and his police escort. In the meantime, the scandal of "tangentopoli" or "bribesville" exploded in Italy; arrest warrants became convictions, striking both the honest and the dishonest, bringing the entire political system to its knees. The Mafia was not a simple bystander in the events which were upsetting all political balances and could not have been indifferent to their outcomes. There was a certain gathering of various storms, perhaps even tsunamis, about to erupt on Italy. Being aware of this, I launched a warning in March '92, even before Mario Chiesa[20], was arrested on bribery charges. In those months, the Mafia was working to defeat the "party of war against the Mafia" and was resorting to massacres to create disorder and demonstrate its unassailable power.

In 1993, the European Monetary System was under the very serious threat of speculation: the lira and the pound were withdrawn from the system. Faced with a crisis of this magnitude, Giuliano Amato's administration was forced to enact financial measures which cost Italians dearly. The "Mafia galaxy" expanded its global scope, taking advantage of a deregulated financial system, stripped of any real controls due to the fact that for years there were those at the chancelleries of various States and international supervisory bodies who believed blindly in liberalization and deregulation and had made of them their banner. According to this new doctrinal orientation, banking and financial agents were to be totally free to operate without the legislative restrictions put into place around the globe after the world crisis in 1929; first

---

[20] A member of the Italian Socialist Party.

and foremost, the distinction between commercial and merchant banks.

2.2 Change is possible: weakening the Mafia

At the beginning of the '90's, the war strategy explicitly replaced the opportunistic attitude of co-existence by which Mafia members were prosecuted for the single crimes they committed, just like other citizens. There was no effort to strike the "association" directly, by dismantling the organization nationwide, opposing its ability to control institutions and politics, intercepting the flow of dirty money, and thus, uprooting an anti-state organization and culture. In short, there was no effort made to implement the strategy so desired by the Parliamentary Investigative Commission of the V legislature.

"In other countries, they wonder with astonishment why the Italian State has still not managed to weaken the Mafia. They wonder and we wonder", wrote Falcone in 1991. *"There are numerous reasons. First of all, besides the power of the Mafia organization, its peculiar structure makes it impenetrable to investigation".* The anti-state is contrasted by the State, weak and recently formed, still split into many power centers, which makes it difficult to organize a war, as we were able to see when we created the DNA and DIA. *"There is more,"* added Falcone, and referring to the limits of the entire ruling class of the Republic, included also the historic opposition, *"in that the fight against the Mafia has not always shown itself equal to the task, confusing the political struggle against the Christian Democrats with judiciary issues related to "cosa nostra" members".*

2.3 Putting an end to emergency and extraordinary reasoning

Thus, in 1990, we were convinced that we needed to definitively put an end to reasoning in terms of emergencies, not only by replacing extraordinary with so-called ordinary institutional measures, but also by ending the practice of making decisions under the emotional duress following each tragic event. For this reason, we refused right from the start to resort to the implementation of a series of juxtaposed regulations conceived in the absence of a unifying plan.

Changing institutions without changing the culture and qualifications of the men charged with managing them has always been a weak point of many reforms. This is why I asked the police force to set up specific and effective training courses for the maximum number of people and strongly pushed for the creation of an inter-force school, as the struggle against the Mafia would require increasingly more collaborative power based on a common culture. I also knew that it was essential to establish a real dialogue between people in key positions, first of all, the prefects, the police commissioners, and the various heads of police forces. It was a question of making them aware of the overall plan and also engaging them in its design, motivating them to make an exceptional commitment at a moment in which Parliament had introduced significant changes to our system.

In the summer of 1991, following a series of meetings with all of the prefects and heads of police forces throughout the country, I decided to change the seat of almost all of the prefects (there were about ninety involved in this operation) to induce them to deal with new situations. As recalled by the Anti-Mafia Commission, I avoided discussing this with my colleagues in parliament, let alone with political parties. Prime Minister Giulio Andreotti gave me complete freedom of action and was presented with the list of the various moves just before the Cabinet of Ministers. After a few months, I went back to visit the same prefects throughout the country and we were able to assess the results together.

Gerardo Chiaromonte[21], had urged me from the onset of my government appointment to send a clear message to the outlying provinces on the need for a general mobilization in the functioning of offices. A few years later, in Chiaromonte's notes which were left incomplete, he wrote: *"the attitude of prefects was – and in my opinion still is – closely tied to the wind that blows from the Ministry of Internal Affairs, the example set by the government. This statement may seem obvious and banal, and in part it certainly is .... When MP Scotti took over as head of the Ministry of Internal Affairs, and in the period in which the collaboration and agreement between him and the Minister of Justice Claudio Martelli, and between both of them and the Anti-Mafia Parliamentary Commission was at its most evident, I noted, quite visibly, that there was a change in the outlying areas. It seemed like everyone had suddenly become braver, and more active, less bureaucratic and cautious, more alert to what was going on in the provinces"*. And, apart from the people themselves, Chiaromonte stressed how: *"the first and perhaps most important principle in the rapport between the Mafia and politics is precisely this: in the practical attitude and conduct of the Government of the Republic and, in particular, those of some ministers"*.

Falcone always used to also remind me that, *"laws serve no purpose if they are not upheld by a strong and steadfast political will"*.

---

[21] Italian politician and writer.

2.4 In harmony with Gerardo Chiaromonte

In Chiaromonte's memoirs, I rediscovered the harmony of political orientation which we tried to establish between the Government and Parliament, which we were occasionally able to achieve, making it possible to transform some intuitions and experiences into important reforms. No other statement could have better explained the direction which, together with Martelli and Chiaromonte, we decided to pursue: *"In these years, I have become increasingly convinced of the fact that the Mafia and other forms of organized crime cannot be defeated unless two conditions are met: a re-awakening of the civil dignity of the people of southern Italy and the unity of democratic forces or those parts of them that intend to really fight the Mafia, widespread illegality, and the lack of democratic security. This unity must be made strong through the participation of groups, associations, new movements, and the consensus of a part of the younger generations. On the other hand* – added Chiaromonte – *I immediately realized the absurdity of the distinction which is nonetheless often made between a political society which is entirely corrupt and colludes with the Mafia – thus unsalvageable – and a civil society that is potentially healthy and willing to fight for democratic legality. This is not true, above all in Southern Italy. ... I am convinced that the new facts themselves that have emerged over these last few months and which in some way demonstrate symptoms of the disintegration of the Mafia (which we should observe with great attention, but also with great caution and without illusion) also have their origins in the activities of the Anti-Mafia Parliamentary Commission I head. Especially in this latter period, in which there has been a convergence in viewpoints and initiatives between the Minister of Internal Affairs, Scotti, and the Minister of Justice, Martelli. This has led to a productive period for the Commission in terms of new laws and measures. The collaboration between myself and important members of Government and the political orientation which has resulted have also had a strong influence on a sizeable part of the Public Administration and State bodies, even though objections and criticism have not been lacking".*

2.5 Giovanni Falcone and Paolo Borsellino

Falcone and Borsellino were two figures who, far removed from the political struggles of their time, and more than any others, believed strongly in institutions, their functions, and the importance of politics in fighting organized crime. Over time, they have come to symbolize that vast number of judges, members of security forces, politicians and figures of society who have contributed to radically changing the concept of how the Mafia should be fought. Their brutal assassination also had an impact on the evolution of the political crisis of that era.

Falcone and Borsellino, together with their "teams", had set themselves the task of fighting the Mafia in harsh and cogent terms, carrying out extremely targeted, almost microsurgical operations which were not meant to and did not harm the healthy fabric of the economic and social tissue. This was one of their characteristics. This approach, which was strictly institutional and was never swayed by bias, was once again confirmed in my eyes when the regulations governing the collaborators in justice were approved.

Some time after the work of the Interministerial Commission of Internal Affairs and Justice had come to an end, Falcone expressed to me some of his deep concerns. I asked him why he was so reluctant to have Minister Claudio Martelli sign the regulation, after having pushed so strongly for its approval into law. He answered that informers were an essential tool in fighting the Mafia, but that dealing with them would require judges and expert police investigators that were not only intelligent and qualified, but above all, steadfast believers in institutions. If this were not the case, the tool would become an opportunity for the Mafia to misinform, deceive, and "eliminate" enemies within their organization.

In his book "Cose di cosa nostra", Falcone wrote: *"Professionalism means above all taking action when one is sure to obtain results. Prosecuting someone for a crime without having indisputable proof of his guilt means doing a terrible disservice. The Mafioso will be set free and the credibility of the judge will be compromised, while that of the State will come out even worse"*. Falcone had a strong sense of the magnitude, but also the risks, of using the various regulatory and institutional tools we were gradually adopting.

After his death, the bill we introduced dated June 1992 establishing the principle that arrests could be made on charges of false testimony and withholding evidence, were based on a conversation with Falcone. He affirmed that if an informer, or a person pressing charges, did not provide reliable information, the public prosecutor should have the possibility of incriminating them for false testimony, or should even be able to arrest them, that is, have the coercive power to say to them, *"either you tell the truth, or I'll put you behind bars".*

2.6 It was not just an Italian problem

At the Central American summit on the security of democracy held in 2011 in Guatemala City, with the participation of the Presidents of Mexico and Colombia, as well as representatives from all the countries involved in fighting organized crime such as the United States and Italy, there was general agreement on the fact that, in the weaker States, criminal control over the functioning of political and institutional systems had become more pervasive.

Indeed, organized crime represented, and still represents, the first and most important danger to stability and democracy. Synergies exist between organized crime and forms of guerrilla warfare and terrorism. In March 2010, at a similar meeting in Rome between the Ministers of Internal Affairs and Justice of Central American countries and Italy, with the participation also of the ministers of Mexico and Colombia, there was total agreement on the risks that the Mafia represented for a State ruled by law.

At least on this point, there was continuity of reasoning!

Regardless of the continent, organized crime tends to acquire the same culture and organizational and operational methods characteristic of the Italian Mafia. It always needs to penetrate the systems of the State, the judiciary, and the police, and to take control over the country and the functioning of Government and local municipalities. This is how its strength grows at a global level. Furthermore, it transforms itself, in a sense, into a sort of "service" agency, with two faces; a legal and an illegal one, at the disposal of political and financial activities. Among the numerous and diverse effects of globalization, certainly the most evident is the one summarized in the title to Anthony Giddens' book, *Runaway World: How Globalization is Reshaping our Live*[22]. It is obvious, however, to experts and non-experts alike, that this process is not yet complete. It will take several more decades to perfect it, that is, to achieve that level of cultural homogeneity implied by the concept of the "global village", referring to the sum total of human activities and not just knowledge.

For almost twenty years now, one of the most important unresolved challenges of globalization, which the world system is losing, is the battle against the plague of transnational organized crime. Indeed, from the very start, organized crime has succeeded in using globalization to its advantage, seeing the opportunities for criminal integration. The activities of transnational organized crime have planted corrosive seeds in the process of globalization, in that they gain entry into legal markets and alter the way they function, creating a large gray area.

To give some idea of the evolution taking place, I thought it would be useful to include in this book a focus paper I wrote on this topic (Appendix 1), which will help readers to understand the anti-state system and the danger which it represents to the security of present and future generations.

---

[22] Published by il Mulino, 2000.

2.7 The forgotten documents

To fight this type of wealthy and transnational crime, there was, and is no other alternative, other than that which I have defined as an "all out" war. There was, and is, no alternative to rejecting the use of extraordinary measures and tools, and providing the State with ordinary systems with which to deal with this challenge. One often under-evaluates the fact that this war meant making a clean break with the traditional approach, as was highlighted in the final report of the work carried out by the II Parliamentary Commission of Inquiry on the Mafia in Sicily in 1972. This report, without overdue emphasis or demagogy, highlighted how the under-evaluation of the Mafia ranged from a deep-rooted conviction that the Mafia itself didn't exist to accepting the phenomenon as an ordinary problem of ineradicable crime.

These were the years in which the High Court of Appeal had ruled that the phenomenon did not exist. At the most, the Mafia was acknowledged as an ancient and rural organization, considered good, capable of ensuring continued social balance in poverty, founded and guaranteed by ruthless rules of conduct and managed by a "cupola" yielding "benevolent" and "fair", if violent power.

The Cattanei Report provided a very clear description of the culture and conduct of co-existence with the Mafia, evident not only in Sicilian society, and its various manifestations, beginning with institutions (parliament, government, judiciary and security forces, administrative, productive, and trade union organizations), and contrasted them with the need, as we will see, for a radical change dictated by the need of freeing those territories from this oppressive weight.

Twenty years later, it was my turn as Minister of Internal Affairs to present Parliament with a report, the first one on the activities of the DIA and on the State of the Mafia phenomenon. Similar to the Cattanei Report, it became an opportunity to assess the results of the war on the Mafia which, in those latter years, had progressively broken with the forms of co-existence described in the 1972 Report.

In the history of the fight against various forms of the Mafia, when it had not yet become the global octopus endowed with the organizational, technological, economic, and financial strength it now yields, and when it had not yet penetrated the vital organs of government institutions, there was always an alternation of these two choices, pax mafiosa or war, with the undoubted predominance of the former. By analyzing, from a historic point of view, the various emergency regulations and extraordinary systems, and above all, the government's conduct, we can clearly see signs of concession and indifference. Political decisions, during the course of national history, starting from the unification of the country, have demonstrated this deep-rooted ambiguity and have often stopped short just at the threshold of adopting radical strategies suited to meeting the challenge head-on. These underlying uncertainties can also be seen in the language of international documents and become more evident in their inadequacies, especially at a time when the Mafia was increasing its anti-state power and was strengthening its particular ability to adopt new computer and information technologies. In this way, the Mafia used the opportunities offered by globalization in unregulated financial markets and tax havens to launder huge amounts of money deriving from criminal activities. The delay in the reaction of States created a dangerous gap between the intensity of the criminal attack and the tardiness of reaction strategies.

When making decisions, legal powers are incapable of breaking with the ambiguity of past solutions, and respond with timid and emergency-driven and, therefore, inadequate reactions. Particularly serious was the delay in accepting that the Mafia had infiltrated areas that were supposed to be immune from Mafia aggression. How could they not have realized that the existence of a huge demand for drugs would create a distribution network which would rapidly result in the widespread presence of criminal organizations throughout the country? Even in recent times, a blind eye has been turned on this phenomenon. There has also been a delay in realizing that the Mafia has penetrated many Eastern European countries, and in Italy's case, the central northern regions of the country. It is only as a result of the findings of many legal investigations that the truth has been acknowledged. I remember that when I exposed the Mafia infiltration of northern Italy, armed with substantial investigative evidence in Milan not only of local criminality, but also of so-called white collar crime, and even within local public institutions, I met with a wall of irritation from figures beyond suspicion, starting with my friend the Minister of Justice who, at that time, had an important role in the fight against the Mafia.

"The Mafia spilled over the boundaries of the Island due to drugs", wrote Cattanei in 1972, *"indeed, the requirements of drug trafficking resulted in the territorial expansion of the interests pursued by the Mafia organization and also resulted in the movement of people, even in places outside Sicily, of operative centers. ... In these new locations, its increased ability to disguise itself and the absence of proven instruments of social defence, favour the reproduction of a phenomenon once believed typical of the Sicilian territory. ... Numerous incidents studied*

by the Commission have shown how the Mafia, moving from its traditional base, has settled into other areas, and in particular, large urban centers, such as Milan, Rome, Genoa and Naples and their outskirts.... As the investigation proceeded, it became increasingly clear that the Mafia is not just a circumscribed phenomenon with clearly defined contours, but is instead in constant evolution both in terms of its structural components, and also in terms of its aims, its means of operating, and finally, its locations throughout the country. ... The contents of the investigation are indicative of the evolution of the phenomenon and the first findings of the study confirm that constant features of the Mafia are the profits derived from forms of mediation and parasitical infiltration, the systematic use of violence and, above all, ties to public powers".

Almost twenty years later, I launched practically the same alarm regarding the existence of a Mafia network in northern Italy.

The topic has recently become once again the object of public debate and the tone of reactions has been different. This time it is the "Northern League" that has defended the status quo, notwithstanding the gravity of the facts. Compared to 1972, the Mafia phenomenon of white collar crime was not yet so evident and we had not yet fully understood the consequences of a banal fact: not even the money resulting from criminal activities is invested in the South, but in areas where profits are higher, that is, in the North. In reference to this current disconcerting turn of events, just think of the City of London, where, in the elegant offices of shipping insurance companies, pirate "brokers" negotiate the amount of ransom to be paid to guarantee the immunity of hostage ship crews.

Chapter 3

3.1 The first explicit signs of a war strategy

The transformation of the Mafia into a destabilizing force, as described in the Cattanei report, should have been cause for concern and required, as of then, the adoption of a suitable war strategy. Fortunately, at the start of the '70's, there was at any event a shift in awareness accompanied by, unfortunately, the murders of key institutional men. Indeed, the brave efforts of men in the police force and judiciary came to constitute the core of the strategy which was to emerge later, at the beginning of the '90's.
In 1992, one of the worst years "lived barbarously" with heads decapitated, children massacred, judges assassinated, and almost two thousand gunned down – a tragic record – Falcone was interviewed by Francesco La Licata. *"What's happening"*, he

said, *"is that we are realizing the enormous danger represented by the mob and its potential for crime. And not just in Italy; other European countries are not better off than we are. We have finally arrived at a turning point with respect to the past, which is the acknowledgement of the great importance of a team, that is to say, pools. A complex phenomenon such as the Mafia, with such an extensive reach, cannot be tackled with outdated instruments. To give an example, a single judge cannot know the thousands of forms, or the thousands of trades an organization such as "cosa nostra" is involved in. Especially if there is not a centralized coordinating body that can give a global vision of the phenomenon, with access to investigations taking place anywhere in the country".*

These statements did not refer just to the Mafia in Italy. They also referred to all of the areas in the world where the Mafia existed and was developing forms of crime which had not only penetrated legal economic and financial markets with huge amounts of capital, but was affecting the political and administrative life of democratic States themselves. Therefore, the need to attack it head on at a global level became increasing crucial; to render the strategies of each single State effective, taking into consideration the existing interconnections between the various Mafias around the world. Every delay in adopting a common strategy at a global level made it increasingly more difficult to eliminate the Mafia in each single country.

However, it seems to me that in many parts of the world today, what still prevails is a policy of mere containment, or rather, a balancing of the rapport between legal and illegal forces - even in the knowledge that the playing field is not level, but favours organized crime precisely because of the delay in putting together a shared battle strategy among the countries involved. At a distance of ten years from the Convention in Palermo on organized crime, we still have not achieved a satisfactory harmonization of national legislature and a synergy between various tools of repression: which makes it difficult, if not impossible, to establish true investigative and judiciary cooperation. In most recent years, I have wondered if we have really put behind us the ambiguity of a battle, which to be effective, needs to be fought at the global level, with sufficient clarity of purpose and determination. We cannot falter in the face of obstacles that are continually being placed on the path of common action and cooperation on a worldwide level. We can and must do more to educate public opinion, hitherto inattentive, to raise awareness that it is on this field that we must win or lose the decisive battle for democracy.

As it did in the case of conventional wars and terrorism, perhaps NATO could also play a significant role, since it is becoming increasingly difficult to distinguish the boundaries between terrorism and Mafia organizations.

3.2 The Mafia – Institutions complicity

I realize that I have made constant reference throughout this book to the Cattanei report; indeed, I believe that it is a forgotten document which should receive more attention. The Cattanei Commission, through its investigations on various tragic events such as the Via Lazio massacre, Luciano Liggio's escape, journalist Mauro De Mauro's kidnapping, Candido Ciuni's murder, the assassination of prosecutor Pietro Scaglione, the kidnapping of Vincenzo Guercio and the Vincenzo Rimi case, presented a collection of conclusive evidence, *"of the existence of virtual complicity, beyond just co-existence, with the Mafia not only in ample sectors of society, but within public institutions themselves, including the judiciary, political parties, and local entities".*

Referring to the economy of the '60's, in describing the rapport between the Mafia and politics, the report asserted that, *"it is now generally accepted that the construction sector and the speculation surrounding it, in large urban areas of western Sicily, are among those activities most contaminated by the Mafia, which is able to take advantage of the crucial and operative conditions of support and complacent laxity, depending on the circumstances, of some representatives of public powers ... In spite of this, no preventive measures have been taken by the authorities, even though they have been repeatedly urged to do so, to control and restore such a sensitive and exposed sector".*

Before the boom in drug-related activities, town planning and public works formed the core business of the Mafia in urban areas. *"At this point, the discussion inevitably comes back to the conduct of public administrations, especially local administrations, to their links with the Mafia world, ... to the various types of influence, in practice, sometimes exerted on security forces .... even on the functioning and conduct of the judiciary".*

With great courage, the report does not hesitate to enter the halls of the Palace of Justice and goes straight to the heart of the problem, stating with extreme clarity that: *"the frequent acquittals confirm – apart from any other opinion on the work of magistrates – the impression of permanent impunity granted to important Mafia members, through a mechanism which escapes the control of laws, of Parliament, and all the other entities and powers of the*

State. ... And it is also once again confirmed that, notwithstanding periods of calm, also prolonged ones, in Mafia delinquency, the danger of the Mafia must be considered constant and capable of sudden and extremely violent manifestations until that time in which we identify and destroy the ties between the Mafia and some public areas which, above all at the local administration level, by not implementing the necessary controls, have allowed Mafia members to continue their parasitic activities in important economic sectors".

3.3 The mutation of the Mafia

I remember an afternoon in which, strangely enough, Falcone had both the time and the will to talk, and we spoke about the mutability of the Mafia, its ability to change shape in order to preserve its power. Besides recalling "The Gattopardo", I mentioned the Cattanei report which had cited, as an example, the rapport between banditry and the Mafia, emphasizing the speed with which the Mafia had contributed to the destruction of banditry. This is the same strategy we continue to see today, when winning clans consign losing ones to State powers. Even the disclosures made by collaborators in justice have served, in some cases, to help it shed its skin, sending to slaughter, and "serving up" the losers.

Falcone substantially agreed with Cattanei's theory. Indeed, he wrote *"Social changes have not yet succeeded in getting the better of the Mafioso phenomenon, precisely because the Mafia has always known how to adapt its methods and actions to the environment in which it operates"*. Cattanei had analyzed the tools adopted by the Mafia to survive the break up of large landed estates and, more in general, the transformation of Sicilian society which had taken place over the past few years, including industrialization and the building of large-scale infrastructure.

In recent times, at a global level, the Mafia has done nothing but confirm this opinion of the anti-state's ability to transform itself to withstand changes in the economy, society, and institutions. In the appendix to this book, I have included some references to an important work by Professor Jorge Luis Garay, on "how illegal networks of narco-trafficking and organized crime not only change themselves, but *reconfigure* States[23]." (see Appendix 8)

3.4 How to perceive the anti-state

Cattanei identified, with extreme precision, the nature and activities of the anti-state, as they were perceived not only all over Sicily and Italy, but in vast areas of the world. *"From the memoirs of famous Mafiosi, we can see that the Mafia carried out constant coercive activities in western Sicily, to the extent that the free and legal expression of social and political dynamics were obstructed, and without the State being able to prevent the population from confirming its opinion that, in general, it was the Mafia that always won out, swift in meting out vengeance against anyone who denounced their misdeeds, and deft at pulling themselves out of even the most compromising situations. ... No one forgets the examples of brave and wise deeds and no one minimizes the difficulties the police force face ... at the*

---

[23] *Jorge Luis Garay and Eduardo Salcedo Albaran. Criminalità e Stati. Come le reti illecite riconfigurandole Istituzioni di Colombia, Messico e Guatemala. Eurilink Edizioni srl, 2012.*

same time, no one thinks that the Sicilian judiciary is (or has been) characterized by Mafia infiltration ... In Mafioso memoirs (without distinguishing between Mafia and politics) the names of politicians who had dealings with Mafia members often appear. It is undoubtedly true that preventive and repressive measures carried out by police forces have not always been up to the task and that dysfunctions and toxic conditions have often ended up favoring the Mafia, ... and that, faced with the interminable series of the acquittals of notorious Mafia members, public opinion has been led to form negative opinions of the men and means by which justice is administered....that in all Mafia affairs, they read the protection and complicity of the authorities".

3.5 The gray area

In 1991, Falcone, in collaboration with Marcelle Padovani, summarized the gray area of co-existence in this way: *"The ruling class, aware of the problems and difficulties of every sort linked to a frontal attack on the Mafia, and in the absence, for that matter, of any guarantee of immediate success, realized that in the short term, it had everything to lose and little to gain from engaging on the battle ground. And it presumed to fight a phenomenon of such gravity with "hot compresses", without the general mobilization of conscious, lasting, and continual repressive measures, and without the support of civil society. The politicians' only concern was to pass emergency laws and create special institutions, which, on paper, should have given a boost to the anti-Mafia fight, but which in practice turned out to be a shifting of responsibility from the government to a structure lacking adequate means and devoid of anti-criminal coordinating powers. The famous high commission to fight the Mafia, created in the wake of the emotional reaction to the assassination of General Dalla Chiesa, is a clear example".*

Re-surfacing from time to time was the old debate on criminality, the issue of whether prohibition is the determining cause of the creation and prosperity of criminal powers, in which case the liberalization of consumption would become a handy panacea. The question is neither simple nor banal and cannot be solved by a referendum proposing a cut and dry alternative. There is already much studious and ideologically unbiased literature written about this subject. This should be kept in mind if we want to avoid falling into the trap of extreme simplification whereby there is an easy solution capable of bringing about the rapid elimination of crime and reducing the consumption of forbidden substances. We know all too well that this is not necessarily true or automatic, as has been documented in many studies on liberalized sectors, such as gambling.

In the Congressional session records dated 10 April 1883, there is an enlightening and pragmatic debate on the lottery, with a speech made by Giustino Fortunato on the relationship between legal and clandestine lotteries, the need for the State to increase its revenues, and the potential for citizens to become addicted to gambling.
It is a revealing debate, that sheds light on the brave battle fought against gambling by a group of senators led by Raffaele Lauro; today it is the battle against organized crime.

During the National Conference on Legality held in Rome in 1991, which I strongly pushed for and which was organized by my Cabinet, we tried to initiate a period of reflection also on these issues, which perhaps should be taken up more frequently at a United Nations level. It is true that many conferences have been held on various forms of harmful consumption. However, we should tackle this issue with our eyes wide open, with an awareness of the values at risk, as well as an awareness of our responsibility towards weaker sectors of society. Perhaps we do not fully realize the importance of education, and in a more general sense, of prevention, because we continue to think in terms of the miraculous virtues of repressive prohibition or of mere liberalization.

3.6 Consciousness raising

When we decided to adopt a war strategy to fight the combination of issues I have mentioned, we were fully aware of the need to establish a rigorous and inflexible policy of repression, without yielding to emotions or emergencies. However, we were also certain that this strategy needed to be accompanied by a call for the total commitment of various forces in society involved in education and prevention.

A consciousness raising appeal is not an exercise in rhetoric; without one, there is no way to make the results of repression long-lasting. The results of a moral revolution cannot be achieved in the short term, and thus, politics is tempted to leave these topics off the agenda. A comprehensive long-term approach would make it actually possible to defeat the anti-state and for Falcone's vision of an end to the Mafia to become anything but far-fetched. A choral effort on the part of society and the State would make everyone stronger, above all, those fighting in the trenches who have to face not only enemy, but "friendly" fire.

Falcone, denouncing some ostracism he encountered in the judiciary, said to Padovani: *"One generally dies because one is alone or because one plays a game that is too dangerous. One often dies because one doesn't have the necessary alliances, because one is lacking support. In Sicily, the Mafia strikes the servants of the State because the State has not succeeded in protecting them".*

3.7 The "treasure" of the Mezzogiorno and the Mafia

If this book has the ambition of contributing in its small way to making the dream of a world without the Mafia a reality, it must not be forgotten that the economic development of Southern Italy has become increasing more difficult to pursue over the last few years. Half of the youth in the south are unemployed with no prospect of entering the workforce. Global economic changes, the emergence of new economies and the decline of many older ones, and changes in geopolitical balances, offer the Mezzogiorno new opportunities for growth within the context of the transformation of the Mediterranean basin, from the Balkans to the Straits of Gibraltar, linked to new trade and integration exchanges with the Far East. At the moment, not more than 20% of these trade transactions affect the growth processes of Mediterranean countries.

Europe and Italy risk letting also this great historic opportunity for the Mediterranean area to slip by due to the short-sightedness they have shown these past few years, notwithstanding all the empty statements regarding Euro-Mediterranean integration.

A short-sighted vision has prevailed also in the choices made regarding the realization of large-scale infrastructure, both material and immaterial, which have been oriented solely towards integration with Eastern Europe, forgetting the Southern Mediterranean and transatlantic integration with the two Americas. The serious national debt crises of European countries has focused efforts on containment measures, naturally recessionary ones, closing the door on hopes for the important Euro-Mediterranean project announced in Paris in 2008 with the new Union for Mediterranean policy. Even the attempts to make a plan for European infrastructure as a symbol for growth seem to be once again aimed at programmes concentrated on integration towards the Urals.

We certainly cannot put the war on the Mafia on hold while waiting for a change in the productive economic system to automatically bring about the elimination of Mafia crime, which is said to be the fruit of underdevelopment. Development is an essential goal, but we must clearly keep in mind that the Mafia also evolves along with changes in its surrounding environment, while still remaining the criminal organization that it is. The Mafia must be blocked today, also because it represents, in any event, an obstacle to development.

This is, however, not the place to delve into an in-depth reflection on these issues. Two years ago, I wrote a short paper on the "Treasures of the Mediterranean" and on the way in which they could contribute to stimulating economic recovery in our country and in Europe, within the new global context[24].

---

[24] L'Italia corta. Le miniere del Mediterraneo, di Vincenzo Scotti, Datanews 2010.

So, you may ask, why I have apparently digressed from the specific topic of the Mafia?

The destruction of the Mafia and the restoration of a widespread situation of legality in the Mezzogiorno, or better, of the sovereignty of law and the State, also remain the preconditions for the "treasures of the Mezzogiorno" to be discovered and valued, attracting investments from abroad. The solution to the problems of the Mezzogiorno must begin with the decision to make war on the Mafia in order to lend credibility to invitations for investments to exploit these "treasures". And this necessity becomes a further reason to understand how strong a destabilizing force the anti-state is; if the economic situation should worsen and unemployment increase further and reduce even the transfer of income to families in the south deriving from grandparents' pensions, the potential for an actual connection between the Mafia and social malaise would make for a terrible combination. For youth, the Mafia would risk becoming a concrete job prospect and act as a social security cushion, as has already happened, for example, in some Central American countries.

3.8 Caution serves no purpose

During my months at the Ministry, I was often advised to exercise caution and be careful not to aggravate the conflict. I was urged not to use language which was overly harsh. These urgings also came from figures beyond suspicion who wanted to fight the Mafia but, fearing violent reprisals, felt it was necessary to proceed with less severity and without introducing incendiary innovations.

I was uncertain whether to expose in this book the resistance and obstacles I encountered to these innovations, to provide a more realistic vision of the evolution of anti-Mafia policy. For the most part, the objections were not backed by solid argumentation; at times, they simply stressed the objective difficulty of waging a war within the bounds of the constitutional guarantees granted to all citizens. However, we did find ourselves faced with biased opposition and political prejudice that favored the status quo.

The aim of this book, however, is certainly not to assign guilt or merit, but rather to shed light on how difficult it was, above all for the pioneers of the '80's, to promote a policy that would mean a clean break from the situation Cattanei described with such clarity. We should not forget that it was a question of breaking with deeply-rooted resignation which, in practice, had induced entire generations to accept the existence of the Mafia as an immutable fact and to strive for co-existence, settling for the maximum containment of its criminal powers.

From time to time, we commented, also with Falcone, on the fact that the war we were fighting was not just against the Mafia, which responded with campaigns of violence and direct retaliations. We also had to fight against "allies" hidden among white collar workers and, unfortunately, also against those who, often in perfectly good faith, did not realize that they had become guardians of the interests, culture, and mentality reinforced by ancient co-existence with the Mafia. If this resistance had not been so widespread, there would have been no explanation for the rulings on the inexistence of the Mafia, the acquittals due to lack of evidence, the lax conduct of so many politicians and administrators, the acquiescence of businessmen, citizens, and even sometimes, of moral authorities, almost as if they were unaware of the danger the Mafia represented.

It is very difficult, given the tangle of prejudices and preconceptions which are so plentiful in literature about the Mafia, to undertake a calm and objective analysis. It will be many more years before historical research will be able to interpret, with objectivity, those works which are also full of contradictions. I was struck when I read, just a few hours after the Capaci massacre, a note on that *"so acclaimed and then so denigrated judge"* written by one of the sharpest minds of the left, Emanuele Macaluso. At a certain point of his analysis, Macaluso is incapable of abandoning some of the preconceptions of Communist jargon and writes of Falcone: *"If I had to comment on the choices of this judge in Palermo and in Rome, I would note a certain Jacobinism in his attempts to adapt and modernize legal systems without changing political orientations and the people in government"*. Falcone had already replied to him one year earlier; when speaking of the opposition and the fight against the Mafia; he had accused him of harboring prejudices such as this: *"Nothing can be done against the Mafia, as long as this government and these men are in power"*.

During even the bitterest moments of conflict over Falcone's proposals, which later became decrees triggering violent reactions, Gerardo Chiaromonte maintained a serene and objective attitude, fuelled by his culture rooted foremost in the great tradition of Neapolitan enlightenment and only later in Marxism. In the midst of conflicts over new legal and investigative institutions, he wrote an editorial in the "L'Unità[25]" on January 5, 1992. After expressing his harsh opinion of the events in Gela and Palma di

---

[25] Italian Communist Party official newspaper.

Montechiaro, he wrote, *"this harsh opinion has not prevented us from appreciating and supporting those government initiatives which were moving in the right direction: the decree to dissolve corrupted local councils, the law on ineligibility for office, the decrees establishing the Direzione Investigativa Antimafia and district public prosecutors (with the related National Public Prosecutors)"*. And, in reference to a more sensitive issue, he spoke in these terms: *"I believe the bitter conflict that has arisen over issues of autonomy and the independence of the judiciary is quite dangerous for democracy. I feel I have the right, as Chairman of the Anti-Mafia Commission, to be able to speak frankly on these issues. I have always reacted negatively to the game of shooting darts at judges, (their slovenliness, their experiences as children, their negligence in keeping evidence tucked away in drawers) and I have argued with the President of the Republic, the Minister of Justice, and others, such as Leoluca Orlando. I also understand the deep-rooted motives of judges (that perhaps go back to the referendum on justice) and their diffidence towards the government and politicians. But the defence of the autonomy and independence of judges, which are pillars of our constitutional systems, cannot be transformed into the mere preservation of what now exists and the rejection, which can become biased, of every type of innovation"*.

Together with Luciano Violante, Chiaromonte was determined to achieve the ratification of the two decrees establishing the DIA and the DNA.

Chapter 4

4.1 Attacking the Mafia

On October 1, 1991, the "La Repubblica" news paper published excerpts of a conversation between Martelli and myself, bearing the headline: *"Attacking the Mafia" : "Would you like to know what we're talking about? We're talking about the Mafia and the Italy which has become accustomed to co-existing with the Mafia"*. Martelli: *"..so what worries me the most about the opposition these past days is the air that's blowing from various protests and the skepticism, that hidden but ever so widespread de-legitimization of the possibility of change"*. I added: *"..as Minister of Internal Affairs, I have the duty to offer my support and hope for a moral revolt that exists even in the South, the duty to make sure that the wretched businessman who accuses his extortionist in court doesn't seem like a desperate fool, the duty to put in place men and systems that look for and find evidence to throw that extortionist and those bosses in jail"*. The journalist from "La Repubblica" underlined that: *"This is how Claudio Martelli and Vincenzo Scotti expressed to Repubblica their anger and desire to give body and soul to what they call the State's counter-attack on the Mafia"*. The conclusion: *"Rebelling against the Mafia has to be possible, co-existing with the Mafia has to be problematic, not to say, suicidal"*.

With the passing of months, but still in 1991, the increase in the number and brutality of the massacres carried out by the Mafia incited quite a few to openly raise objections and criticism against many of the measures. Substantially, they suggested greater caution in adopting repressive measures, on account of the fact that it was not advantageous to force a criminal adversary into carrying out massacres to defend itself from attack, like a hunted animal that has no choice but to resort to extreme violence.

Looking back today on these urgings to exercise caution, we might be tempted to interpret them as a request for a form of "truce". Those urgings for caution and moderation are attributable to that tradition of under-evaluating the Mafia anti-state phenomenon which, however, is the antechamber to an objective yielding to a form of co-existence. Martelli and I continued to believe that the State must absolutely never show weakness by sending the Mafia ambiguous messages and appearing, thus, almost willing to surrender to forced realism instead of reinforcing a strategy of firm opposition.

4.2 The fear after every massacre

After every new Mafia massacre, however, the information organs of public opinion tended to assign responsibility, in some cases rightly so, to the lack of protective systems or on the complicity linked to so-called corrupted elements in the force. Apart from any possible capacity to prevent acts of real terrorist warfare, or of succeeding in eliminating every form of corruption in intelligence services, we had to ask ourselves if there was not, in the sequence of the massacres, a direct link between the victims and the single acts of our war.

On several occasions, I have invited reflection on the fact that, at the end of the period of massacres, the people most responsible for the implementation of that war: the courageous judges, members of security forces and citizens, were either killed or discredited. The Mafia messages to political leaders were clear, and without a shadow of doubt, were perceived as such. The sequence of Falcone's various investigations and the massacres was significant. His contribution to establishing the repressive measures was followed by the Capaci massacre. The bill dated June 8 asserting the State's will not to loosen its grip, blocking any hypothesis other than that of war, was followed by the via D'Amelio massacre. And finally, the conversion of the decree into law was followed by the attack in 1993. Even the hypothesis put forward by the judiciary regarding the specific motives for the Borsellino murder, that is the judge's firm determination to prevent any attempt at negotiation, can be linked to the adoption of the June 8 measures, and in particular 41bis, regarding prison regimes.

In the sequence of massacre events, it can be noted that to every Mafia reaction to a State decision, there was an immediate reply, on the part of the State, in the form of even more repressive measures. So it is not inappropriate to ask ourselves why, at a certain point, the chain was broken and we found ourselves in a situation where there was a mitigation in the repression, an autonomous decision in favour of convenience, or perhaps, of realism. A frank analysis of these decisions and actions could help us to evaluate with more transparency the effectiveness of each action taken, both in the short and medium term, assessing both costs and benefits. I fully realize these discussions and debates are extremely sensitive! However, this path is certainly better than silence and ambiguity.

What was our opinion and what did we think we should do under those circumstances? It is impossible for me to write about these events without also recalling the difficulty we had in having to assess such a situation and take proper measures. On more than one occasion, I found myself wondering if it wouldn't have been better, faced with the possibility of being able to save a man's life, to reconsider our whole strategy. Together with Martelli, and the authoritative advice of our collaborators, including, of course, Falcone, we tried to remain steadfast to the decision we had taken that, when faced with a massacre, we would not, in any way, lessen the intensity of repression. We would, instead, have looked for more efficient techniques, improved our investigative tools, and had the courage to correct any errors we had committed.

Chapter 5

5.1 Servants of the State

In the chronology of events, the initiatives of the '90's were preceded by the approval of the Rognoni-LaTorre Law. Subsequently, as a consequence of the activities carried out by the pool of investigating prosecutors led by Caponnetto, we arrived at the legislation pertaining to the 1990/1992 period, which marked a discontinuity in the fight against the Mafia. The process of drafting and approving this legislation was neither easy, nor fast. The lapse between the urgency to intervene, and the time needed to obtain the approval of measures, highlights how much determination was required to achieve our goal.

The first legislative decree, which I presented together with the Minister of Justice Giuliano Vassalli just a few days after my appointment as Minister of Internal Affairs, was called: *"Urgent measures for the fight against organized crime and the transparency and proper functioning of administrative offices"*. Legislative decree n. 324, dated 13 November 1990, was not converted into law within the obligatory sixty day period, and was re-introduced by the new decree n.5, dated 12 January 1991, which was also not converted and, which in turn was re-introduced by legislative decree n. 76, dated 13 March 1991, which was also not converted and was then re-introduced by decree n. 152, dated 13 May 1991, which was finally converted into Law n. 203 dated 12 July 1991.

In the first decree, presented in November, and in its subsequent re-introductions, we proposed the first modifications to the Gozzini law, which later, at the end of June 1992, resulted in the famous Article 41bis on prison regimes. Its aim was to cut all ties between Mafia bosses behind bars and members of clans working on the outside. This was a decisive crossroad that clearly indicated the direction we intended to take. These were the first changes that triggered the Mafia's immediate reaction, which was to raise the level of the conflict. The list of victims remains as a warning, even to future generations. Among them all, I would like to remember the young judge Rosario Livatino for his great symbolic virtue, not only civil, but also moral. He fought without fear, with regulatory and investigative tools that were still inadequate, against an enemy that grew stronger by the day.

5.2 The weight of political circumstances

Many times, after spending frenetic days in Parliament, I would ask myself when an important decree was passed, how we had ever managed to achieve a broad consensus when the general political situation was so fraught with conflicts from both within and outside the government majority. Our political system was displaying great difficulty in dealing with the technological and socio-economic global challenges, and above all, the political ones, created by the fall of the Berlin wall.

The parties seemed unable, and did not even attempt, to tackle the important constitutional reforms that would have made our country's system of government more efficient and thus, fairer. It was a question of changing the form of the State and government as set out by the constitution in 1948. This constitution had been created at the height of political turmoil, when the freedom and democracy of our country were at stake, and above all, in a period in which it was still unclear which of the two alliances, or better, which of the visions of democracy, liberal or totalitarian, would win the first decisive general elections held after the Fascist dictatorship. The second part of the constitution had given rise to the parliamentary system and a form of government that demonstrated its weakness in dealing with the rapidity of the domestic and international changes which required precisely what it was impossible to achieve, that is to say, political stability based on a democracy in which the ruling party and opposition alternate in governing the country.

The Communist Party showed no interest in putting its hands on the Constitution, since it could continue to take advantage of the political benefits granted by important laws and parliamentary regulations. Together with the Communists, there were the great vestals, not only, and rightly so, of the important principles set out not only in the First Section, but in the entire Constitution, and also therefore, norms clearly deriving from the political climate of the constituent. Siding against a change were powerful figures who, precisely for that reason, wielded substantial weight in blocking the path to any innovation. I remember that back in 1990, when I was the parliamentary group leader of the Democratic Christian party, the sessions in the House very often ended with a request from Oscar Luigi Scalfaro, the Speaker of the House at the time, to take the floor in protest against President Francesco Cossiga's comments on constitutional reform, in defence of the intangibility of the Constitution.

These cultural and political differences gave rise to Ciriaco De Mita's and Bettino Craxi's conflicting plans of action, with differing visions of the possible evolution of the political system, and subsequently, with proposals for institutional and electoral reforms which were ultimately irreconcilable. Italy lost an exceptional opportunity to modernize, free from the ideological conditioning of the past century, and the historic parties of the Democratic coalition hurtled headlong towards suicide: the disintegration of the First Republic pursued through judiciary probes. These legal proceedings were not only aimed at prosecuting penal crimes and misdeeds, but at destroying the existing political balances; in practice, at decapitating the ruling class and leading our country towards the Second Republic.

Without the self-destruction of politics and political parties, no legal action could have brought about the political revolution that followed.

5.3 A necessary parenthesis

Recent historical studies, free from prevailing jargon, have begun to analyze the political events which led to the end of the First Republic, highlighting the weight of the short-sided opinions expressed by major political leaders, above all after the kidnapping and murder of Aldo Moro. They included mistaken strategic evaluations of the historical impact of the fall of the Berlin Wall and the end to the bi-polar world order, and the emergence of globalization processes. Certainly, the "Clean Hands[26]" trials, not to mention the Mafia massacres, led to a rapid acceleration of the institutional crisis. Nevertheless, the deep-rooted reasons for the crisis must be looked for, above all, in the lack of a response to the political challenges which the global changes had brought about.

Many in those years met the fate of Erasmus of Rotterdam who, in the period of conflict between the Pope and Martin Luther, asserted that since it was impossible to cite the Gospel truth, it was better to remain silent. Later, doubts slowly began to emerge about the real reasons and origin of the entire ruling class' flight from responsibility which allowed the judiciary to transform a legal action into a political one, as effortlessly as cutting butter with a knife.

---

[26] "Mani Pulite" was a judicial investigation into political corruption held in the 1990's led by Judge Antonio Di Pietro. It involved many top politicians and industry leaders in a system of corruption referred to as "tangentopoli" or bribesville.

It is quite impossible in just a few pages to deal with such a thorny issue of recent Italian history; nonetheless, I think it useful to stimulate further reflection from the point of view of one who had the fortune to be a part of these events.

Everything started with the political crisis of the center-left and the project initiated by Democratic Christian statesman Moro with his government of "national solidarity" which ended soon after his assassination. These events marked the end of a historic cycle which had ensured the stability of governments formed by center and center-left party coalitions. These parties, in spite of differences in culture and traditions, gave rise to coalition governments, not only to implement a common platform, but to pursue the plan to defend freedom, and present an alternative to Communism. This governability was borne out of necessity, but was nonetheless capable, due to its choice of programs and the stature of its ruling class, to lead a country which had come out of the war on its knees and lacked raw materials, to become the fourth most industrialized country in the developed world, overtaking even the British Empire which had come out of the war victorious.

In carrying out their activities, the various coalitions showed no lack of conflicting solutions or differences of opinion over the adoption of specific policies or single measures. However, though these conflicts led to changes in the composition of governments, they were always overcome in the end by the prevailing political reasons behind the coalition. When the differences reached the point of irreconcilability, the resignation of the government in charge and, often, a new Prime Minister and Cabinet facilitated a solution to the conflict. In particularly tense periods, a sort of interim neutral government was formed until the path to collaboration could be taken up again. To give an idea of the type of contrasts, I can give two examples, among many, that were the subject of conflict within the coalition: the agrarian pacts, during the period of centrism, and the legislation for the accreditation of private schools during the centre-left period. When more complex reasons for crises arose, recourse was made to the so-called short-term "seasonal" governments led by Deputy Giovanni Leone.

With the death of Moro, the political idea of De Gasperi and other party leaders of Democratic coalition governments, was definitively set aside. In reality, that model had already ceased to exist with the initiative of Socialist Party Secretary Francesco De Martino. In January 1975, he declared that the coalition model based on a common political strategy was at an end since the Socialists already had a higher political objective in mind, that is, governments that included Communists. De Martino's decision opened up a new phase for an alternative left-wing government, which however, with the advent of Craxi, became less attainable. Nevertheless, it still remained the Socialists' strategic and ultimate objective. Indeed, according to the Craxian Socialists, this alternative could only be achieved with a different balance of electoral power between Socialists and Communists.

In the meantime, the Socialists continued to form new governments with their traditional allies. However, in the absence of a unifying political foundation, as had existed in the past, it became increasingly difficult to hold together diverging programmatic visions and reach acceptable compromises. The weakness of the governments strengthened the influence of the

Communist opposition in Parliament, which was alternately interested in a rapport with the two main alliances of the coalition, the Christian Democrats and the Socialists. We should never forget that the Communists governed the central Italian regions and large urban areas with the Socialists, both in the north and in the south. Pact-building was not a free political choice. It was the result both of constitutional structuring, focusing on the crucial role of Parliament (the regulations of the two Chambers made the position of the executive and its majority weaker) and on the internal conflicts between the two main political parties which encouraged them to look for outside support in the Communist opposition.

Starting in 1975, there was a long phase of government instability which, however, did not lead to an institutional crisis. In spite of everything, we were still in the Yalta era. And we were in a phase of growth sustained by the national economy, with a political financial situation that was still able to fulfill the electoral requests of each party by resorting to a further expansion of the public sector of the economy. However, in 1978, at the end of a long negotiation for the formation of his national solidarity government, in Moro's last speech before his kidnapping, he urged his friends in the party to look beyond present circumstances, saying that for the Christian Democrats, nothing would ever be the same and that it was necessary to observe the evolution of international events to understand the sign of the times. It was necessary to work towards a more balanced political system that could ensure the stability of Italian governments, called to deal with another stage of its development within the framework of the new international context. Moro was not aiming for an alliance with the PCI (Italian Communist Party), the historic compromise envisioned by Enrico Berlinguer, but was trying to create a convergence of all constitutional forces on the strategic decisions regarding issues of liberty and democracy, and coherent international alliances to bring about, over time, the conditions for a true democracy based on alternating governing coalitions. His horizon had already widened beyond Yalta. Indeed, we should not forget that an attempt to create a government of national solidarity had a precedent in the Andreotti-Jotti motion of 1975 referring to the keystones of Italian Atlantic and European foreign policy, which was also approved by the PCI. After all, the American atomic umbrella defended the same liberties and freedoms that were enjoyed by Italian Communists.

The political project that Moro was defining was abruptly brought to an end with the kidnapping of the Christian Democrat statesman. So ended the possibility of an evolution towards alternating governments and, with it, their stability. At that point, stability was one of the fundamental conditions needed to deal with the challenges of new global systems and the multi-polar economic and political world order.

5.4 A majority without a common political strategy

In 1980, when the "preamble" proposed by Carlo Donat Cattin stating the impossibility of any alliance with the Communists was approved at the Christian Democratic Congress, a new form of alliance between the Democratic parties was formed. In contrast to the past, this led to governments with a fragile composition, based on the political platform of the interests represented mainly by the Christian Democratic and Socialist parties. These were no longer strategic coalitions founded on a common political cause. De Martino's new political balances faded into the background and failed to take shape due to serious strategic errors on the part of both the Socialists and the Communists. The absence of a political dialogue between Berlinguer and Craxi had a negative impact on the evolution of Italian politics, also due to the weight the moral issue would have on the relationship between the left-wing parties.

On the other side of the alliance, there was the bitter conflict between the Christian Democrat leader De Mita and the Socialist Party leader Craxi, both of whom, even while governing together, were trying to weaken each other. This made it increasingly difficult to govern the country at a time when Italy was coming to grips with a global economic situation which was dictating a radical need for a more competitive productive system, more attuned to the dynamics of the market and less weighed down by the oppressive State apparatus. Craxi worked hard to build consensus in the Socialist Party and tried to corner a position at the center, traditionally belonging to the Christian Democrats, and then tried to form an alliance with the Communist Party from a stronger electoral position, following the example of François Mitterand in France. De Mita, on the other hand, worked to limit the effects of the "Craxi factor" on the government, resorting to the rules of turnover and by looking for possible constitutional agreements directly with the Communist Party, considered the mainstay alternative to the Christian Democrats. Craxi accused De Mita of supporting the proposal made by the director and editor of the newspaper "La Repubblica" for a government led by "honest men", untainted by party influences. Craxi believed that this proposal was part of a strategy aimed at weakening the

Socialists and strengthening the Communist hegemony of the Italian left. Not all Italian Communists shared the Berlinguer line against Craxi and the Socialists. Many Communists, over the course of years, had deemed Craxi's demonization an error. Many years after the "Clean Hands" revolution, in an interview with Barbara Palombelli published in the "Il Corriere della Sera" daily, De Mita stated that at the beginning of the legal assault, he had followed the judiciary proceedings of the Milan investigative pool with interest, as they were considered useful in containing Craxi's expansionism.

5.5 They didn't see the hurricane coming

The conflicts between the two major governing parties continued to fill the front pages of newspapers every day and public opinion perceived this as the result of a coalition founded out of necessity. The general feeling was that the parties were only carving out more power and privileges for themselves, heedless of the important issues of modernization the country was facing. This was an uncommon phenomenon with the old coalitions: the party apparatus had become more important than the ministers. The ministers were summoned by party executives not only to be given general guidelines, but specific instructions on how to administer their mandate. The most powerful party leaders became heads of the "appointment offices" of State controlled sectors. The Socialist ministers were to be found on Via del Corso and the Christian Democrats in Piazza del Gesù: in the eyes of the public, the country's government appeared to be involved in relentless allotment of power. And the relationship between the Christian Democrats and the Communists which, in

De Gaspari's vision was meant to be a stabilizing element in the Cold War era, and which, in tough times, had prevented a violent conflict bordering on civil war, had become just a form of pact-building, and in the language of political jargon, what Italians call an "inciucio", or system of underhanded agreements.

An analysis of the political events of those years naturally leads us to ask ourselves why distinguished members of a political class, who were certainly not incompetent, did not want, or were unable to see the signs of the crisis of trust between Italian society and political parties (there were signs of anti-politics which the Aldo Moro follower Giovanni Spadolini described in "Il Corriere della Sera", even after he had left as director of the newspaper) and the advance of a hurricane which would sweep them away with such ease. Many of their actions seem incomprehensible, or to say the least, puzzling. I realized this in 1992 after Mario Chiesa's arrest, when my warning, as well as that of the Milan Prosecutor, was met with a refusal to acknowledge its destabilizing influence on institutions. The results of the first referendum vote was another example of a signal that was completely under-estimated. It would not have taken much for savvy politicians to realize that the votes to abolish the multiple preferential voting system were votes in favour of a change of a totally different nature. There were many events that confirmed the saying, *"Deus dementat quos perdere vult"* (those whom God wishes to destroy he first drives mad). I would like to recall a few incidents which are among the least well known, but most significant.

There are two emblematic events I can recall from when I was group leader of the Christian Democrats in 1989 and in 1990: episodes among many that demonstrate the short-sightedness of the political class in evaluating the situation.

The first one, in 1990, dealt with the extremely timely issue, then and now, of political party funding, its nature, its scope and its punishability. I made a proposal to various parliamentary groups not to limit the amnesty, established by the introduction of the new penal procedural code, to crimes of illegal funding committed up to that date, but to take advantage of this opportunity to carry out a whole-scale and transparent regulation of party funding. They replied that it was better to limit the amnesty to crimes that had already been committed. No one wanted to be the first to go out on a limb and propose a limit to the public funding of campaign expense reimbursements (real ones), or to de-penalize the crime of illicit funding from the private sector with substantial monetary sanctions, with effective funding transparency and disclosure, with strict limits on amounts, not to mention the obligation of itemizing all political contributions in personal income statements. Former administrative secretaries and party secretaries had their crimes exonerated and it was above all Bettino Craxi and Arnaldo Forlani who paid the political price. But they were to realize this only when it was too late.

The second event concerns Law n.223 dated 6 August 1990, regarding the licensing of frequencies for what was then a television duopoly. From a certain point of view, this is also a timely issue. The conflict focussed on whether to assign three networks to Mediaset. This could have been an opportunity to regulate the limits of media power concentration - not just for television - but for all forms of media and guarantee real freedom of information. It could also have been an opportunity to regulate conflicts of interest: not only in reference to the rapport between politics and media power, but also the (negative) rapport between the latter and other financial and productive activities. I called a meeting of the party steering committee and proposed the introduction of a set of anti-trust laws that failed to find consensus among other groups and was received coldly even by my own group. On both the right and the left, there were specific interests that had to be defended, in favour of businessmen who had entered the media sector with the specific aim of using that power to increase and consolidate their business affairs. The takeover of "Il Corriere della Sera", during the time of the Loggia P2[27] should have taught politicians something. At that time, no one was interested in safeguarding the autonomy and liberty of politics. No one realized that the media would become the real "boss" of politics, dictating its agenda and solutions. Their vision was short-sighted: they saw only what was happening at that moment. And how did the duellers act? De Mita tried to establish a television empire for the Christian Democrats with Calisto Tanzi and the Brazilian Globo network; Craxi thought he already had one created for him by Silvio Berlusconi; the PDS (Party of Democratic Socialism) on the other hand, concerned itself with building power by appointing its own men to head state-run authorities.

---

[27] It was a Masonic lodge that, under the guidance of the businessman Licio Gelli, constituted a sort of shadow government. It was implicated in many criminal activities, including the collapse of the Vatican affiliated Banco Ambrosiano and several corruption cases within the "Tangentopoli" scandal.

Chapter 6

6.1 Getting back to the Mafia

I have allowed myself what may seem to be a digression to recall some aspects of the political scene at that time, above all to underline how it was almost a "miracle" that the anti-Mafia legislation proposed by the government was approved through the progressive consolidation and growing convergence of forces broader than the governing majority. On more than one occasion, this convergence blocked the initiatives of across-the-board opposition that would have easily impeded the adoption of important measures. Indeed, without this convergence, it would have been almost impossible, or at least much more difficult, to overcome existing corporative objections to the decisive provisions of the strategy adopted to fight the Mafia, such as the establishment of the DIA (Direzione Investigativa Antimafia) and the DNA (Direzione Nazionale Anti-Mafia), or the legislative decree dated 8 June 1992. Time has erased the memory of the opposition we had to face, making it seem as if the establishment of these bodies and the introduction of new regulations were simple and effortless. This memory could be refreshed by a re-examination of the heaps of newspapers articles from that time and an analysis of the long timeframes required for the parliamentary approval of these measures.

The political crises in trust fed prejudices against government initiatives; we had to win over, one by one, the consensus of public opinion and citizens. Even if the government's proposals were objectively valid, they were strategically weakened as a result of the "general political climate" and the scarce credibility of the government majority on these issues. It was presumed that the government would be incapable of providing a guarantee of a continuity of action and even of the content of the proposals themselves. Rearing its ugly head once again was the old and popular question regarding the alleged complicity of interest, in the southern regions, between government parties and the Mafia.

We were aware of our weak points which had already been exposed by the Cattanei Report in 1972. We tried to regain margins of credibility through a constant and unyielding approach, resorting to an effective media campaign *"liberi di vivere"* (Free to Live) to overcome widespread resignation to the belief that the phenomenon was invincible. Just like Cattanei in 1972, we never hesitated to render public any case of ascertained complicity. From the reports motivating the provisions to dissolve town councils as a result of Mafia corruption, it was easy to glean what this complicity was, with the specific details of each corrupted environment. In this way, the dissolution decrees conveyed a picture of the complexity and variety of interwoven connections;

although there were varying degrees of severity, we were faced with a pathology that involved all the political forces.

In Poggiomarino, in the Campania region, I had the Council of Ministers dissolve a DC–PCI town council. Faced with criticism, even from friends and fellow party members, Chiaromonte and I decided together to meet the citizens in a public assembly to discuss the reasons for the decision. The debate was not easy because the dissolution had been interpreted as an affront to all the town's honest citizens and administrators. We were able to calm the waters and win over a hard-line group of protestors only after a long discussion. As we explained to the citizens of Poggiomarino, the Mafia had tried to influence, by every means possible, the town council's decisions, above all on issues of town planning and it had succeeded, a fact which had been ascertained by the investigative commission.

6.2 The conditions of the "war"

Experience has taught us that the war on the Mafia must be founded on strong institutional, political, and social unity. There has to be convergence and pact-building; an awareness of the efforts that will have to be made, not blind heroism that is ignorant of the perils ahead. A war on the Mafia that involves, as comprehensively as possible, the entire community has been, and remains, a necessary pre-requisite to ensure the normal functioning of the public life of a democracy.

A moral revolt, the unfaltering respect for legality, and the absence of acquiescence remain, therefore, unalienable requirements for the fundamental cohesion of society. These should never be the instruments of division or discord among a country's citizens.

In times of war, all citizens must cooperate in isolating those who, directly or indirectly, provide support to criminals. It is the judiciary's job to repress every violation, without political prejudice or prejudice of any kind. Democracy must be nurtured: using judiciary means to strike political enemies creates a breach which leads to the degradation of human and political relations. In carrying out its duties, the judiciary must be careful never to become the instrument of political conflict. It must persecute crimes, not cure the ills of society; the job of educating rests with others. When one wavers from these basic principles of civil life, the strength of repression is weakened and the institutions that guarantee the rights of all are rendered fragile.

6.3 Signs of a turning point

Around the 1980's, signs began to appear, more forcefully than in the past, of initiatives on the part of the judiciary, security forces, and some political figures. These initiatives were accompanied by a new awareness in civil society of a need to oppose the encroaching subculture of the Mafia which had favoured the entrenchment of the Mafia in southern Italian society, to the point where it had become part of its image. The "revolt", if this is what we can call it, came precisely from within the judiciary and the first maxi-trial of the Mafia marked the turning point in anti-Mafia jurisdiction.

Prior to the establishment of the Direzione Nazionale Antimafia, in referring to a university text which was being used to teach new generations of judges and lawyers, Falcone noted that: *"in the Treatise on Italian penal law, the jurist Vincenzo Manzini States that even if the Mafia is a criminal organization, it is still necessary to demonstrate the concrete crimes for which its members have formed the organization. It is a subconscious refusal to accept the reality of a legal order within the State legal system"*.

Chapter 7

7.1 A surprise nomination to Palazzo Viminale

Taking up once again the thread of the war strategy against the Mafia, I would like to now explain its evolution in a more systematic fashion, starting from my nomination as Minister of Internal Affairs, going on to an account of the measures adopted, and ending in June 1992 when I left Palazzo Viminale.

The Christian Democratic convention of 1989 ended with the termination of De Mita's dual role as Prime Minister and Party Secretary and with the re-election of Arnaldo Forlani as Party Secretary, consolidating the alliance between Craxi, Andreotti and Forlani. In just a few months, Prime Minister De Mita would be replaced by Andreotti. De Mita had attempted to maintain his dual role until just a few hours before the convention started and had made no contingency plans for a successor that would guarantee continuity at Palazzo Chigi: he had trusted, above all, in his allies in the center. These latter, however, had reached an agreement with Forlani, who had assured Mino Martinazzoli that he would be the successor. In his speech, Martinazzoli made practically no mention of these agreements and Forlani's re-election to Party Secretary, limiting himself to a train of thought that was highly suggestive, and which made daring leaps into the future. He received a standing ovation.

With the arrival of Forlani, I considered my commitment to the party at an end and proposed my candidature as parliamentary group leader. In July 1989, when I was elected, it never entered my mind that during the course of that legislature I would be called to hold the post of Minister of Internal Affairs.

In mid-August 1990, we received the unexpected news that Antonio Gava had suffered a stroke while vacationing in Sardinia. The first reports were worrying, but we soon received more reassuring news. At the beginning of September, Gava invited me to lunch at his house in Arcinazzo to tell me that he had decided to step down as minister and to ask me if I would be willing to take over the position. Even though he had recovered from the stroke, both mentally and physically, Gava believed that the Minister of Internal Affairs had to be in total possession of his faculties. This was proof of his sense of institutional duty of the highest order! The change would not take effect immediately; Gava thought that mid-October could be a possible date, after the center faction "Azione Popolare" convention had taken place in Sirmione. I expressed many doubts about accepting the nomination.

I put my trust in the passage of time and his possible change of heart, thinking there would be time to reflect. In the meantime, knowing Gava's reputation for discretion, I was sure the news would not leak into the public domain. I continued doing my job as before and made no changes to my calendar. Together with the entire executive of my parliamentary group, I left for China; a trip that held great interest. This was the first delegation from a Western country to visit Beijing, at the peak of the embargo, following the tragic events of Tiananmen Square. The trip lasted almost ten days and we met with the country's most important political, cultural, and religious figures. We had a long and very frank discussion with Jang Zemin lasting over an hour and a half, touching on also the most sensitive human rights issues, the rapport with Catholics, and with the Soviet and Italian Communist Parties. The Christian Democratic group had submitted a parliamentary motion to end the embargo.

Almost a month of silence had passed since I had met with Gava in Arcinazzo. This was quite incredible, given the Italian traditional lack of discretion! On the evening of October 16, while I at a meeting with some friends from the parliamentary executive, I received a phone call from President Cossiga, in the presence of Andreotti, who told me that he had signed a decree nominating me as Minister of Internal Affairs and that he would be expecting me the next day at Palazzo Quirinale for the swearing in ceremony. I never spoke to the Prime Minister about my nomination. On the other hand, when I was nominated Minister of Labour in 1978, even though I had helped Andreotti prepare the list of minister's names, which was modified several times over the course of a few hours, the Prime Minister never told me anything about my own imminent nomination.
I was to learn only later that the decision to nominate me as Gava's successor to Palazzo Viminale had met with considerable, and unaccountable opposition. In Gianni Cipriani's book on

"Lo spionaggio politico in Italia" [Political espionage in Italy] he States that, in the house of a SISMI (Military Secret Service Agency) general, Judge Rosario Priore had found some service papers about me which had been circulating on the eve of my nomination. They contained clearly false and defamatory information about me gathered from informers, which, who knows for what reason, was taken seriously by intelligence services, unless their intent was to create an obstacle to my nomination.

This type of operation did not surprise me, and it was not the only one, if I think back at whoever produced the false police document on my alleged visit to Raffaele Cutolo at the Ascoli Piceno prison during Ciro Cirillo's kidnapping. This document led to the Unità newspaper management's resignation, an apology in parliament from PM Giorgio Napolitano, and a journalist's arrest. The accusation of libel, instantly ascertained, led to a judiciary decision after over twenty years, and was settled by an agreement between parties.

At the time, it was customary for the SISDE[28] to contribute a monthly sum to the expenses earmarked for the Ministry of Internal Affairs. In my opinion, this practice, which was entirely legitimate, created a strange situation whereby an entity, which depended on the ministry, contributed to the expenses earmarked by the Administration. I put an immediate end to this practice, and, as the Ministry Treasurer told the judges, I spoke about it to my colleague Guido Carli. A modification was made to the budget, and a specific sum was allotted to be administered by the Ministry offices.

There was a further incident which I learned about towards the

---

[28] Italian Secret Service Agency.

end of my mandate at Palazzo Viminale which I found even more disconcerting, especially considering the legal repercussions it had after I left my post as minister. On the evening of October 16, the same day I was nominated as Minister of Internal Affairs, some Guardia di Finanza (Military Tax Police) agents had gone to a hotel under judiciary seal, which had, therefore, already been searched thoroughly as part of the patrimony belonging to a person accused of business dealings with the "Camorra". They confiscated some photographs that had been taken in the spring of 1978 at the award ceremony for Carnacina, a famous chef. At the ceremony, to which I had been invited by the local senator Peppino Manente Comunale, a distinguished member of the Senate Labour Committee, there were not only the Prefect (whose opinion I had consulted regarding whether I should attend, given that I had been nominated Minister of Internal Affairs a few weeks previously) and the Police Commissioner, but all the representatives of the judiciary and security forces. At the time of the ceremony, the owner of the hotel had not been under any kind of investigation and those photographs, as could easily be proven because it was a public ceremony, had been widely published in newspapers and shown on local TV stations. Therefore, after twelve long years, there was nothing new about the photos and they could never have been used for blackmailing purposes. The murky and inexplicable side of this affair, for the security forces of a State ruled by law, emerged later, after I had left the ministry, precisely in those years in which there was an attempt to discredit Martelli and myself. The legal proceedings ended up being filed away during preliminary investigations, after being transferred from one ministerial court to another. In any case, it is a fact that until 1992, no head of a security force had ever spoken to me about this incident.

In reference to my nomination and contacts he had with President Scalfaro in those days, Paolo Cirino Pomicino wrote[29]: "I saw him one evening, just at the moment in which we had to decide a replacement for Gava. ….. He was chomping at the bit. He could think of nothing but the Viminale. And he repeatedly asked me to put pressure on Andreotti on his behalf. That was fine by me... so I told him I would do my best. The morning after, however, when I called Andreotti, I found out that they had already decided on a new Minister of Internal Affairs. That was a position the dorotei [Christian Democrat faction] wanted and Gava had already chosen Vincenzo Scotti as his successor. The news spread quickly. So when I arrived at the Commission, I was faced with an infuriated Scalfaro."

7.2 The rapport with the left

After my nomination to the Minister of Internal Affairs, my first priority was to open a dialog with the opposition in order to reach a broad consensus on the strategy to fight the Mafia.
In the hours preceding my swearing in, I had met with some of the exponents of the Democratic Left Party (PDS), from Luciano Violante to Ugo Pecchioli, but, in particular, I had a long conversation with Chiaromonte, who I respected highly as a politician, and above all as a man. He was loyal and logical, with a tough and intransigent manner, but was always willing to listen and analyze facts objectively. At that time, he was Chairman of the Anti-Mafia Parliamentary Commission. In our meetings, I felt that his courtesy masked strong scepticism that I would be able get things moving in the right direction.

---

[29] Strettamente riservato, Geronimo, Mondadori, 2000.

Indeed, Chiaromonte believed that the general political scenario would have made that impossible. Notwithstanding this underlying diffidence, he assured me that the PDS would judge the merits of my proposals and that he would be prepared to support them if he thought they were useful in fighting the Mafia. I appreciated Violante's and Chiaromonte's frankness and, above all, their opinions concerning the gravity of the situation, as well as their suggestions and precious advice on legal initiatives that could be adopted and on which the Anti-Mafia Parliamentary Commission had been working for some time. With Chiaromonte, in particular, I had already had the opportunity to discuss and exchange opinions back in 1965 when I was a young Secretary General of the Committee of Ministers for the Mezzogiorno. Pastore had assigned me the task of collecting the opinions and decree proposals to extend the "Cassa per il Mezzogiorno", and the coordinating plan from the heads of the PCI in Southern Italy, Chiaromonte and Napolitano. From our very first encounters, I admired not only their political astuteness but their extraordinary skill.

I had met with Chiaromonte and Napolitano several times at the house of politician and trade unionist Luciano Lama during the government of national solidarity in order to try to find, this time together, the most opportune measures to bring down inflation, reduce the national debt, and re-organize the social security system. The Minster of Treasury, Filippo Maria Pandolfi was also present. We had negotiated a pension reform plan with the three trade unions which, had it not met with corporative opposition from the Confederation of Industries (Confindustria) and company managers, not to mention journalists, judges, and diplomats, led by the PSDI Secretary Pietro Longo and many other parliamentarians, would have brought about, way back then, a single public social security system for all workers, with standardized regulations and a single contributory and pension ceiling with many public/private supplementary pension fund systems. With a view to reform, the unions had accepted as a necessary measure, structural cuts to the system in effect (two thousand four hundred billion annually), reducing by 50% the increments on all pensions and on the salaries of employed workers resulting from cost of living adjustments.

In return, the trade unions were expecting an end to the jungle of pensions and the financial fragility of the system.

7.3 Looking for a broad consensus

In an interview with the Repubblica newspaper after I was sworn in, I stressed the need to look for broad parliamentary consensus, not only to approve new bills, but above all, to oppose the Mafia with a solid front of national political forces. The contents of the interview reflected my train of thought, but the headline, *"Me, a second Gava? Wait and see"*, could have led to a futile and unintended misunderstanding with my predecessor and party. In the interview, I mentioned the need for a different rapport with the opposition, in contrast to the head-on confrontations they had always had with Gava. The young journalist Giovanni Maria Bellu wrote: *"Vincenzo Scotti, the new Minister of Internal Affairs, was sworn in exactly at noon before the Head of State. It's four o'clock in the afternoon and the neo-minister, escorted by two plainclothes policemen, is walking from Montecitorio to Palazzo Chigi. He still has to officially take charge, but Vincenzo Scotti, hands planted in the pockets of his dark jacket, has accepted* to talk here on the imaginary doorstep to the Viminale. Just a second ago, coming out of the group's headquarters, his answer to an MP asking him how he was feeling was: How's it going? "No, not very well", he said. But this was only for superstition's sake. ... He is ready to agree to the PCI request for a debate on the resignation of his predecessor and friend, Antonio Gava. ... His nomination has been interpreted as a succession ploy made according to criteria within the DC. Does that bother him? Some have called him a second Gava. "On this point, whatever I say is of little value. I hope I can prove wrong those who criticize me, by doing what I can within my capabilities. But certainly, political solutions, I think all over the world, are achieved by finding a balance. And these balances depend on the rapport between the forces within the parties and the institutions. Therefore, I'm not scandalized, nor upset by opinions like yours. I just wish there weren't opinions made "a priori", judgements made with a view of not taking into account what a person does, or tries to do". Does he mean he will let his deeds speak for themselves? "I hope to succeed. Every office is difficult, there are no easy tasks in this world. We'll see. I hope, however, as Minister of Internal Affairs, to speak little. On the other hand, that's what I've thought for a long time: in a government, the Ministers of Internal Affairs and the Treasury should speak less than anyone else. That is to say, they should intervene only to give indications based on a solid foundation, not just to express ambitions or wishes. ..." You have a reputation as a great mediator. Your ability to reconcile contrasting interests is, actually, proverbial in your party. But how can this help you in your current role? "Let's just say that, being from the south, I hope that a little luck comes my way. Because sometimes, all the good intentions in the world aren't enough and in the situation we find ourselves in, we certainly *can't make miracles, neither rapidly, nor in a significant way: above all, we have to arm ourselves with a large dose of humility and make the machine work, providing serenity to all those who are fighting in the trenches. And here on the doorstep to the Viminale I would like to say this: that I will do everything within my power to give people in the trenches the certainty that the minister wants to enhance their work and eliminate any obstacles that make their job more difficult. ... I hope there can be a broad consensus of forces in this direction. I can guarantee that I will spare no effort to make this possible". Of all the problems waiting for you behind that door, which is the one you fear the most? "The spread of a culture of illegality. And the fact that this culture tries in every way possible to infiltrate the workings of public institutions." What, instead, gives you some hope? "The fact that the people in southern Italy, the great majority of people in southern Italy, have nothing to do with all of this and want to be helped to live in a different way".*

The next morning, I called Gava immediately to explain my point of view and what I had meant in the Repubblica interview and, above all, to apologize for the headline that could appear critical of him. He reassured me immediately, saying that he shared the sense of my words, and wished me success in avoiding the bitter clash with the opposition which had made it so difficult for him to implement a series of initiatives against the Mafia. With the parties of the majority, I established a running dialog: with the Minister of Justice Christian Democrat Enzo Binetti, I shared a longstanding friendship. As for the Socialists and the Liberals, I could not forget that in January 1983 I had received their fundamental support in finalizing the agreement on the cost of labour, an agreement which opened the way to a politics of consultation, and on whose necessity and validity I debated at length with Professor Mario Monti in the columns of the "Il Corriere della Sera" newspaper. The rapport with the Republicans was at a particularly tense stage due to general political reasons, especially after they had been "excluded" from the majority. However, even under those circumstances, my friend Giorgio La Malfa wrote me, praising my conduct and renewing his longstanding friendship. In agreement with President Cossiga, crossing the confines of the parties formulating Italy's post-war constitution, I met with the Secretary of the right-wing "Movimento Sociale" led by Gianfranco Fini, from whom I received a resounding *"yes to a turning point in the fight against clans"*, as the headline read in the "Secolo" newspaper on October 18, 1991.

Chapter 8

8.1 Security and freedom

There has always been debate on the need for special laws to fight crime effectively. Even during the period we were battling terrorism, there were many in favour of resorting to extraordinary measures, with the temporary suspension of some constitutionally protected rights. This also took place at the beginning of the '90's.

In 1992, in his speech at the funeral of police officer Aversa, killed together with his wife in Lamezia Terme, President of the Republic Cossiga stated: *"Today we are faced with a dramatic question. Will we be able to defeat crime without resorting to an extraordinary regime which allows for exceptions to procedures established by the Constitution?"* And a few days later, in an interview in the newspaper "Il Corriere della Sera", he reiterated his question and expressed his opinion more clearly: *"If crime cannot be defeated by these means (ordinary laws), we have to consider special laws which – mind you – can be one of two types. Laws allowing exceptions, that is special ones, not to the principles of the Constitution, but to the legal system, ... or "special" ones that allow exceptions to the Constitution; that is to say, that would thus be unconstitutional if there weren't a specific regulation authorizing such an exception... Of course, the adoption of special laws threatens the foundations of the State ruled by law, especially in the minds of those less informed from a liberal-democratic profile. But it is also true that if we keep on going like this, we risk being swept away by the State; whether by ordinary, special, or other laws. This is why I say that our constitution cannot include a clause permitting the suicide of the State".* He ended these considerations with this comment: *"It is better to have well-planned special legislation (as in the example of Northern Ireland...)".*

I was unable to attend Aversa's funeral because I had undergone a hip fracture operation just a few days previously. It would have afforded us a valuable opportunity for a direct, and undoubtedly lively, discussion. Instead, we had to carry out the debate at a distance through interviews and statements.

Cossiga's provocation was by no means banal, nor futile, even though it was not wholly embraceable. When asked by journalists what I thought of Cossiga's proposal, I answered: *"The exceptional thing we need is the application of existing laws".* A similar position was taken by most members of the majority and the opposition, from Andreotti to Spadolini, to Craxi, to Nilde Jotti, to Macaluso, and to Violante, in addition to many authoritative members of the judiciary. The dissent of the judiciary was almost absolute, if we consider the two opposing poles. Gian Carlo Caselli (*"An exceptional reply would be to succeed in applying ordinary tools to fight the Mafia with a normal degree of efficiency"*) and Marcello Maddalena (*"All the judges need are extremely ordinary laws"*). An aspect of Cossiga's proposal has once again gained relevance as the result of some recent Supreme Court of Appeal rulings. Is the offence of association with the Mafia regulated by the penal code constitutional and in what way should this offence be punished? I remember that when Violante, Chairman of the Anti-Mafia Parliamentary Commission at the time and I, met our colleagues from a similar Parliamentary Commission in Paris, the latter strongly disapproved of the idea of introducing a similar offence on the books of countries belonging to what was then the European Community.

From the very start, the introduction of norms regulating association with the Mafia, as well as those related to collaborators in justice, gave rise to thorny questions about their application. This is because, as Falcone suggested, if a judge was not extremely steadfast and well-qualified professionally, his investigation could become untenable. The problem is not one of raising doubts about the investigative approach of the Palermo pool, strengthened over time by new norms regarding evidence gathering, but to proceed with extreme scrupulousness, resisting the eagerness to read newspaper headlines about the results of one's work, above all when this work contains holes and contradictions. In these pages, I have allowed myself to repeatedly warn against the risk one takes when one proceeds without allowing evidence to be deposited properly, and without verifying whether this evidence will hold up in hearings and appeals, up to highest Court of Appeal. As I am trying to demonstrate, this is not a matter of siding with opposing positions, but of preserving, to the very end, calm analysis and judgement. The risk is that not just a specific investigation will be called into question, but the entire regulative system on which the single investigation is based.

When I took on my duties at the Ministry of Internal Affairs, I had already read many documents about the maxi-trial and had formed an idea of how we could and should gather these strategic insights and transform them into regulations and organization. Notwithstanding the obstacles arising from the general political situation, which made it practically impossible to imagine the necessary changes urged by the judges in Palermo, we identified some conditions that would allow a change to take place. Among these was full agreement for a war strategy among the ministers institutionally involved in fighting the Mafia (Internal Affairs and Justice), the support of the President of the Republic and the Head of Government, a positive rapport between the Government and Parliament, the work of the Anti-Mafia Parliamentary Commission and the decisions of its chairman, Senator Chiaromonte. The Commission's activities had dodged a double temptation: that of stopping short at a simple sociological study of the phenomenon, and that of delving into an investigation parallel to the one being carried out by judges. Instead, Chiaromonte had directed his efforts towards the aim of drafting a set of anti-Mafia laws clearly ascribable to a proper and total war against the Mafia. A later and further favourable condition was added with Falcone's arrival in Rome, in a high position of responsibility and in harmony with the top echelons of the Department of Public Security.

The turning point was triggered and sustained by the seeds of moral revolt planted in important sectors, though still in the minority, of civil society and the ecclesiastic communities of the Mezzogiorno. We need only recall the sermon of Cardinal Salvatore Pappalardo and several other priests in the outskirts of Palermo and other areas, both in southern and northern Italy.

Giovanni Paolo II's sweeping condemnation of the Mafia removed any excuse for the caution shown in some Catholic areas and incited people to fight without hesitation. However, changes in the civil society of the Mezzogiorno came but slowly and were still a far cry from the clear-cut position taken only recently. It was 1991. We were coming back from Palermo with Falcone after having taken part in an embarrassing session of the Provincial Committee of Public Order and Security following the murder of the industrialist Libero Grassi, who had refused to pay protection money. I had noted his silence during the meeting, interrupted only by some brief words of courtesy. I asked Falcone his opinion of the behaviour and speeches of business and union representatives at the meeting. Falcone answered dryly that the Mafia had a great ally in the conduct of important members of associations at the meeting, and above all, in their complacence.

8.2 Falcone at the Ministry of Justice

I first met Giovanni Falcone when I was Deputy Secretary of the Christian Democrats and I was invited to join a round table on the fight against the Mafia at the Palace of Justice in Palermo. We sat next to each other and thus were able to comment frequently on the speeches that followed one another. Therefore, I did not hesitate to contact him when President Cossiga and Minister

Vassalli informed me that they had initiated the paperwork for his transfer to the Ministery of Justice in Rome. At first, I thought his transfer to the capital would not be very useful and I told him so quite frankly. I thought the same thing when Martelli took the initiative of nominating Falcone as director of Penal Affairs. I believed that, at that stage, his presence in Palermo was indispensable, especially after the new penal code procedure went into effect which posed quite a few problems to Mafia investigations, in particular to public prosecutors who would become its masters. At the core of the problem was the gathering of evidence and its defence during hearings, not to mention the rapport between the police and judges in their search for notitiae criminis (notification to a prosecutor that a crime has occurred) and their preliminary investigations.

When Falcone was transferred to Rome and we started seeing more of each other, I came to appreciate his great intelligence and moral and intellectual rectitude, and above all, his ability to go straight to the heart of the problems we were facing Martelli and I both know how essential his contribution was to the work of defining the new laws. Falcone had a special talent for seeing the concrete consequences of a penal regulation and for giving an extraordinary contribution to the drafting of laws, which was not common in the legal offices of Roman ministries. The lucky thing for me and the Ministry of Internal Affairs was that both Prefect Raffaele Lauro, my cabinet head, and Prefect Sabato Malinconico, head of the legal office, as well as Prefect Carlo Mosca, head of the special secretary office, demonstrated similar qualities.
Even before Falcone's transfer to Rome, we met at the ministry for a meeting with Rudolph Giuliani and Gianni De Gennaro.

The three of them had worked together on the preliminary investigations for the maxi-trial in Palermo. The time was ripe to put in place a war strategy, and thus overcome the inadequate culture of emergency measures and special bodies. It was time to modify ordinary institutions and equip the police and judiciary with new anti-Mafia laws and instruments that were more efficient and effective than in the past. Falcone warned us of the obstacles we would encounter and on the need to arm ourselves with patience and perseverance. We had to abandon the liturgy of great Mafia crimes which normally triggered a great emotional public response (in that climate, it is easy to accept emergency type measures and institutions which, later, are swiftly stripped of any real substance!) They only serve to overcome the critical phase of emotionalism!

Modifying existing balances is always very difficult. The Florentine secretary Macchiavelli's admonishment regarding the innovative principle has stayed with me all these years. And, in June 1992, I came to understand well the meaning of the term "unarmed prince".

8.3 The first laws

On the very same day I was sworn in at the Quirinale, I met with Andreotti to define a set of laws which the two ministries, Internal Affairs and Justice, had been working on for some time: this would constitute my first legislative decree. First with Vassalli, and above all, later with Martelli, we agreed on the urgent need for a better understanding of the nature and scope of the enemy we were facing and of devising a strategic plan on the basis of which we could decide what to include in the innovative measures to be introduced in Parliament. I was firmly convinced of the need to start out on the right foot: we needed to adopt a coherent policy and instruments with a state legal system that was fully "in effect". We needed to change the legal system based on the need to destroy the anti-state completely. We couldn't just superimpose special entities and laws on it which would have prevented the state from fighting an all out war on the Mafia.

On my desk, apart from the documents prepared by the Department and various security forces, were some reports on the work that the public prosecutor's offices were doing or had done in Palermo and in the Calabria, Campania and Puglia regions. Among the many documents I read in my first days at Palazzo Viminale, I found those submitted to me by General Luigi Ramponi on money laundering and the criminal economy to be of particular interest. It was time to act and Ramponi gave me a big hand in establishing procedures, above all in the realm of the economy and illegality. At Palazzo Viminale, I had the good fortune to be able to rely on a pool of Cabinet and law office functionaries with solid legal grounding and a strong sense of the State and its institutions. With them, as well as with Prefect Lauro, Prefect Malinconico and Prefect Mosca, we were in perfect agreement over the basic strategy we had decided on and which I wished to pursue. The three of them, working in admirable harmony, carried out my directives, setting into motion the great machine of Palazzo Viminale. The functionaries of my secretarial office, directed by Nino Gargiulo with Cinzia Ceracchi who, for years, shared in the joys, disappointments, and frustration of the long and hard work days with ready smiles on their faces, even in the toughest times of times, were particularly supportive. Maria Di Fazio and Paolo Naccarato were the most vulnerable as they were the ones who had to face media pressure and attacks when dramatic events came hard on the heels of one another, resulting in significant repercussions on government policy and public opinion. And there were also the invaluable men of the Viminale "battery" who represented an extremely efficient link between the top levels of institutions, who preserve with utmost confidentiality, the memory of the complex network of relations on which I was able to build solidarity and consensus.

Chapter 9

9.1 Probing deep into the Mafia: the Report on the DIA

Two documents illustrate quite clearly what our aims were in changing the strategy to fight the Mafia. The first, which was the last in terms of chronology and which was written almost at the end of my term at the ministry, was the half-yearly report submitted to Parliament in June 1992 on the activities of the DIA (Direzione Investigativa Antimafia). I decided to add an introductive chapter to these reports, prepared by the various offices on their progress, which I wrote personally, having discussed a draft prepared by analysts including Pino Arlacchi.
The second is a communiqué written by the Anti-Mafia Parliamentary Commission after the assassination of Salvo Lima: a study paper, albeit a succinct one, containing at its core a request for a clear response from Parliament on how they

intended to reply to the Mafia attack.

I will start with the DIA report which, although it was the last document I signed, expresses in a more systematic way the reasons behind the decision for war, revealing the convictions that upheld me in those two brief, but intense years I "lived" at Palazzo Viminale.

In introducing this document, I think it would be useful to cite the comments of a distinguished journalist at the "Repubblica" newspaper, dated 12 July 1992, when I was no longer Minister of Internal Affairs: *"The real danger, the gravest threat to Italian democracy is "cosa nostra" – writes the Minister of Internal Affairs – who is performing his last act in the battle against organized crime by submitting the dossier on the first six months of the activities of the DIA, Direzione Investigativa Antimafia. It is an alarming report, different from those traditionally submitted to the House. For the first time, it contains an accurate analysis of the Mafioso phenomenon, with specifications, distinctions, and considerations which are most certainly not secondary. "cosa nostra" - says Scotti's report – constitutes only a segment, the most hidden, deep, and dangerous level, of what we call the Mafia: due to its capacity to challenge–contrast authorities directly, due to the specific and savage nature of its members, and due to its tradition of territorial control, it represents the most serious danger of all. An important distinction must be made: "cosa nostra" is not synonymous with the Mafia; they are two aspects of the same phenomenon. Therefore, a distinction must be made between the two, a distinction which emerges from the important investigative work done by the anti-Mafia pool led by Giovanni Falcone. The Capaci massacre has confirmed the validity and strategic importance of such a distinction. The main feature of "cosa nostra" is its tendency to challenge the State on an equal footing, not to mention, to infiltrate it by means of obscure relations with members of the State apparatus or its elected bodies, to the point where whoever tries to oppose its enormous power is neutralized".*

Moving on to the text of the report: "The massacre of 23 May 1992, in which Judge Giovanni Falcone, his wife Francesca Morvillo, and three of his bodyguards, Vito Schifani, Antonio Montanari, and Rocco Di Cillo were killed, marked an end to a ten-year cycle of Mafia activities and the State's efforts to oppose them. This cycle, which started in Palermo on 3 September 1982 with the assassination of General Dalla Chiesa, his wife Emanuela Setti Carraro, and a bodyguard, has been characterized by a dual tendency for growth, both in the power of criminal groups and in the opposition to them on the part of civil society, public opinion, and institutions of security and social defence". The report continues: "The expansion of Mafia power during the 80's has manifested itself in a general increase in the number of criminal groups and their members, in the spread of the territorial base of clans at the local and inter-regional level, and the closer ties between the Mafia and other forms of national and international organized crime .....The State's response has expanded in multiple directions".

The so-called maxi-trial, which started with Caponnetto and ended with Falcone, took place in 1985/1986. It brought charges against the most important members of the clan federation headed by the Greco–Corleonesi families.

"During the entire decade lasting from 1982–1992, exceptionally effective investigative and fact-finding activities were carried out, allowing security forces and judges to define in a much more detailed way than before, the features and forms of

the phenomenon of organized crime in our country. These investigative activities have not been painless, in that they have cost the lives of many representatives of institutions who discovered some hitherto unknown traits, characteristics, and details about Mafia ties to the economy, society, and public institutions. These findings included the renewed interests of the Palermo-based Mafia in the Atlantic heroin route, as well as the killing of Police Commissioner Boris Giuliano, the prominence of the Corleonesi in the Mafia power structure, the assassination of Counsellor Terranova, the importance of the "Catanese" clan in the Mafia organization and in the illegal economy of Sicily, the murder case of Prefect Dalla Chiesa, the role played by the Salvo cousins in "cosa nostra", the death of Counsellor Rocco Chinnici, and finally, the innermost workings, the secret architecture(and its subsequent level of dangerousness) of "cosa nostra" and its allies, such as in the assassination of Judge Falcone".

What were the keystones of the turning point? Above all, the understanding of a crucial point gained through Falcone's investigative efforts: the distinction, from an operative point of view, between the Mafia and "cosa nostra". Secondly, the practice of modifying ordinary state institutions instead of resorting to emergency procedures and measures, and extraordinary institutions, as had occurred since the unity of Italy. This process of improvement was guided by the findings of the Court of Palermo investigation office. What leaps out from the pages of these official documents, is the collaboration between Palermo and Rome, the rapport between Falcone and Martelli and all of us at Internal Affairs, always shielded from the press and the media spotlight.

Keeping these facts in mind, the statement at the beginning of the Court of Palermo's warrant-sentence against "Abbate Giovanni

+ 706" becomes enlightening:«*This is the trial against the Mafia organization called "cosa nostra", an extremely dangerous criminal organization that, using violence and intimidation, has sowed and continues to sow death and terror (..) The danger lies in the "cosa nostra's" tendency to challenge the State and its representatives on an equal footing, not to mention its infiltration of the State by means of secret dealings with members of its apparatus and elected bodies, using corruption or violence against anyone who stands up to their enormous power. (...) Other important criminal organizations, such as the "camorra" and "'ndrangheta" and other Sicilian clans, not belonging to "cosa nostra", demonstrate the same tendency to challenge and manipulate legal institutions, but only "cosa nostra" is capable of doing this systematically and with implacable efficiency, to the point of adopting tools and tactics that are subversive*».

In the cited DIA report, I wrote:«*Statements made by the most important collaborators in justice, from the top echelons of the Sicilian Mafia–Tommaso Buscetta, Salvatore Contorno, Antonino Calderone and Marino Mannoia – and the cited investigations of the anti-Mafia pool are in total agreement about the existence of a formal and secret association among members of the Sicilian Mafioso organized crime, equipped with clearly defined rules of conduct, decision-making bodies, operational roles, plans of action and admission procedures*».

The difference between the Mafia and "cosa nostra", which our strategy aimed to destroy, did not consist in a difference in social and economic organization or in a difference in cultural context. The findings on the Mafia, as an important "economic and political entity" in Italy, were no less sound, because "cosa nostra" was an integral part of the set of non-values, powers, behaviours, endeavours, and ways of acting that could be summed up under the concept of the Mafia phenomenon. "Cosa nostra" constituted just a segment, the most well-hidden, deepest, and most dangerous decisional level of what we call the Mafia. This is due to the Mafia's capacity to directly challenge legal authorities as a result of its effective and proven approach to manipulating and gaining power over men and institutions, not to mention, due to the specific and savage nature of its members and its tradition of territorial control. "Cosa nostra" represented, therefore, the most serious threat to democracy and liberty in Italy. The rejection of "pax mafiosa" in favour of a "war" strategy was aimed at eradicating this form of criminality from its strongholds and its territorial criminal networks and, above all, at identifying and destroying its national and international links. If the war strategy attempted to strike at the heart of the criminal organization, it was clear that the Mafia would react violently and try to strike right back, to kill or wipe out the institutions and its representatives responsible for the war.

9.2 Speech at the Anti-Mafia Commission in March 1992

The second document, which I mentioned previously, is the text of the Anti-Mafia Commission hearing on 17 March '92, after the murder of Salvo Lima and before the Capaci and via D'Amelio massacres. In that speech, I reiterated clearly and unambiguously exactly what I had asserted on my first Parliamentary appearance, the day after my appointment as Minister of Internal Affairs in October 1990. At that hearing in Parliament, my intention was to openly state the sacrifices we would have to make if we declared war on the Mafia. The Parliament had to make a decision in the full knowledge of the consequences they would be deliberately accepting.

«Since October 1990, when I took on my political role as Minister of Internal Affairs, I have always felt that we are facing a long and difficult war. I don't think we have any alternative, unless also during this election campaign, (we were right in the midst of the 1992 campaign to re-elect Parliament) *we want to settle for a climate of calm and normality, that is to say, exactly what pax mafiosa has made possible, if you like, with the acquiescence of state bodies. This would have the negative effects on civil life that we have all witnessed and continue to witness. Let me add, moreover, that the risk represented by the moral crumbling and collapse of civil society which criminality would thus obtain, would be by far more serious than the political price which we must be ready to accept if we want to avoid extinguishing that breath of life and yearning for renewal that has been germinating in increasingly vast layers of the community and which, in part, owe their origins to the furious reaction of the Mafia; it's enough to remember what happened in Sant'Agata, Militello and Tortorici. If Italian democracy wants to save itself from increasing subjugation to criminality, then we must all be ready to face a painful ordeal, marked also by extremely troublesome events».* I concluded: *« Today, we find ourselves in the presence of a phenomenon which does not aim to destroy institutions, but rather bend them to its purposes, which are not ideological, but are ones aimed at profit and the accumulation of wealth. Thus, the risks have increased, from the moment organized crime, seeing the impossibility of adopting its usual methods, has resorted to terrorist techniques, as we are seeing increasingly frequently».*

I would like to underline once more that this realistic analysis was made two (two!) months before the Capaci massacre and almost four (four!) months before the one on via D'Amelio.

More recently, on 28 October 2010, when I recalled these statements at a session of the current Anti-Mafia Commission, Chairman Senator Giuseppe Pisanu asked me:«*During the Anti-Mafia Commission hearing on 17 March 1992 concerning the Lima crime, you said the Mafia conflict was and would be one of a certain nature. What information did you have that allowed you to ascertain that the conflict would develop with those types of events?*»I answered: «I realized that the stronger the State's reaction against the Mafia, the easier it would be for the Minister of Internal Affairs to openly say to the Anti-Mafia Commission: look, this is the nature of the fight; if you want to choose an alternative, I'm out; for me, the only possible course is the one we have taken, so we have to be prepared for a battle». The battle was the one we are all familiar with».

When I spoke at the Anti-Mafia Commission in March 1992, I had already initiated the procedure to declare a state of alarm due to the events we foresaw and which, to a great extent, came to pass. Why did I speak in those somewhat threatening terms to the Anti-Mafia commissioners? The killing of Lima had created a sense of fear and uncertainty, even though it was never expressed blatantly. I heard growing criticism against an excess of repression that would carry a high price, also in terms of human lives. A more cautious approach, would perhaps, have achieved better results. I never avoided discussions on this issue, also because I would have preferred that the criticism be clearly and openly stated. But the criticism, at times also harsh, was always limited to single measures, and never went beyond that to criticizing the underlying strategy.

This is why I wanted to provoke, first and foremost, a clear response from those who had given the government to which I belonged, their vote of confidence.

On more than one occasion, I had tried through the press and in Parliament to trigger a debate and obtain an alternative proposal to my strategy, ready to leave Palazzo Viminale at a moment's notice. On 2 September 1991, many months before the Capaci and via D'Amelio massacres, the "Il Corriere della Sera" newspaper published a six-column front page interview I had granted to Maria Antonietta Calabrò with the double headline: «*Scotti: against the Mafia, words, the war on the Mafia is not made on TV*». "*I'm tired of being the imaginary scapegoat of my political colleagues and public opinion. I'm fed up with the typically Italian schizophrenia whereby when there is a killing, we hear the same tiresome refrains: "The State should raise the ante, the State doesn't exist." The Mafia is a pyramidal and hierarchical organization. It is an act of war. It's as if "cosa nostra" were using cannons, the Air Force, and the Navy simultaneously and in coordination, while instead, this is something I can't do. That's the difference between us and them. Either they give us the tools to fight this war, or otherwise, I can just as well go home tomorrow morning, they would just be doing me a favor*". "*So speaks Minister of Internal Affairs Enzo Scotti, who proposes taking a decisive course of action immediately, and once and for all, against the Mafia. Yesterday, «Il Corriere della Sera» decided to publish, as background, an anthology of ten years of political promises regarding the Mafia. What did you think of it?*" "*I agree completely, it's just unbelievable. It's always the same story after each death*". "*Yes, but it's not just that; we change tactics after each new crime*" "*There's the circus of the moment, which feeds on clichés which the public has had enough of for some time now. The most abhorrent aspect is this schizophrenia of proposals and suggestions made in the TV spot light or under emotional impulse which are then followed by radically different behaviour the day after. I've always done what I thought was right: when we decided to send bosses back to jail on the basis of a High Court of Appeal ruling, I asked for a legislative decree. Enough crying: Corrado Carnevale[30] (the "Sentence-slayer" judge, A/N) does it or doesn't do it. If we are convinced that it's wrong, let's modify it.... but, let's adopt a line. The only possible line is: the Mafia is a pyramidal organization. The instruments we use have to take this aspect into account. So let's just adopt these measures and put an end to it. I've raised the issues under my jurisdiction: above all, that of coordinating and reinforcing security forces. By the end of September (the time needed to conclude the preliminary investigations) all the town councils that have been corrupted will be dissolved. But all of this is just one ring; if I can't count on the other ring, the judiciary, I can't do anything. Otherwise, it's all just demagogy". "How strong is the State in territories controlled by cosa nostra?" "The reinforcement of territorial control has already been initiated but has to continue and possibly with more sophisticated technical tools. Simple patrols and road blocks, on their own, are not very effective. We can't go so far as to militarize the country, we can't become a Police State, but we can do something more substantial, with more suitable tactics. I've asked for them to be studied and put into effect". "But isn't it maybe true that the real problem is the institutional and social control of the Mafia phenomenon?" "Yes. There is the problem of creating a completely different*

---

[30] He earned this nickname because of the high number of Mafioso convictions which he overturned on appeal due to small technicalities. Out of the over 200 convictions of Mafioso obtained in the maxi-trial led by Falcone, only a few dozen were still behind bars by 1990 due to Carnevale's role in appeals court.

climate. Confindustria has urged for more means, and that's fine, but when we ask the banking system to do away with secrecy and to carry out more stringent monitoring on money laundering, they absolutely refuse to provide banking information. The money, the money paid for protection, is used for something, it's not as if they spend it every night in clubs...The municipalities should be very careful in checking any modifications in licenses and property transfers. Notaries and intermediary agents are asked to collaborate, but ultimately, they just wash their hands of it. How many national companies, ones involved in public works, are under the Mafia's yoke? I haven't asked traffic wardens to act as policemen, but for heaven's sake, I would expect them to report on Mafiosi that are buying construction or commercial licenses, and so on".

Getting back to the hearing in 2010, Chairman Giuseppe Pisanu asked me some other questions: *"Can you tell us your interpretation of the Salvo Lima killing? You stated – albeit in general terms – that it was a warning to the political class. Did you discuss this with Giovanni Falcone? What opinions did you form?"* I replied: *"I spoke with Falcone in-depth and at length about the Lima killing and my statements on 17 March '92 accurately reflect our shared opinions. Falcone did not consider Lima to be a person inside the Mafia organization, differently from Ciancimino, who he believed to be an inside member of the organization, and he believed, as I did, that the killing of Lima was most definitely a warning – a very precise and specific one – to Sicilian politicians and the regional secretary of my party, who were supporting the war strategy".*

Chapter 10

10.1 The Mafia in the era of globalization. The Italian semester of the European Community Presidency

A change from "pax" to war in Italy would have been weak and ultimately ineffective in the absence of international cooperation to harmonize legislation, enabling counter-measures to act rapidly and create a unified front. A few weeks after my appointment to Palazzo Viminale, I presided over a meeting of the European Community Ministers of Internal Affairs and Justice. Part of the Italian presidency program of the European Community (Trevi Group) was held in Naples, but organized crime was not an item on the agenda because security was not yet part of its mandate nor a part of the European agenda. However, in my introduction to the work session, I took the opportunity of calling my colleague's attention to the need for strong, and at that time, voluntary European cooperation to fight the "octopus", from which no country could consider itself immune.

Years would pass before common action was adopted, and it is thanks to the efforts of Franco Frattini, acting as Deputy Chairman of the European Commission, that the first concrete and comprehensive initiatives regarding security and organized crime were taken. We were very far from the decision taken in recent times by the European Parliament to establish the Anti-Mafia Commission, headed by the resolute Italian parliamentarian Sonia Alfano. Indeed, from the reaction of the majority of my colleagues in Naples, I realized that it was necessary to push forcefully for a change, at both the European and international levels.

10.2 International cooperation against the Mafia

From the very first day the judges in Palermo started their preliminary investigations for the maxi-trial, they made recourse to international cooperation. On the other side of the Atlantic, they were able to rely on the helpful collaboration of Rudolph Giuliani, who had high esteem for the professional skills of Giovanni Falcone and Gianni De Gennaro, the Italian judge's collaborator at the time.
Falcone's insistence on international cooperation was significant if we consider how long it took for many States to become aware of the scope and power of organized crime, not to mention the need to take important steps towards implementing adequate counter-measures.

In 1994, the United Nations conference on organized crime,

which is only remembered because the presiding Prime Minister Silvio Berlusconi was served a notice of investigation at it, was held in Naples; in 2000, in Palermo, the International Convention on organized crime was ratified precisely in acknowledgement of Falcone's efforts to organize the conference in Naples. In the brief period that I was Minister of Foreign Affairs, I urged for the establishment of a special ministerial office, charged with the task of pursuing international judiciary cooperation and named Giusto Sciacchitano, a judge who had worked in Palermo in Falcone's time, to head it.

If we look back today at the progress made in those years, notwithstanding the conferences, the statements, and the framework agreements, we have to admit that we were still very far from achieving the fundamental conditions necessary to make investigative and judiciary cooperation functional: this is due to the indispensable need for homogeneity in the anti-crime laws of various States, a prerequisite for investigative and judiciary institutions to be able to work together. And it is also for this reason that we were not able to carry out a sufficient number of joint investigations with respect to the number called for by the global dimension of organized crime.

The current status of international cooperation is the result of a delay in realizing that the Mafia - and more specifically "cosa nostra" – were not "ordinary" criminal organizations that could be fought using normal investigative and judiciary cooperation agreements, or simple extradition agreements. It was a widespread, global system that required a common network of protection comprised of shared laws and reliable and credible institutions. The traditional Mafia organization, challenged by the process of globalization, had acted more swiftly than legal institutions in transforming and adapting its organization and network of cooperation among the various Mafias, thus expanding its threat to the functioning of free society, the market economy, and democratic institutions in many States around the globe. The lever used by organized crime was to concentrate on some weak States and selected tax havens to constitute its logistical base from which it could contaminate countries with stronger institutional structures that made them potentially more difficult to penetrate. If there was an error committed by these latter countries, it was precisely that of under-evaluating the role that weak States and tax havens have had and still have today in attacking healthy systems. To give an example, the history of relations between the United States and Central American countries is characterized by just such delays and under-evaluations. There was, however, another error: the belief that the problem could be solved directly between the United States and these countries, while it was imperative instead to act on a global level and work together with Europe to create that network of protection I mentioned previously.

Over the last few years, Italy has pushed strongly for a triangular form of cooperation between the United States, Central America and Europe in order to create a more effective and realistic international effort. The Central American security system has proposed that some friendly States, starting with the United States, implement a set of projects to strengthen institutions and adequately train the security forces of weaker States. Certainly, on their own, these projects are all interesting, but without a common strategy and, I insist, without harmonized institutions and laws, we risk wasting resources and obtaining only partial results, those "hot compresses" of which Falcone spoke. It's not a secret that the police forces of stronger States cannot trust the police and judges of many weak or corrupted States. A sore spot is constituted by global financial markets with weak regulations and controls. In the last few years, starting from the explosion of the 2008 financial crisis, we have repeatedly heard statements of good intentions to regulate international markets, tax havens, and the most sophisticated forms of dirty money laundering more effectively. The concerns over the consequences of restrictions on the free movement of capital have, until now, rendered these attempts both timid and tardy.

I have often asked myself whether, when tackling these problems, we risk under-evaluating their dangerousness due also to the link between drug-trafficking, arms trafficking and forms of terrorism and revolutionary guerrilla warfare in many parts of the world, from Central America, to Afghanistan and Pakistan and many regions of the Caucasus, the Middle and Far East. Even the trafficking in human lives, prostitution, gambling, and more recently, pirating, are all controlled by a criminal network, whose strength lies in the widespread corruption of public bodies, as well as financial institutions, indifferent to where the money comes from and, consequently, to the risks of becoming prey to blackmail. In order to manage their affairs in the new economic and political configuration of the planet, criminal organizations need, even more than in the past, to infiltrate economic and financial institutions, to manipulate their operations and bend them to their criminal thirst for power. This criminal strategy takes advantage of weaker States and tax havens and then branches out and also penetrates those countries that think they are immune to the presence of organized crime or think they can easily control it.

The Mafia is a criminal agency potentially at the service of speculators and unscrupulous brokers as well as corrupted politicians, to whom it turns for protection and the possibility to operate. It adopts violence and massacres, and, according to the geo-political context, also uses terrorism and guerrilla tactics; but it does not resort only to these violent criminal actions. Indeed, it has learned how to launder its illegal revenues in legal markets. In these markets it appears as a normal financial agent, who, in a very short time, operating online, has been able to erase all traces of its activities. For this reason, it operates through "white collar" workers beyond suspicion.

Chapter 11

11.1 The Mafiosa society?

It is difficult to avoid a misunderstanding which contributes to justifying the excuse that the Mafia is impossible to destroy. The opinion that is often expressed, also in good faith, is that the Mafia is a manifestation of the culture and society of the Mezzogiorno, and in particular, of Sicily. For this reason, when we hint at the possibility of a society without the Mafia in southern Italy, the spontaneous reaction is that this dream can only come true if there is a radical change in its economic, social, and cultural organizations. The dream is subordinate to this rebirth and any repressive action, no matter how harsh, is not capable of achieving this aim. In the meantime, we have to wait, and learn how to live with it! This has always seemed to me to be just an excuse to ennoble the strategy of co-existence.

Thus, I refuse to be swayed by these arguments, even though I have always thought that repression should go hand in hand with economic and social reform policies.

While we were working on the new anti-Mafia legislation, I took the initiative of calling the Minister of Education's attention to the role schools should take in the fight against the Mafia. To start with, the focus of attention was on the implementation of systems to monitor and support obligatory school attendance, above all in the areas where the Mafia presence was strongest. The high drop-out rate constituted one of the most serious shortcomings of the educational system, especially in the South: promoting school attendance was part of an effective educational campaign for legality and respect for laws.

Together with this education towards legality, I decided to promote awareness raising in the entire Italian society, also by means of a yearly event, to be held simultaneously in Rome and in all Italian provinces. Unfortunately, we were only able to organize the first event on 8 July 1991 in Rome, where we invited Pope John Paul II to kick off the National Conference on Legality with a meeting at the Vatican. The work then continued at Palazzina Treviat the Police Academy, with speeches by high ranking government figures, starting from the President of the Republic, from the House, the Senate, the Cabinet, and the Anti-Mafia Parliamentary Commission, and ending with representatives from business and social sectors, trade unions, and the political parties represented in Parliament.

The Holy Father began his speech with: "The meeting organized by your ministry with the aim of reflecting on the topic of "The culture of legality" is opportune and offers a contribution to the promotion of a new quality of life in Italian society". He continued*: "In analyzing the causes that have produced a sort of eclipse of the sense of legality itself in the consciences of so many, we must look to a more general decline in the sense of values that sociological studies have been observing for some time. The crisis of the "idea of duty", both in public and in private life, the contestation of the "principle of authority", sustained by mass ideologies, the blurring of the distinction between moral good and evil, accompanied by a growing concession to permissiveness, are also factors that influence in a fundamental way today's crisis in legality and civil co-existence. He went on to say: "Indeed, we must never forget that a mere "formal" assertion of legality without effective reinforcement in concrete action ends up favoring a form of illegality made up of compromises and corruption resulting in a widespread sense of malaise that chips away at the foundation of social cohesion, which as is well-known, is the basis of civil coexistence itself. Even though these problems, to which your attention is drawn, are primarily political, social, and economic ones, there is, however, no doubt that their roots are ultimately of an ethical and spiritual nature. Indeed, these are, perverse "mechanisms" that belong to those "systems of sin" based on personal guilt, in that they are the result of the concrete deeds of people who introduce them, consolidate them and make removing them difficult". "It is clear, therefore, that every action aimed at re-establishing legality must necessarily start from a reaffirmation of those fundamental values, without which a man's original dignity is wounded and society is undermined at its core.*

... in this perspective, it seems opportune to stress the urgency with which anyone in a position of responsibility should work to

heal the fracture between morality and society, with an awareness of the enormous weight that political intervention has acquired, which often results in a profound deformation of the foundation of social life". "*Regaining personal and social morality requires substantial effort and a renewed sense of the responsibility of public conduct. Everyone must feel implicated, from various social organizations, to public and private ones, each making their contribution by educating their members and enhancing the many forms of volunteer service".*

11.2 Not yielding under any circumstances

The memory of Falcone and Borsellino, twenty years after the massacres, should not be cause for commemoration, but rather for a rigorous analysis of what was a turning point in the fight against the Mafia, with its light and shadows. But, above all, what we need to do today is to move forward on that path, fighting the new international Mafia networks, their links to terrorism, and their ability to penetrate legal markets and the functioning of public institutions with effective means.

These new developments are at the heart of a particularly lively debate taking place in the headquarters of important multi-lateral organizations, starting from the United Nations. This concerns not only countries that consume the products of organized crime, but also those where the actions of the anti-state have produced devastating effects and where the adoption of a war strategy has been deemed indispensable, with varying success, for example in Columbia, Mexico, and other Central American countries.

Once again, we come back to the decision we took in 1992, on the terrible night of the Capaci massacre. Martelli and I, faced with the bodies of Falcone, his wife and his bodyguards, while acknowledging the high costs we would have to pay, decided we would never let down our guard, or modify our strategy, and that, on the contrary, we should strengthen the defences and intensify our activities with more decisive instruments. Notwithstanding the fact that we were an outgoing government, due to constitutional time limits, we decided to proposed to our colleagues in government, the President of the Republic and Parliament, a legislative decree containing measures which, in part, we had already examined with Falcone. This resulted in Legislative Decree n. 306 dated 8 June 1992,(converted, with amendments, into Law n. 356 dated 7 August 1992 – Urgent modifications to the new penal procedural code and measures to fight Mafia crime).

Chapter 12

12.1 The Mafia – political parties

The first step I took, just a few weeks after my swearing in at Palazzo Viminale, was to write a letter to all the mayors of the regional capitals in Sicily, Calabria, Puglia and Campania to stress how the Mafia, the "camorra", the "'ndrangheta" and the "Sacra Corona Unita" were not the organizations they used to be: *"Having grown precisely due to the proceeds from drug trafficking, they have become a bloodthirsty criminal organization and a sort of anti-state power"*. At the end of the letter, after calling attention to the need to intervene at the grass roots level on some of the causes which, under the responsibility of local governments, constituted a ripe terrain for Mafioso culture and a form of co-existence with it, I addressed the mayors directly, referring to their specific role as head of local communities and stressing that, *"widespread illegality, we must admit, has caused problems for institutions. But today, there is a strong desire to free citizens from its oppressive influence. This desire could become even stronger if it were accompanied by a genuine commitment, your personal heartfelt support and that of every local administration. I would be grateful if you would ask your local and town councils to act, within their respective jurisdiction, on these concerns of mine"*.

I addressed the political parties during my presentation in Parliament of the legislative decree to dissolve town councils corrupted by the Mafia. My urging started with the assertion that the State had had to intervene to fill a void created by the parties' negligence in selecting a local ruling class and monitoring their conduct. If the political parties did not act to re-appropriate their guiding and monitoring role, the State's substitutive intervention would not fully achieve the desired effects, which in practice is exactly what happened. As a result, it was necessary to dissolve local administrations again shortly after the re-integration of politicians in power. This is why I asked the secretaries of all the parties to make an exceptional commitment. The renewal of democratic institutions would be possible only with the support of political forces throughout the country, working together towards the common goal of transparency and legality. This is the only way we could raise a unified resistant barrier against infiltration from the anti-state, impeding the Mafia from using, time after time, one or the other political party in local government, influencing the proper functioning of elected institutions. A pre-condition for free democratic dialectics was and remains the creation of a healthy obstacle to Mafia infiltration.

12.2 The Mafia – businessmen

I addressed business associations on two separate occasions. The first was during the revolt of business owners in Capo d'Orlando, led by the unyielding Mayor Tano Grasso; the second was in Palermo just after the, killing of Libero Grassi, a brave businessman who had refused to pay protection money. In those years, the reactions of civil society and organizations representing social forces were, in most cases, very generic and tended, above all, to isolate and assign responsibility solely to public institutions. This was a far cry from the position taken recently by the Chairman of the Sicilian Confederation of Industries, Ivan Lo Bello, and the National Confederation of Industries (Confindustria), that provides for expelling businessmen who do not report on racket activities to the police and pay protection money.

12.3 The Mafia – the Catholic Church and religious communities

Action against organized crime is not on the political agenda of nations and international organizations, starting from the United Nations, but they affect all aspects of society. This comprises also religious institutions, including the Catholic Church, due to its moral weight in the civil and political spheres of many countries. The ample space the Episcopal Conferences worldwide dedicated to important ethical issues and also to specifically political ones, not to mention the ample mass media coverage of these opinions, confirmed my belief in the irreplaceable contribution the Catholic Church could make to the fight against the Mafia.

In 1991, in addition to inviting Pope John Paul II to inaugurate the National Conference on Legality, I involved, as Minister of Internal Affairs, not only mayors, leaders of political parties, trade unions and business confederations, but also, and especially, the Italian Catholic Church.

Therefore, I turned to the bishops of the Mezzogiorno expressing my thoughts and asking for their support, availing myself of John Paul II's important message at the inauguration of the National Conference on Legality: a global war on the Mafia could not be carried out without the scathing condemnation of the incompatibility between the sub-culture and traditions of Mafioso society and the evangelical message. Southern Italy was a land where Catholics were in the absolute majority and, therefore, it was up to priests to take on the most important role of eradicating these customs and sub-culture. I encountered some powerful, and quite (still) inexplicable incomprehension from the Secretary General of the CEI (Conference of Italian Bishops) and the President of the Calabrese Bishops' Conference. My letter was interpreted as the attempt of a State, incapable of guaranteeing safety and legality, to dump its responsibilities. I was very embittered! The objective of my appeal was to ask for the educative support of the most important moral authority of southern regions, who were also dealing with Mafia pressure. I have never under-evaluated the great progress made by the ecclesiastic communities in southern Italy, nor the bravery of so many priests in the outlying areas who have paid with their lives, in Sicily and in the Campania regions, for their pastoral work against the Mafia.

Therefore, John Paul II's solemn and scathing condemnation,

pronounced in Sicily with extraordinary vigour, was decisive. Even today, the press reports on tension between Bishops and priests, and the ancient traditions of local communities, exploited by the existence and sub-culture of the Mafia.

1

Chapter 13

13.1 Putting bosses back in jail: an act of war

The steadfastness of institutions is a crucial factor in fighting the Mafia. Among the many measures we implemented, the one that made its mark and triggered a violent reaction from the Mafia was the legislative decree regulating the terms of preventive detention, which put many Mafia bosses back in jail. These were bosses who had been serving time as a result of a first instance[31] conviction in the Palermo maxi-trial, but who had been released by a High Court of Appeal ruling based on an interpretation of precisely these terms of preventive detention.
In fighting the Mafia, any act capable of making the enemy

---

[31] The Italian penal justice system provides for three levels of trial. The Inferior courts of first instance, the Appellate Courts, and finally the High Court of Appeal. Double jeopardy does not exist and both defendants and prosecutors have the right to appeal.

understand exactly how far the State was willing to go was of utmost importance. And that legislative decree was a most eloquent and clear statement of the State's new strategy, taking on operative as well as symbolic meaning. On the basis of an interpretation of the laws governing the maximum period of preventive detention, the High Court of Appeal had released all the bosses convicted during the Palermo maxi-trial, even though for the most part, they had been sentenced to life imprisonment in the first instance. I didn't want to enter into the merits of the basis for the High Court's decision: I realized, however, that for Mafia members, this decision was proof of the organization's invincibility in relation to the Palermo trial and of the evident weakness of the State in conducting the war. The most vulnerable to attack were the judges who had prepared the case for the maxi-trial and those who had issued the sentences convicting prominent "cosa nostra" bosses in the first instance.

Martelli and I both realized immediately the consequences of that sentence. Whatever we may have thought of it, and quite apart from merely the legal aspects, it would be perceived as a defeat for the State and capitulation to the Mafia. Together with our collaborators, we studied what could be done to repair the damage. As Minister of Internal Affairs, I was very concerned, also in light of comments coming from the top echelons of security forces. Furthermore, it was necessary to find a rapid solution which would allow us to put those convicted at the maxi-trial back in jail, and keep the list of most wanted criminals from getting any longer. The difficulty was not in persuading the Cabinet of Ministers to approve a legislative decree, nor in getting the President of the Republic to sign it: the real problem was that we needed to act quickly, and in total secrecy, to adopt the provision which would prevent bosses from turning into fugitives once they realized the government intended to adopt such a measure. This is why we had rumors circulate that adopting the decree would be impossible. Then, keeping the adopted decision top secret, we gave security forces the time to call bosses into police headquarters where they could hold them in temporary detention until the decree was published in the Official Journal and the Appeal Court had decided to re-open prison doors.

Our strategy succeeded: Prime Minister Andreotti assumed responsibility for approving the decree without convening the Council of Ministers, specifying that this had been justifiably requested by his colleagues at Justice and Internal Affairs. The President of the Republic signed the emergency measure, even though he considered it *"an arrest warrant by legislative decree"*, dictated out of sheer necessity. The silence surrounding the government's and President Cossiga's decision until after the publication of the decree in the Official Journal, and the Court of Appeal's decision, allowed security forces to detain the bosses, certain no decision would be taken by the government.

"It was kept secret for hours, guarded jealously in a drawer at Palazzo Chigi", wrote Silvana Mazzocchi in "La Repubblica" on 2 March 1991: *"Even though it had been approved by the government in the early hours of the morning, the legislative decree on facilitated releases was struck from the usual official communiqué yesterday and remained an object of speculation until late yesterday afternoon while waiting for convicted Mafia members, released some day ago,to arrive at Palermo police headquarters for their daily check in. A package of laws aimed at reinstating preventive detention .... And a plan was mentioned by the head of the Viminale, Vincenzo Scotti, in Malta yesterday morning, while at Palazzo Chigi, Nino Cristofori stated at the press conference that this decree had not been presented at the*

Council of Ministers and that a technical committee had had to be called in to iron out and revise the text. You will have more news this evening, said the under-secretary to the Prime Minister's office, addressing journalists who wondered what glitches had blocked the long awaited measures at the last moment. In the meantime, the anti-release decree, approved and signed, was on its way to press, to come out in a special edition of the Official Journal this evening, thus giving the green light to the warrant for the Palermo lower Court of Appeal, which had hurriedly gathered to meet in the meantime. On the other hand, once it was published, the measure drafted by the ministers of Justice and Internal Affairs, in complete accord, would become effective at the stroke of midnight yesterday".

The government's decision thus had the effect of demonstrating the State's strength and its capacity to overcome any obstacle. The Mafia high command realized that the government would hold firm to its decision and that doubts about its power had been raised in the eyes of its members. The Mafia high command decided to respond immediately, also as a warning to whoever had turned their backs on them, by resorting to terrorist and guerrilla strategies aimed at innocent citizens as well.

Reading the news stories on the *"black Friday of 50 godfathers"* and listening to the reaction of their lawyers, it was possible to glean then and understand today, how violent their reaction would be. *"The longest day for "cosa nostra" bosses started by chance on a sidewalk of a street in Calatafimi. This was the town chosen by Giovambattista Pullarà, the place selected for forced residence by one of the bosses of the Santa Maria del Gesù clan after his triumphant release from the Ucciardone prison. The encounter took place at about nine in the morning. The Mafioso was taking a stroll and window shopping, about to go into a café* when two plainclothes agents blocked his way. Mr. Pullarà, the Police Commissioner of Trapani would like to speak with you. He would like to meet you....... Would you mind getting into the car? The 'commendatore' has something he would like to tell me? Why not exchange two words with him since I don't have anything else to do today. How could he suspect, at nine in the morning on his fourteenth day of liberty, that twelve hours later he would still be sitting in a small room at Police Headquarters? How could Giovambattista Pullarà ever imagine that, in Rome, they had already signed that cursed decree? The police operation, perhaps for the first time in the history of anti-Mafia blitzes and round-ups, was actually carried out in total secrecy - in the whole of Sicily, even in the channel islands of Pantelleria and Lampedusa. All of the Mafioso released by the Court of Appeal over the past few days were called in for checks and detained by surprise while a very lengthy meeting of the Appellate Court in Palermo was taking place. The meeting started at five in the afternoon and lasted until late in the evening. During the night, about fifty arrest warrants were signed. ... A knock-out blow to bosses that had been rounded up in their villages, a move that has triggered a storm of controversy among lawyers in Palermo - Sicilian penal experts are on the warpath". ... "And one of them, Aldo Caruso, Senator Salvatore Greco's defence lawyer said this is a South American type measure that calls to mind the notorious "privilegia odiosa' of Neronian times. All the rules of law have been violated, once more we are forced to make note of heavy-handed and inadmissible executive interference in judiciary matters".

This is how the bosses came to realize that they were facing a tough war.

The climate was changing: from *pax mafiosa* to declared war!

Chapter 14

14.1 The six "pillars"

The repression strategy devised with Martelli hinged on a package of six initiatives which included various legal measures and guiding acts. The bills proposed and approved by Parliament, albeit after undergoing several modifications as a result of pressure from many apprehensive opponents, constituted a comprehensive vision so that the effectiveness of each single law depended on its cohesiveness as a whole. The cohesiveness of the various measures was the result of positive integration between the two ministries and their ability to take advantage of the synergies created by the joint efforts of security forces and the judiciary, not to mention the ways and means by which they were coordinated on the field.

14.1.1 The first pillar –The problem of Mafioso in prison (art. 41bis)

The first package of initiatives dealt with the so-called "prison problem", that is the links between bosses in prison and clan members on the outside. These links allowed the Mafia to maintain its chain of command and the efficiency of its whole organization intact. As we will see, there was the same problem with links between fugitives and active members of clans. This issue also required more efficient and effective intervention, both in order to re-capture fugitives and to intercept communication, which was entrusted in part to "pizzini[32]".

I have already mentioned that I had just been sworn in at the Quirinale and found myself having to face the final draft of a legislative decree on which the two ministries, Justice and Internal Affairs, had been working. The most complicated and thorny issue turned out to be the regulations regarding the detention of Mafioso convicts. The investigations carried out by the Anti-Mafia Parliamentary Commission, the legal and journalistic inquiries, not to mention the reports from the Anti-Mafia High Commission and later, those of the DIA-Anti-Mafia Investigative Division, have always highlighted the role that prisons play in the *modus operandi* of Mafioso clans. The criminal organization has always been active in prisons: to guarantee the privileges of bosses, to recruit members, to intimidate other prisoners, to maintain its organizational links on the outside and to demonstrate that imprisoning its bosses doesn't hinder, but rather reinforces, the organization's operational dynamics. The power of the Mafia, therefore, manifests itself even when its members are

---

[32] Pizzini are small slips of paper which the Mafia uses to communicate in code from prisons and hide-outs.

in jail. If we intended to dismantle the organization, it was essential to untangle this knot as well.

The dramatic situation of Italian prisons, especially in the past few decades, has always focussed on the need to improve, above all, the physical conditions of prisons, to humanize internal relations and respect the constitutional requirements of punishment. In 1986, Italy adopted a prison law[33] named after an extraordinary figure, Senator Judge Mario Gozzini, a friend of mine from my "Azione Cattolica" days. If this law had been put into effect in any environment other than the hell which prison over-crowding had produced, it would have been instrumental in bringing about the implementation of constitutional rules of a particularly ethical nature. This opinion was shared by an important Italian judge, Adolfo Beria D'Argentine, who stressed the *"difficult but indispensable task of conjugating the rights of individuals with those pertaining to the need to ensure the safety of the collectivity"*. The degradation of prisons has favoured the use of these places by the Mafia to increase its power and operations. The hell pits of Ucciardone and Poggioreale have cast a terrible shadow on our country's respect for human rights. Not surprising, Italy is under investigation by the Council on Human Rights in Geneva and the International Court of Justice at the Hague. It was not easy, therefore, to adopt measures that would reduce the privileges enjoyed by Mafiosi in Italian prisons and to cut off the criminal links between bosses behind bars and operative members on the outside.

In November 1990, when, on the occasion of the legislative decree, we tried to tackle the Mafia prison problem in light of

---

[33] Law n. 663, dated 10 October 1986 – "Modifications on the law governing penitentiary systems and the implementation of measures for the privation and restriction of freedom". (Gozzini)

what was actually happening in those places, I personally had the conviction that some of the privileges envisioned by the Gozzini law could end up being used to favor criminal activities. How could we deal with the issue of granting privileges to ensure that they would not become tools to facilitate the anti-state's activities? In reply to this question, we introduced some laws aimed at limiting Mafia inmates' eligibility for some of Gozzini's privileges. The debate on these proposals, both in Parliament and in the general public, was heated. It focussed on the need not to backtrack on the provisions of the law, except in rare cases, but did not take into account the real situation and the need to keep prisons from continuing to act, in many respects, as command and dispatch centers for incarcerated bosses. Opposition to the introduction of the new laws obtained objective and paradoxical convergence from, on the one hand, the defenders of human rights and the rehabilitative aims of punishment, and on the other, those opponents more interested in maintaining the status quo of *pax mafiosa*. I followed the debate at the Commission of Constitutional Affairs and Internal Affairs personally, and was able to get a sense of the difficulty we would have encountered if we had tried to introduce even more radical changes. The procedure for the ratification of the law decree was particularly long and tortuous, to the point where the government had to re-introduce the decree a stunning six times!

After the Capaci massacre, when we decided together with Martelli to introduce some restrictive measures to the prison regimes of Mafia criminals in the legislative decree dated 8 June 1992, we considered, above all, its temporary (if not brief) application, linked, in any case, to the results achieved in the complex war against the Mafia. Above all, we were targeting links with the outside and the need therefore, to prevent bosses in jail from continuing to run their organizations. We were absolutely not thinking in terms of punitive measures as an aim to themselves, nor of impinging on respect for the personal dignity of inmates. What worried me the most, and I stressed this many times during preparatory meetings, was that once these restrictive laws were approved, opposition from many quarters would force us to retract before having achieved definitive results in the battle against the Mafia. The implementing decrees of 41bis, at the disposal of the Minister of Justice, were not acts at his total discretion and would always necessitate close collaboration between Internal Affairs and Justice: the entire management of the war on the Mafia, including the application of 41bis, necessarily depended on the crucial collaboration between the two administrations, police forces, and the judiciary. It was unimaginable that we could set up self-referring potentates without putting in place reciprocal checks. The entire repressive system had to operate together in unison.

Regardless of what the findings on the investigations and trials on so-called Mafia "bargaining" will be, it behooves us to provide some political considerations and just as useful clarifications on the decisions made regarding the application of 41bis. Minister Conso has taken full responsibility before inquiring judges and the Anti-Mafia Commission for some of these decisions, stating that he acted totally on his own, without informing the government or the State. Up to now, however, the testimony of those responsible diverge on who took the first initiative in asking for restraint in the application of this law, that is, for not implementing the plan which provided for Mafia inmates to be isolated from other inmates, and for not renewing the decree for some bosses. The issue is certainly not the administrative legality

of these decisions, but rather, the lack of clear and transparent motives and a shared choice of action which, in any case, would have a significant impact on the whole strategy to fight the Mafia. A change of policy could have been legitimately adopted, but it would have been useful and compulsory to hold at least a preliminary parliamentary debate.
The Anti-Mafia Commission's investigation, introduced by Chairman Pisanu's noteworthy report, on the massacres in 1992 – 1993 and alleged bargaining could provide a positive contribution, shedding light on the distinction between political responsibility and judiciary bearing on the matter.

I think that this would be a way to help our fellow citizens (and historians) understand more clearly the evolution of events and to assign responsibility, without forcing them once again to passively accept the traditional "official line" on the inexplicable mysteries that shroud the dramatic events that take place in our country. The effectiveness of the future battle against the Mafia would be reinforced if we could finally reach agreement on a political-historical evaluation of the light and shadows of the past. By doing so, the message to organized crime would also be much stronger and the deterring effect of the penal code, more effective.
I have asked myself repeatedly over the last few months, if political forces have not just continued to look on the investigative and repressive activities of police forces and the judiciary as spectators, waiting to be able to put these findings to use in an internal political battle. The job of politics and the parliament is not to carry out legal investigations parallel to judiciary ones so much as to re-establish an institutional image of transparency and credibility in the fight against organized crime. We are not

discussing dogma but rather the strategies, more or less effective ones, of public institutions. Quite apart from violations of the law, which should be ascertained in the serenity afforded to judges without transforming trials into competitions, there is still the political issue of the clarity and linearity of conduct of those, in seats of power, who are called to perform institutional functions independently of their political leanings. In a certain way, this issue is just as relevant as determining any possible individual penal responsibility.

Twenty years after the deaths of Falcone and Borsellino, we should try to overcome political rifts on the significance, and consequently, on the anti-Mafia strategy represented symbolically by the dispute between Sciascia and Falcone. This would not only be useful in assessing the current status of the war, but also in determining the extent to which it was attenuated and, therefore, how much it should be reinforced, also in light of what has been tragically demonstrated by events.

Art. 41bis, the Anti-Mafia Commission's negotiation and work

The problem today is not that of awaiting the judiciary's verdict on whether some decisions could have been dictated by a direct or indirect rapport with Mafia members, but of dissipating the mist that risks preventing us from properly ascertaining the facts and possible responsibility. This is precisely the role politics plays, and, in particular, the parliament's monitoring function. To this aim, the work of the Anti-Mafia Commission is important, as it must fulfil its supervisory and investigative role by making a political assessment that looks to the future. What this means, in reality, is that it must in some way balance the costs and benefits of the choices made: only such an analysis can trigger the need to re-examine some aspects of the strategy in place.

It's not a question of yielding to a cut and dry distinction between truth and error, or of entrusting oneself to "God's judgement", but of carrying out a serene evaluation, in the light of what was or wasn't done, and of what should be decided today. When the silence on such important issues has lasted over twenty years, bits of truth emerge in bursts and only when the topic of "bargaining" and fear for our country's security arise. We have a duty towards all those who lost their lives in this war and we cannot allow even the slightest suspicion to insinuate itself into people's minds regarding the propriety of the conduct of public institutions and the men who represent and lead them.

Democracy is fragile, but what erodes it is a weakening of the rapport of credibility and trust between citizens and institutions. And trust is founded on truth and transparency.

At a distance of twenty years, examining the anti-Mafia legislative code would be a useful endeavor, in that a real confrontation on a possible strategy, that is the one adopted in 1990, and on the way it was or was not implemented, could finally reconcile Sciascia with Falcone, on the basis of an agreed evaluation. I don't think re-proposing the ancient debate on a strategy of war or a strategy of co-existence would convey a strong will to weaken the Mafia phenomenon. We risk sending the Mafia a hesitant message and, thus, a "reassuring" one on their future. What is important is to choose an effective strategic policy and, subsequently, not to waver from it, ensuring the State's continuous and constant action. What we are learning today from the judiciary investigative findings is the need to maintain, at all times, even when Mafia violence erupts against the systems of security, the constant and transparent conduct of institutions.

The justifications published here and there by the press over the past few months, supporting the discretionary actions adopted in 1993 to limit the scope of the application of prison regimes established by the so-called article 41bis, substantially reiterate the same arguments which, at the beginning of the '90's, were used when we proposed the first modifications to the prison regimes of those convicted of Mafia crimes. Even then, those justifications couldn't override the need we had to keep prisons from being, in a sense, ruled by bosses, and also to prevent bosses from continuing to manage clan affairs from within prison walls. It is useful to read the statements, after the introduction of 41bis, of the director of penal institutions at the time, Nicolò Amato, in response to a journalist: *"The Mafioso is an enemy of the State. Therefore, it is right to affirm a principle of seriousness and certainty. On the other hand, the decree says to Mafiosi: you can hope to obtain privileges if you repent. This is the philosophy behind the Gozzini law, which grants privileges to inmates who mend their ways".*

14.1.2 The second pillar – Collaborators in justice and "informers"

In logical sequence, the second of what I have called our pillars of strategy and surely the most complex to legislate and deal with, was the introduction of "reward" measures for so-called collaborators in justice to our penal system. In the language of the media, these are often called "informers", a term which has altered, quite significantly, public opinion and that of experts on the nature of this tool and the results that can be obtained from it. The information we wanted from collaborators in justice was on the Mafia organization, its activities, and its men, keeping fully in mind that the collaborator was always a member of a criminal organization and that the Mafioso was only interested in obtaining financial aid for his family and a shorter sentence for himself. The treatment for collaborators in justice can never be considered an incentive to repent and collaborate with justice on the heels of a religious or moral impulse, following an act of repudiation for crimes committed: what it is, clearly, is an invitation to make a ruthless calculation based on expediency. For this reason, every piece of information always has to be checked scrupulously, to avoid any risk of providing a means to carry out across-the-board revenge, to settle scores between criminal clans and, above all, to carry out acts of revenge against institutional figures.

We had already used collaborators during the fight against terrorism, but that was a radically different phenomenon from the Mafia's. In that case, the legislation occurred in the context of a historical phase in which a breach had opened up within the terrorist movement, especially after Moro's kidnapping and murder, and there was a confrontation, quite a bitter one, on whether armed struggle could bring about a revolution and the establishment of a communist regime destroying capitalism. Under those circumstances, using the word repentance had meaning. Using that word for the Mafia was a mistake which would cause many misunderstandings. These differences did not result in the identification of substantially different reward measures, but required investigating judges and criminal investigation divisions to approach and apply them differently. The difficulties arising from dealing with collaborators were evident from the drafting of regulations to their adoption as laws. An *ad hoc* inter-ministerial commission, headed by Senator Giancarlo Ruffino, undersecretary to the Minister of Internal Affairs, was set up to draft the regulations. Falcone took part in the work and was the main framer of the text.

When the work was finished, I asked him to explain its contents to Minister Martelli, in order to get him to sign the measure. Since more than two weeks had passed since the work had been concluded, and the Minister of Justice had not yet sent back the provision signed by Martelli, I called Falcone to find out the reason for the delay. He asked me to meet him and told me, confidentially, that he nurtured some doubts about the law. Even though it was a fundamental and extraordinarily important tool for the future of the fight against the Mafia, it required an investigative and judicial system capable of preventing the Mafia from manipulating collaborators in justice into setting investigative and legal activities on the wrong track and settling scores within the organization. Experience has confirmed not only the validity of all of Falcone's concerns, but also the extreme importance of this investigative tool, since most of the results obtained by judicial actions against Mafia crime have been achieved thanks to the intelligent use of collaborators in justice and the skill of government departments in verifying and using this information.

14.1.3 The third pillar: DIA and DNA, a tough choice

I have already mentioned how, in Falcone's view as well, the effectiveness of collaborators in justice depends in part, if not above all, on how the police and judicial forces are organized and on the professional skills of criminal investigation divisions and government departments. The investigative activities for the maxi-trial had already led Falcone to believe that, in fighting the Mafia, changes needed to be made not only to the normal organization of investigating judges, but also to intelligence and investigative activities. The aim, as I have already mentioned, was to abandon the logic of setting up emergency entities whose tasks were not clearly defined, and which, when they overlapped with those of ordinary bodies, ended up creating operational confusion. The establishment of the Special Anti-Mafia High Commission was just such an example of this emergency reasoning.

Therefore, a proposal gained ground for a nucleus of government departments specialized at the district and national levels, in charged with investigating Mafia crimes as crimes which, although committed by individuals, had been masterminded and carried out by an organization operating over vast national and transnational territories. Only by gaining an understanding of the organization as a whole and its structural base, would it be possible to prepare a case capable of producing concrete results in Mafia investigations, taking on the whole criminal network. The goal was to create a complex structure with a national anti-Mafia public prosecutor's office and district prosecutors, providing them with coordinating powers, and in some cases, also powers of assumption. The issue of taking cases over from lower courts immediately turned out to be the most sensitive one.

When I met Giuliani in Rome, we discussed the need to carry out significant changes in the judiciary organization while simultaneously creating a single national intelligence unit dedicated to the Mafia, capable of providing government departments with investigative input and also of acting as criminal investigation divisions. With Martelli, we came to rapid agreement on the need to follow the course traced by Falcone and Giuliani. We began to exchange concept papers, even before Falcone became General Director of Penal Affairs at the Ministry of Justice.

It was a tough battle, but in the war against the Mafia, the third package of measures turned out to be a key one. In the summer of 1991, I was forced to slow down my efforts to draft measures and, specifically those related to the DIA, due to the unexpected Albanian "invasion" - over 25,000 Albanians had landed on the coast of Puglia. We had reached a deadlock stage in which opposition to the new entities was growing and it seemed increasingly more difficult that we could overcome it easily. Cossiga was following our work attentively. We spent an entire day, far from institutional premises, in Alta Badia, at the Wieser's hotel in Armentarola, analyzing all of the reasons for the opposition. It was at this meeting, with the prefects Enzo Mosino and Paolo Naccarato, that Cossiga proposed using the acronym DIA to name the new body.

We reached our goal, but had to renounce something which we considered important for the operative governance of the DIA and the DNA. We were not able to appoint the "couple", as the press called Falcone and De Gennaro, to head them. The hostility against the two most important figures in the fight against the Mafia was strong and widespread: on 29 October 1991, in "Il Giornale di Napoli", Lino Januzzi expressed clearly the reasons for this extreme opposition which, as we will see, was shared for other reasons and expressed in more subdued tones, by opposing sides: *"This is a couple whose strategy, after the initial euphoria over Mafiosi turning informers and the maxi-trials passed, has resulted in total failure: Falcone and De Gennaro are the ones most responsible for the State's fiasco in dealing with the Mafia ... If politicians are willing to entrust to the two men defeated in Palermo, the management of the nation during the most serious emergency of our lives, it's, within certain limits, their business. But the affair is starting to get dangerous for everyone: from today or tomorrow, whenever these nominations are made, we will have to protect ourselves from two "cosa nostra", the one that has a cupola in Palermo and the one who is about to take office in Rome".*

This type of language disappeared from newspaper stories as of 26 May 1992, the day after the Capaci massacre!
It is well to remember that the first person to refer to the National Anti-Mafia Public Prosecutor's office as a "Mafia cupola" was not the journalist, but none other than the chairman of the National Judges' Association, Raffaele Bertoni, who was subsequently elected as a Senator of the Republic.

Before talking about the barrage of criticism we had to overcome in establishing the two new institutions, it is incumbent on me to recall some of the attacks on Falcone that preceded that barrage. Substantially, there were three of them. The first was the harsh assessment of his preliminary investigations for the maxi-trial, the second was his failed nomination to head the Palermo Office of Investigating Judges, and the third, the proceedings before the Commission of the Magistrates' Internal Board of Supervisors for allegedly holding back information relevant to possible trials against the Mafia. On 25 June 1992, a few days after Falcone's murder, in the entrance hall to the Palermo City Library, Paolo Borsellino referred to the events of the maxi-trial and the Palermo Court Office of Investigating Judges when he made his famous statement to Antonino Caponnetto: *"Falcone started dying in January 1988!"*

The main reason for the ostracism against Falcone had to do with the preliminary investigations for the maxi-trial in Palermo and his "irregular" investigative procedures. That evening in Palermo, Borsellino painted a clear picture of the situation: *"Because I exposed this truth* (the ostracism from the Magistrates' Internal Board of Supervisors as a result of Falcone's and also of Borsellino's work A/N) *I risked suffering serious professional consequences, and maybe that was to be expected, but what is worse is that the Internal Board revealed immediately what its real aim was: taking advantage of what I had exposed, Giovanni Falcone had to be gotten rid of as soon as possible. And maybe I had expected also this, because I was convinced that they would have gotten rid of him anyway; at least, I said, if he has to be gotten rid of, the general public has to know about it and realize it, the anti-Mafia pool has to die in the open, it can't be left to die in silence. Public opinion worked a miracle, because I remember that in that hot summer of August 1988, the general public got mobilized and forced the Magistrates' Internal Board of Supervisors to take back a part of its previous decision made at the beginning of August, so that on September 15th, even though it was limping, the anti-Mafia pool was back on its feet".* And moving on to the issue of Falcone's failed nomination, he recalled how: *"The race for the nomination of successor to the Investigative office of the Palermo Court was on. Falcone was running, a "Judas" immediately took it upon himself to trip him up, and on my birthday the Magistrates' Internal Board of Supervisors gave me this present: they chose Antonino Meli".*

With regards to the Magistrates' board's position on the

investigative office pool and the maxi-trial, the astute journalist Giampaolo Pansa, documented how Falcone, ten months before the "cosa nostra" trial had started in Palermo, had described the environment surrounding him: *"The climate is such that you often have to be careful of the people around you"*. And as for the issue of collaborators in justice, Falcone added: *"Some people even object to the expediency of keeping informers in security outside of prisons. What a lot of rubbish has been said and written! That they live a life of luxury, dining with champagne ... when Buscetta was in Italy, we were under pressure to lock him up in a regular prison"*. And on the same issue, in an interview published in Panorama magazine in 1985, Falcone stated: *"The press has played along with some of these tactics. When low ranking informers began talking, there was an attempt to discredit them by saying they were crazy. Then the "important informers" arrived, such as Buscetta and Contorno. So then the concept of the protection of civil liberties was invoked. A concept which sounds, to say the least, odd in a city like Palermo, that holds the world record for the number of acquittals due to a lack of evidence"*. In the period of the maxi-trial and, to be more precise, just before it began, the lawyers and university law professors in Palermo went wild. *"Trials are becoming inquisitions ... Mammoth trials give no great guarantee that the truth will emerge ... in the maxi-trial, the investigating judge is confusing his role with that of the accuser... informers produce an aberrant situation in which the penal process is degraded to a police tool, to be used at police stations, where you can find spies, whistleblowers, and police informers, that is to say, criminals promoted to collaborators in justice"*. Falcone felt he was being cornered and stated: *"What astonishes me in particular, is a high level statement that the maxi-trials constitute a rudimentary response to the phenomenon of organized crime. I'm surprised, and I have to say, also embittered".*

On 31 July 1986, the "Giornale" described the pool judges in this way: *"Super judges, super protected and super specialized in destroying clans… a select and impenetrable club of judges… judges cloaked in special anti-Mafia merits. Reigning over them all is Falcone, or rather the Myth, the phenomenon, Falconcrest. His police escort is legendary".*

Therefore, I wasn't surprised when the CSM (Magistrates' Internal Board of Supervisors) chose Meli over Falcone as head of the Office of Investigating Judges. On 14 September 1988, CSM councillor Vincenzo Geraci, one of Meli's supporters said to "La Stampa": *"Due to their division into compartments, these pools can easily turn into many separate and isolated bodies within the judiciary".* And a senator added: *"Judge Meli's commitment to the law is the only reassuring point in a period in which we are used to judges who instead theorize on violations of the law"*, clearly referring to Falcone.

As I mentioned, a third attack brought Falcone before the CSM, on the initiative of Leoluca Orlando, with the accusation of having shelved trials against the Mafia, of having hid evidence of complicity between the Mafia and politics, and finally, of having informed Andreotti by telephone of revelations made by the informer Giuseppe Pellegritti. This phone call was used on several occasions to discredit and neutralize Falcone and was referred to, in a subtle way, by his enemies when rumors of his candidature for National Anti-Mafia Public Prosecutor began to circulate.

That story is worth remembering. During one of his preliminary investigations, Falcone had to deal with the informer Pellegritti, who had accused Andreotti of being the instigator behind some high-level political crimes in Sicily. Falcone immediately asked him what proof he had for such accusations, stressing that, in the case of unreliable testimony, Pellegritti would be incriminated for slander. Since Falcone ascertained that there was no foundation for the accusations against Andreotti, he did not hesitate to incriminate Pellegritti. Falcone spoke about this in response to a question during the CSM disciplinary hearing. A commissioner asked him if he had received a phone call from Andreotti. Falcone replied that he could not answer a question of that type. He would only answer it if the question were reformulated to ask explicitly if Andreotti had called him to talk about the Pellegritti case. In its original formulation, stated Falcone, the question was typical of a culture of suspicion, which had for some time contaminated the life of our country.

It does not appear that the question was ever reformulated.

I have requested several times that various chairmen of the Magistrates' Internal Board of Supervisors make the acts of that disciplinary procedure public, because this would help us to better understand this important moment of national history, as well as the history of the fight against the Mafia.

There is an excerpt from Falcone's cited statements at the CSM hearing which is extremely significant in showing the persecution he was subjected to. Falcone talks about a lunch he had with the mayor of Palermo, Orlando. After the lunch, upon arrival at the Palace of Justice, he found some press releases on his desk containing the mayor's accusations of alleged concealment of Mafia investigations and of his attempts to cover up evidence of Mafia-political complicity. Falcone stressed how, during the lunch, they had spoken amicably on many issues, except those contained in the accusations, which had pre-emptively been submitted to the press. Falcone stated before the Commission that he finally, and only on that occasion, understood what the mayor Orlando meant by "friendship".

The National Anti-Mafia Division – DNA

Before analyzing the reasoning behind the opposition to the establishment of the DNA-National Anti-Mafia Division and district prosecutors, I would like to recall the links between this entity, belonging to the judicial system, and the intelligence and investigative police division: the DIA – Anti-Mafia Investigative Division.
At a distance of several years, Francesco Cossiga, who had closely followed the establishment of the DIA, wrote: *"Having as his advisors Giovanni Falcone and Vincenzo Parisi, Scotti decided to make a radical change, almost at the limits of "formal legality", both at a legislative level and at an organizational one, in the fight against the Mafia and organized crime. It was his idea to set up an inter-force "intelligence" and anti-Mafia investigative coordination center"*. Not without reason, Cossiga noted how, *"after he* (Scotti, A/N) *had left the Viminale, this police body turned into a fourth police force, not only for judicial matters, but also for security and policies of the Prosecutor of the Republic. It conducted, also driven by political motives, devastating investigations, such as the one on Giulio Andreotti, often becoming the tool of real and proper political espionage and activities of legal persecution ..... and if he (*Scotti, A/N*) had stayed longer as Minister of Internal Affairs, this certainly would not have happened"*, concluded Cossiga. This tendency inherent in the DIA, which Cossiga highlighted, apart from its merits, was due to a certain ambiguity in the political-parliamentary

compromise establishing the aims of the body and, above all its links to the Anti-Mafia High Commissioner, the special corps taken from the three existing police forces and, finally, the new professional profiles to be selected through specific competitions and undergoing specialized training. Opposition from the police and judiciary, which became more substantial after Martelli and I announced we would present a single legislative decree, succeeded in preventing this result, making it more difficult in parliament to define the operational links and synergies between the two bodies more clearly.

The legislative decree establishing the DIA was converted first, and was followed by the DNA.

The district Anti-Mafia Prosecutor's Offices

As recalled by Borsellino, opposition to the DNA's approval came, above all, from within the judiciary. Opposition was expressed in particularly harsh terms by the Chairman of the National Judges' Association, Bertoni, but also by members of the moderate wing such as Maddalena, a judge of great intellectual rigor and civil commitment. In a letter, also bearing the signatures of Borsellino and other distinguished colleagues, he expressed his strong dissent.

A few days before his death, Borsellino spoke about this with great intellectual honesty: *"If we want to appraise Falcone's work at the Ministry of Justice, the appraisal, even if contested, even if criticized, is an appraisal which focuses above all on the creation of an organization which, rightly or wrongly, he thought could work, especially in the fight against organized crime, and on the work he did, the activities of the anti-Mafia pool, which were carried out in the absence of a law providing for them and in the absence of a law, even at its moments of greatest success, which sustained them. This, rightly or wrongly, but in any case in his intentions, was the super-prosecutor's office, of which even I was initially doubtful, signing a letter written by my colleague, Marcello Maddalena, which was substantially critical of the super-prosecutor's office, but never for an instant did I doubt that this tool, which Giovanni Falcone had worked so hard to create, served the purpose, the idea, rightly or wrongly, of going back, above all, allowing him to go back to being a judge, as he wanted".* Even the public prosecutors in Palermo, who were well-acquainted with their colleague Falcone, were against setting up a "Super-Prosecutor's office". Responding to a questionnaire sent out by Falcone as the Director of Penal Affairs for the Ministry of Justice at the time, the public prosecutor Pietro Giammanco, who had signed a document in reply to Falcone together with all of the deputy prosecutors, stated that the proposed new entity would end up becoming *"dangerous new centers of power, which in their complex management, would remain outside the current system of institutional supervision".* In reference to the legislative decree approved by the Council of Ministers, the Palermo public prosecutors asserted that the system for coordinating investigations should definitely not be replaced, but rather rationalized, to obtain improved efficiency. The management of all of the investigations should remain under the jurisdiction of the State Public Prosecutor's Office. Opposition to the project was not based solely on reasons of merit. It was also a personal attack on Falcone; an attack, as we have seen, that began way back when he was conducting the preliminary investigations for the maxi-trial. And, above all, there was a biased refusal to even discuss the proposal, without once wondering why, up until that point, the judiciary, even at the highest levels of jurisdiction, had ruled that the Mafia didn't exist, and what is even more serious, why most trials on the Mafia had ended with acquittals due to a lack of evidence. Apart from the deficiencies highlighted in the Cattanei report in 1972, carrying out investigations on the Mafia was difficult, precisely because of the fragmented nature of organization and the limitations this posed on investigative activities. Notwithstanding any other reasons, wasn't there perhaps a real foundation for the organizational and institutional flaws denounced by Falcone?

Falcone: Anti-Mafia National Public Prosecutor?

During both the discussion and approval stages of the legislative decree, and subsequently, when we had to appoint the first Anti-Mafia National Public Prosecutor, there were two incidents which, like two big boulders, blocked the smooth passage of the legislative decree and, later, prevented Falcone's nomination. I have already referred to these two incidents: the Pellegritti affair, with insinuations about the telephone call to Andreotti, and the issue of Falcone's transfer to Rome, first upon the request of Minister Vassalli and later upon the request of his successor Martelli, who nominated him to head Penal Affairs at the Ministry. These two events constituted the justification for an attack on Falcone, an attack which gained support due to the left's deep-rooted and unquestioning bias against the Andreotti government. There are two speeches that convey a clear picture of the clashes which erupted among colleagues, over Falcone, precisely in reference to the two boulders I have mentioned. The first was made by a member of the judiciary possessing great intellectual rigor, who has often been criticized for her intransigence. Ilda Boccassini, of the Democratic Judiciary association, invoked the memory of Falcone in Milan a few days after the Capaci massacre. *"Two months ago I was in Palermo"*, wrote Boccassini, *"at a meeting of the National Judges' Association. I will never forget that day. The kindest words, especially from the left, from the Democratic Judiciary, were these: Falcone has sold out to political power. Mario Almerighi called him a political enemy. Now let me say this: it's one thing to criticize the Super-Prosecutor's Office. It's quite another to do as the CSM, the intellectuals, and the so-called anti-Mafia front did, and say that Giovanni was no longer free from political influence. Giovanni was prevented, in his own city, from conducting Mafia trials. So he chose the only path possible, the Ministry of Justice, to work towards realizing his project: a single anti-Mafia entity. And this was a revolution"*. And, directing her comments at the Milanese judges she was speaking before, Boccassini made the following scathing comments. *"That revolution of Giovanni's, I defended it against all of my colleagues. But I was swept away. Because I was his friend, because I believed in him. But my colleagues who were in Palermo today, to attend his funeral, were saying up until yesterday that he shouldn't be trusted"*. ... Then referring directly to the prosecutors in the "clean hands" investigation, she said: *"You Gherardo Colombo, who mistrusted Giovanni, why did you go to his funeral? Giovanni died in the bitter knowledge that his colleagues considered him a traitor. And the final injustice inflicted on him was right here in Milan, when they sent him a rogatory request from Switzerland without the attachments. He called me and said: 'They don't even trust the head of penal affairs'..."* The second speech is the one included in Chiaromonte's book of memoirs, which I will cite a few pages further on.

With Martelli, we had to overcome daily the diffidence and prejudiced belief that this government was incapable of conducting a resolute battle against the Mafia. Falcone's theories could never have coincided with those of two ministers in the Andreotti government. In those June days in 1992, Professor Mario Patrono, a member of the CSM from 1990 to 1994, asserted to the contrary that there was convergence between Falcone's ideas and those of the Ministers of Internal Affairs and Justice. The innovative will of the State *"in reality, can be seen in the reply given by the State, not by a single individual, in dealing with the instruments of repression in order to make a radical change in the fight against organized crime: its awareness of having to face the complexity of the Mafia phenomenon in a coordinated, decisive, and global fashion with a level of determination and preparation at least equal to those of organized crime: the new system for gathering evidence, which tends to transform penal trials from parlor games (not an Italian parlor and certainly not a Sicilian one) into a tool that searches out the truth; the laws governing informers, which in the fight against the Mafia constitute a fundamental element; electronic surveillance, and the activities of undercover agents".*

The attack against innovations was not aimed solely at blocking the establishment of the DNA, but was aimed directly at preventing Falcone's nomination as Anti-Mafia National Public Prosecutor in the case parliament converted the legislative decree.

The left-wing councillors belonging to the Magistrates' Internal Board of Supervisors said they had absolutely no intention of voting for Falcone and that they would instead support the candidature of the public prosecutor of Locri, Agostino Cordova. The reasons for their choice were exactly those recalled by

Boccassini and by Chiaromonte. Falcone had become an enemy, he had agreed to come to Rome and to collaborate with Martelli, as general director, to set up a sort of State prosecutor's office dependent on the executive, of which the establishment of the National Anti-Mafia Division was a precursor. Franco Coccia from the Left Democratic Party (PDS), Gianfranco Viglietta from the Democratic Judiciary, and Alfonso Amatucci from the Green Party, had already voted against Falcone in the CSM commission. Alessandro Pizzorusso, a board member of the CSM, who had been elected upon indication of the PDS, wrote an article published in the "Unità" newspaper on 12 March 1992, listing all the reasons why Falcone should not head the DNA. Without mincing his words, he wrote: *"from what has been said, it appears, I think evident, that if in the current situation his professional skills are not rewarded as they deserve, this would not be due solely to viciousness, or underhanded initiative by his adversaries"*. This type of language was clearly intended to act as a warning.

The almost certain failure of Falcone's nomination, and the CSM's encroaching choice, heightened my concerns not only that the wrong choice would be made, but also that the person responsible for launching such a delicate, and at the same time complicated entity, apart from his or her professional qualities, risked being someone sceptical of the DNA's usefulness and potential. I therefore decided to write a confidential letter to the deputy chairman of the Magistrate's Board, Giovanni Galloni, asking him to share it with the Board. In the letter, tried to explain why the Minister of Internal Affairs felt it was his institutional duty to point out, to the entire board, the sensitivity of the choice and the reasons that motivated him to call to their attention to the existence of a certain "reason of State" that pointed in favour of

Falcone's nomination. I would have liked to have made this letter public, but I don't have a copy of it and I trust that the CSM, sooner or later, will do so.

It was necessary to accelerate and intensify repressive actions against the Mafia and the parliament had already approved the government's proposal to establish two new entities that were meant to operate, within full respect of the judiciary's autonomy, in great harmony and convergence. To establish these two new entities, coherently with the spirit, but also with the letter of instituting laws, it seemed to me opportune, within the limits of circumstances, that the CSM's choice for National Public Prosecutor and that the Minister of Internal Affair's choice for director of the DIA should share the same ideas and show a high level of professionalism acknowledged also by the international community, not to mention a person who had already been involved in productive collaboration in anti-Mafia investigations. I was referring specifically to the preliminary investigations for the Palermo maxi-trial, which had helped us to gain insight into the establishment of the DNA and the DIA. Feeling uneasy, also due to the absence of any signs of a change in the CSM's orientation, I thought it would be useful to meet the CSM board members elected upon indication of the Christian Democrats, in a social setting, together with Falcone and Deputy Enzo Binetti. I was motivated strictly by "reasons of State" and certainly not by reasons of friendship since, contrary to many, I have never claimed to be Falcone's friend, even though we worked together. Deputy-Chairman Galloni immediately declined the invitation. The meeting took place at the restaurant inside the Hôtel de la Ville in Rome. All three board members confirmed that, apart from their own votes, Falcone's nomination would never manage to obtain a majority vote. Then, except for Professor Giuseppe

Ruggiero, the other two made it clear that they would not be willing to vote for Falcone, citing reasons that were substantially the same as those expressed by his enemies. Falcone was quite upset, so much so that at the end of the dinner, I felt impelled to apologize to him, above all, for the reasons given to oppose his nomination.

Working against Falcone was the lingering biased refusal to accept the idea of the entity itself. Thus, preventing Falcone from being the first public prosecutor represented in itself a clear indication of who would be chosen for the position. To a great extent, it was an ideological campaign. The day the legislative decree was approved by the Council of Ministers, the judges' board met in Rome for the general assembly. The assembly's comments were concise: *"an illegal entity* (it had been constituted by law! N/A*), incredible, and contrary to principles in force"*. I was extremely puzzled that an outstanding judge from Piedmont such as Mario Cicala, general secretary of the association, with a great sense of State and institutional duty, would go so far as to make a similar statement: *"if we had put forward a simple proposal, we would have justly been attacked by political forces, as being nostalgic for judge sheriffs who don't respect the executive"*. Edmondo Bruti Liberati, from the Democratic Judiciary also warned of: *"the risks of an enormous concentration of power in the hands of the Anti-Mafia National Public Prosecutor"*.

Falcone, showing great restraint, limited his comments to the "Republica" columnist Mario Pirani, to: *"in the judiciary, there are two opposing concepts: those who sustain that each judge is able to carry out every type of investigation and those, such as myself, who believe it is an illusion that by these means they can achieve effective trial results against organized crime on a national or international scale"*.

The Anti-Mafia Investigative Division

The establishment of the DIA also met with substantial opposition from within the system, but this received less media coverage.

During the Anti-Mafia Commission hearing held on 28 October 2010, Senator Achille Serra, the Milan Police Commissioner during the establishment of the DIA, recalled that all of the heads of police forces were opposed to the idea of setting up the Anti-Mafia Investigative Division because, among other reasons, they feared it would jeopardize the continued existence of the special police corps (SCO, RIS and GICO). The criticism, as recalled by Senator Serra, arose at the very first hint of an intention to create an intelligence and investigate body specialized in the fight against the Mafia. At the same anti-Mafia hearing, my Cabinet head Lauro, who is today a senator and member of the commission, confirmed Senator Serra's testimony providing further details.

On the same day the legislative decree was approved by the Council of Ministers, Prefect Parisi asked to see me together with Prefect Lauro, to express his intention of resigning as Head of Police, since he had been called, on my behalf, to mediate between the top operational levels of security forces, precisely due to the establishment of the DIA. I replied to Prefect Parisi, to whom I had always shown the greatest respect due to his exceptional professional skills, that although we may have had our differences of opinion, servants of the State have no other choice than to respect the law and work towards the best possible implementation of the new investigative entity, placing at its disposal the best men available and, above all, remaining true to the aims for which it had been established.

In the days preceding the Council of Ministers' meeting, I had discussed the project with the heads of security forces and had acknowledged some of their concerns by explaining, once again, the reasons for the need and urgency to carry out the project. To avoid further pressure, the final text of the legislative decree was drafted by the Cabinet and the legislative office and kept secret until the Council session. It was sent to the heads of police forces only after it was signed by the Head of State!

While Parisi kept his dissent private, the "La Repubblica" newspaper published an interview, two days after the Council of Ministers' decision, with the General Commander of the Carabinieri Military Police Force, General Antonio Viesti, who announced, without hesitation, the Carabinieri's total opposition to the DIA's establishment. After reading the interview, I immediately called the general, reminding him that he had expressed opposition, as head of the Carabinieri Military Police, to a law of the State. Indeed, the regulations of a legislative decree go into effect immediately after its signature by the President of the Republic and publication in the Official Journal. For this reason, unless the general intended to hand in his resignation, I demanded that he issue an official press release confirming his loyalty, and that of the Carabinieri, to the law and to upholding its application. Less than an hour after my phone call, press agencies were publishing the "scoop" of the General Commander's communiqué, true to the Carabiniere's motto: *"nei secoli fedele"* (Forever Faithful).

During the decree's conversion into law, all of the reservations and concerns, and reasons for the opposition, which had already been expressed in its early stages, were raised in parliament. The most significant criticism was directed at the specific mission of the DIA (an intelligence agency and not a fourth judiciary police force, even though the DIA would be able to carry out investigative activities), and the selection of personnel. In the initial stage, it would necessarily have to rely on resources from the three police forces, but later, it would set up its own autonomous selection and training systems. Furthermore, there was the fate of the three special corps, set up with similar aims, and the need to eliminate the Anti-Mafia High Commission. After some amendments, which did not significantly alter the contents of the provision, the legislative decree was converted into law.

14.1.4 The fourth pillar: follow the money

The growth in criminal revenues progressively forced the Mafia to create for itself a professional organization capable of laundering money and operating on financial markets to manage legal business activities. This evolution in the criminal organization was carried out simultaneously with the great technological and financial changes that brought about the globalization of markets, with increasingly fewer rules and checks. Greatly facilitating the new forms of Mafia operations was the existence of so-called tax havens, indispensable to criminal logistics.

It has taken some time, but sovereign States and international organizations have finally realized the need for adequate measures, to intervene at the crucial moment when money from criminal activities is transferred to legal ones. Indeed, once it crosses the "border", it becomes increasingly difficult for State authorities to intervene.

To strike at the enormous accumulation of criminal wealth, it has been necessary to confiscate Mafioso holdings even before the judiciary has made a final ruling, with the so-called freezing of assets and requisitions. This measure has revealed itself to be one of the most efficient in curbing Mafia power and, in the past few years, has been used effectively in Italy.

With the globalization of financial markets, anti-money laundering tactics represent one of the most urgent items for the agendas of the United Nations, the International Monetary Fund, the OCSE, and the World Bank. What we are dealing with is one of the most important omissions of top level international organizations and the consequences have been increasingly grave. Organized crime represents one of the most important Achille's heels of globalization.

Falcone considered these reasons, motivating us to attack the Mafia's wealth, to be decisive. He always used to say: *"Let's follow the money, let's follow its trail and you'll see that we'll be able to defeat the Mafia better"*.

The measures of the fourth pillar of our strategy were conceived on the basis of this reasoning.

On this front, we had the crucial support of the Guardia di Finanza (Italian Finance Police) and investigations carried out by criminal finance and computer technology experts who had begun to publish important studies in that period, such as Luigi Rey, acting Chairman of ISTAT (Central Institute of Statistics) at the time, and Professor Ada Collidà. General Ramponi, General Commander of Finance Police, who provided me with precious support in those days, informed me that, for some years, the corps had been carrying out a series of studies and had been using computer experts to draft a bill on money laundering. The text had already been submitted to the Internal Affairs and Finance Commissions of the two branches of parliament. Ramponi and I continued to worked together on many other occasions, evaluating various options. I must also mention the decisive contribution of invaluable experts, both in the Carabinieri and in the Police, to the drafting of regulations. We decided to start with a regulation aimed at banning the use of cash, to introduce the traceability of all financial transactions, calling for collaboration from credit institutions, financial institutions, and notaries. We knew fully well that any intervention on the domestic market would be, by itself, weak.

The transfer of money from illegal markets to legal ones was facilitated by the development of computer technologies and the creation of a global capital market. In real time, money could be transferred through financial and banking institutions located in different continents, and above all, to tax havens, without leaving a trace of the transactions by making dozens and dozens of computer transfers. This is why the effectiveness of national anti-money laundering regulations were dependent on the introduction of European and international money-laundering ones that would force States to comply through underwriting international agreements. In those years, we were substantially taking the first tentative steps towards setting up money laundering regulations and computer tools capable of working with one another.

The gray area and white collar workers

What the experts' reports showed, however, was that the Mafia was recruiting a significant number of white collar workers, knowingly or unknowingly, to achieve a high level of professionalism in managing capital transfers and business affairs.

In order to obtain parliamentary approval for the anti-money laundering measures, we had to overcome issues that were more of a technical rather than a political nature, contrary to when we had tried to adopt the other anti-Mafia measures. Most of the problems dealt, above all, with the need not to impose too many restrictions on market freedoms, creating distortions which would be harmful, foremost for our country, if we were not successful in simultaneously achieving the introduction of international regulations, shared by other States. Taking advantage of the prestige and authority of the Treasury Minister, Guido Carli, and the Governor of the Bank of Italy, Carlo Azelio Ciampi, we urged for bilateral and multilateral talks to transform the principles contained in the solemn documents approved at various international conferences into regulations and action. On several occasions, I met President emeritus Ciampi for dinner at my friend Mario Pendinelli's house, to continue discussing this matter.

Some significant progress has been made over the years, but as the recent financial crisis has shown, the regulations and checks on international financial transactions are still too weak, notwithstanding the statements that have been made at various G8 and G20 summits since 2008. For example, even today, transactions can be made on derivatives by phone, leaving no trace. Compare this with the traceability of transactions which, instead, are required of a pensioner with an income just on the threshold of poverty!

After reaching an understanding with the Treasury Minister and the Governor of the Bank of Italy, we agreed on a text for the first anti-money laundering law. To a great extent, we adopted the initial proposal of the Finance Police, except for the creation of a data bank on all banking and financial transactions: what the newspapers in those days referred to as the "brain". In its stead, similarly to the Anglo-Saxon model, we relied on the collaboration of officials at banking and financial institutions to monitor suspicious money transfers by notifying supervisory bodies of any transactions which seemed suspect. This was a voluntary solution which was not very successful, and was a fallback choice with respect to the data bank, which had been demonized in the name of banking secrecy and, in particular, due to its potential effectiveness in fighting tax evasion!

Beyond the money-laundering law

There are still too many interests which hinder the state's efficient intervention on money-laundering and criminal finance. This intervention needs more international rules and regulations on transparency, on the subjective liability of individuals, but also the objective one of society, in the fight against corruption and, no less importantly, in the ban against fighting tax havens.
Banks and financial markets have always prospered in the shadows of secrecy, of silence, of ambiguity, and of widespread negligence. Attempts to introduce restrictions have always been defeated and it has been presumed that every strict law on transparency, necessary for the fight against the criminal economy, should be limited because of its adverse effects on legal financial markets and the economy in general. It has always been claimed that these restrictions represent "fetters and constraints" that hinder the freedom of banking and financial agents to achieve maximum profits. It's been years, since the crisis exploded in 2008, that we keep talking about ethical conduct, transparency rules, and the abolition of banking secrecy and tax havens. But we are still, notwithstanding the good intentions of many leaders, starting from the President of the United States, at the stage of noble declarations which do not lead to the effective regulation

of financial markets.

The need for individual safety, balanced against the dangers of terrorism, led many citizens around the world to accept restrictions on personal freedoms, because they were necessary to guarantee security: from the simplest, such as airport controls, to the most complex, which invade, to a greater extent, the sphere of privacy. But evidently, the protection of the secrecy on money transfers is more important than personal privacy: any restriction on the complete freedom of transactions and economic and financial operations is rendered difficult, if not rejected, as being dangerous. Also the fight against corruption needs more effective tools to prevent the money gained through illicit activities from being put to use. All those wishing to profit from crime covet secrecy, silence, and opacity, not transparency.

Some international findings on criminal financial networks should be read more carefully, to spark a more effective reaction in public opinion against white collar crime.

14.1.5 The fifth pillar: changes to the code of criminal procedure?

I have already mentioned that, after the Capaci massacre, we decided with Martelli to finalize straightaway, without waiting for the formation of the new government following the elections in 1992, the package of regulations we had planned in the war against the Mafia. When Falcone was still alive, we had begun to study some changes to the criminal procedural code, especially with regards to evidence gathering, and to the Gozzini Law on prison regimes for Mafiosi.

In the days immediately following the massacre, we were

supposed to have met with Falcone to propose the changes to the code and the Gozzini Law (the fourth pillar of our strategy), to carry out the establishment of the DIA and the DNA (second pillar) and, at the same time, to verify the applications of laws on the links between the Mafia and politics.

Until that date, 23 May 1992, we thought a further examination was necessary, also in order to overcome growing opposition to any minimum proposal for a change in the criminal procedural code.

In March 1992, the election campaign was in full swing and, for this reason, we decided to prepare the measures and wait for an opportune moment to present them in parliament. Unfortunately, the Capaci massacre convinced us that we could not wait for the new government that would be formed after the election of the new Head of State. We had to provide an immediate and unequivocal response to the massacre and terrorist-Mafia attack. We realized that the Mafia would not stop at Falcone. To the contrary, we had clear indications that the massacres would continue. We had no other option than to proceed with the legislative decree, going even further than the regulations we had discussed with Falcone, to make these measures a more adequate response to the challenge launched by the Mafia on the State. It was no longer a time for consultations and negotiations. With Martelli and our collaborators, we locked ourselves up in a room and decided on the final version of the regulations to include in the legislative decree.

With great insensitivity, ignorance, and maybe even bad faith, some newspapers asserted that those regulations were dripping with blood and that we had just been waiting for the Capaci massacre to be able to adopt them. These cruel comments distressed me profoundly, to the point where I was forced to respond harshly: *"I think that saying our decree is stained with blood is a vulgar and, above all, unjust accusation... These measures are the result of a strategy inaugurated a year and a half ago ...".*

Paradoxically, accusations came from both those, on the one hand, who stated they were against the merits of the measure, and also its unconstitutionality and, on the other hand, by those who judged that it came too late. Incredible!

During the preparatory stage of the provision, at the beginning of 1992, we were urged by political representatives from both the majority and the opposition, during the course of informal consultations, to exert caution and careful consideration in making modifications to the then recently adopted code of criminal procedure. As I have mentioned several times, the Capaci massacre forced us to resort to a legislative decree as our procedure. Realistically, we could not file a bill which would only signal good and general intentions and nothing more, which the Mafia would have interpreted as submissiveness. If we wanted to act, there was no alternative to a legislative decree. Naturally, many negative opinions were expressed about the legitimacy of our outgoing government being able to adopt such a tool.

The powers of the government in charge, strictly speaking, would not have permitted the adoption of such a legislative decree, due to some of its contents which were of dubious constitutionality. Martelli and I spoke with Andreotti, who was willing to call a Council of Ministers as soon as we were ready to submit the text. Andreotti pledged to introduce the measure, urging his colleagues not to open a debate on its merits which would have complicated the urgent approval of the proposals. Indeed, at the Council of Ministers, Andreotti limited himself to stating that the Ministers of Internal Affairs and Justice, in light of the grave emergency, had requested the presentation of those changes by decree and were willing to assume full political responsibility.

The President of the Republic was also consulted to obtain his pre-emptive support for the measure. To this end, I relied on the help of my friend Michele Zolla, Scalfaro's political advisor with whom I had worked at the Commission of Ministers for the Mezzogiorno prior to our reciprocal election to Parliament. His positive reply came immediately, notwithstanding the President's many commitments in tackling the tough job of forming a new government.

As we had envisioned, as soon as the decree was approved and made public, there were numerous objections regarding the constitutionality of some of the regulations and substantial opposition to changes to some important points of the criminal procedure code, which had just recently been put into effect. Some distinguished party representatives from the majority told me, quite bluntly, that they were opposed to the text, and informed me that if the proposed version were not substantially modified in parliament, there was no way it would be converted. My friend Giuseppe Gargani, the DC party responsible for justice, advised me not to insist on a rapid approval procedure and to re-submit the matter to the new government, leaving it up to them whether to insist on that text or, better, to re-formulate it taking into account the criticism coming from the judiciary, lawyers, associations, and representatives from the majority itself. A few days before the via D'Amelio massacre, in an official press release issued by the PDS group, the opposition Senator Cesare Salvi also expressed opposition on the basis of unconstitutionality, because the decree, he said, *"introduces various regulations that are in contrast to the Constitution, in particular for the changes to criminal procedures regarding evidence gathering and the powers of criminal investigation division which are in contrast with the guarantees of defence rights"*. The bar announced a national strike and the lawyer Mario Casalinuovo, vice-president of the penal chamber, claimed that we had *"sunk back to Medieval laws"*. Furthermore, many sectors of the judiciary voiced doubts about the decree's regulations, starting from the National Judges' Association, which pronounced itself against it, limiting itself to comments on some of the regulations. The press in those days continued to publish declarations of war which gave every indication of the rough time we would have in obtaining parliamentary approval, to the point where its conversion could not be taken for granted.

If we were to stop reading the parliamentary acts and the press on the date of the via D'Amelio massacre, we would harbour no doubts that the parliamentary result would be negative. However, it was difficult for us to fully understand why the controversy was so bitter and why there was not the slightest margin for agreement on opportune changes that would not alter the basic aims and functions of the provision. The objective convergence of opposition from various quarters was clearly aimed, this time, at obtaining the withdrawal of the decree or a ruling on the unconstitutionality of some of its regulations, which we considered to be indispensable, and which, if cancelled, would have robbed the provision of any significance.
In this openly hostile environment, we took the first parliamentary

steps towards the decree's conversion, during the course of which, even those who in the previous legislature had been staunch supporters of our strategy, now appeared hesitant. We sorely missed Falcone's wise advice! The Anti-Mafia Commission ended its mandate and its outgoing President, Chiaromonte, advised us against pushing to accelerate the approval procedure, urging us to leave a decision on its merits to the new government.

But when the via D'Amelio massacre happened, just as when the Capaci massacre occurred, the scenario changed and the parliament, converted the decree, in the version presented by Martelli and myself, in a question of a few days.

Chairman Pisanu, again referring to the hearing in October 2010, asked me: *"The decree, known as the Scotti–Martelli decree, that of 8 June 1992, issued therefore before the via D'Amelio massacre, how was it received by political forces for its subsequent conversion into law? Was there opposition?"* I replied immediately: *"I tell you quite frankly that Borsellino's death was instrumental in obtaining approval for the conversion law of that decree; unfortunately, without it, we would never have obtained approval, considering the across-the-board opposition from lawyers, judges, and parliamentarians from both Houses, who had expressed, maybe even in good faith, ... their strong dissent".*

14.1.6 The sixth pillar: control over the territory and the rapport between the Mafia, institutions, and politics

In the press release issued by the National Judges' Association

on 8 June 1992, there was emphasis on a specific point: *"a prerequisite necessary for the effective fight against the Mafia is the severing of links between politics, business, and organized crime"*.
This aspect highlighted by the judges was, from the very start of my work at the Viminale, my greatest concern.

The most sensitive and complex issue we had to deal with in the war against the Mafia, and not only in our country, was, and still is, organized crime's establishment in and control over a territory and its ability and power to infiltrate and manipulate institutions in the management of public affairs.

The power of bosses has always been founded on its ability to rule over a territory, ensuring through violence, *omertà* (the code of silence), and subjection, the loyalty of its members, but also the subjugation of citizens, and the acquiescence, if not the complicity, of public authorities. Control over local institutions, political parties, and their single components, has always been a specific feature of the Sicilian Mafia. Over time, this feature has spread and influenced all types of crime that have links to the Sicilian Mafia, changing their *modus operandi*. The names of the various Mafia organizations differ, but their distinctive nature remains that of a rapport with public authorities to guarantee their ability to carry out criminal operations in a climate of illegality, corruption, and blackmailing. Therefore, the way it controls its territory and the way it influences political and institutional life constitute the minimum common denominator of all criminal organizations, at a global level.

I have already underlined how the repression of crime must go hand in hand with the converging efforts of all components of politics, foremost of political parties, but also of civil society and religious communities, to raise a barrier against every form of Mafia infiltration and manipulation. The selection of the ruling class must take into account the alert vigilance of all concerned to prevent the so-called gray area of legality and illegality from growing and contaminating the life of any community. When vigilance is lacking, the contamination becomes real, planting deep roots in a culture of widespread illegality to the point where the lines between what is legal and what is illegal are blurred, and the Mafia acquires control over the public, and even the private life, of citizens.

This is why it was indispensable for a democratic State to introduce strict regulations to its legal system to combat any form of Mafia infiltration into public bodies and into any aspect of politics. This was a stopgap solution, limited in time, and as such could achieve positive results only if the State's repression was accompanied by heightened awareness and a sense of duty on the part of all those responsible for educating and selecting the ruling class, and all honest citizens.

The starting point, also in order to lend credibility to educational activities and collective responsibility in selecting a new ruling class, was to adopt legislature that would contribute to blocking Mafia control over territorial institutions. It was a tough undertaking to intervene on matters that affected civil liberty rights, politics, and the sovereignty of the people. In the application of regulations to dissolve town councils corrupted and influenced by the Mafia, it was necessary for the DIA to simultaneously carry out continuous monitoring activities, to give local heads of public security the ability to interpret the activities of criminal organizations properly. To achieve concrete results, we decided to strengthen the powers of the Regional Committee for Public Order and Security, delegating powers of the Ministry of Internal Affairs, such as the National Authority for Public Security, to the prefects of regional capitals. In this manner, the committees would be able to implement effective plans of control over the territory taking advantage of the collaboration between all existing police forces, including the local police, bolstered by a higher authority capable of making final decisions.

The provisions

The first provision, and to some extent the most complex, was the legislative decree regarding the dissolution of local councils showing clear signs of infiltration from organized crime. This was a preventive measure, adopted on the basis of an administrative inspection carried out independently from judicial authorities. The crux of the problem was the need to reconcile respect for the sovereignty of the people, and therefore, the free expression of votes, with a guarantee of the freedom of elected officials to act on behalf of their electors. If a town council was not in a position to freely carry out its functions because organized crime had succeeded in corrupting it, it would have to undergo a period of compulsory administration before a new election could be held. Naturally, it was necessary to put in place an administrative procedure capable of carrying out inspections in an extremely meticulous and accurate way, in order to ensure that the President of the Republic's decree rested on a solid foundation of legitimacy and objectivity, free from any type of biased political influence.

It was not an easy issue to resolve and the constitutionality of the solution went under close scrutiny by both Houses and, subsequently, also by the Constitutional Court.

There were many objections to the provisions in parliament and to these were added those regarding the legislative decree on the ineligibility for office and the expulsion of town councillors.

In the brief period I headed the Ministry of Internal Affairs, at the first application of that law, I proposed that the Council of Ministers dissolve dozens of town councils, without batting an eye, even those belonging to my electoral college, and even on the eve of parliamentary elections. I gave strict orders, through my Cabinet head Lauro, to all the prefects of the Republic and, in particular, to the prefects of the Mezzogiorno regions (Sicily, Calabria, Puglia and Campania), to proceed heedless of who was involved. At risk was the credibility of the government's new anti-Mafia policy itself. There were many protests from many colleagues, parliamentarians, and senators, not to mention local political representatives who controlled party membership and voting blocks, directed not only at the minister pro tem, but also at my principal collaborators at the Viminale. In particular, some of my parliamentary colleagues mistook the strict application of the new legislation as an attack on popular sovereignty. Actually, the dissolutions put an end to the consolidated balances of local power corrupted by the Mafia, unscrupulous speculation, and the patronage system.

Events have revealed some of the deficiencies of the regulation, which have been dealt with, for the most part, in subsequent legislation, even though experience has shown that further modifications are needed. The first concerns the activities of the commissioner, called to remove any possible organizational causes for corruption in order to proceed, before going back to the urns, to a re-organization of administrative bodies and the rotation of relevant bureaucratic heads, who have often turned out to be responsible for Mafia infiltration.

This initial flaw in the regulation resulted in many cases in which the council had to be dissolved a second time because, notwithstanding compulsory administration, severing Mafia links entirely had not been possible. The second dealt, and still deals today, with the weakness of the efforts of political parties to renew the ruling class and to apply the anti-Mafia ethical code in their nominations. I immediately realized that these could be flaws and called the attention of party secretaries to this possibility. The dissolution of a town council represented an extreme measure, which should have been accompanied by a plan on the part of political parties to favor the emergence of a new ruling class, with selection procedures capable of preventing possible Mafia infiltration. In the '90's, there were many examples of Mafia intervention when, no longer trusting party representatives, the Mafia had aimed at directly including men under their close control in electoral lists, also making use of civil lists.

Government supervisory bodies could not intervene sporadically or randomly: their efforts had to be effective and targeted. Thus, they had to be based on constant monitoring with a comprehensive vision of the dynamics of organized crime. This is why I stressed the importance of intelligence activities capable of providing prefects with adequate input to access local bodies on the basis of critical indicators.

It was evident that a battle against Mafia control over the territory would be a very difficult path to take, but also the only one possible if we were to succeed in restoring legality to local institutions and not abandoning the political class to itself, impotent in combating intimidating pressure and often, criminal violence. It was difficult for an honest local administrator in a small town to escape from criminal blackmailing, if he could not count on the support of security forces, civil society, and the leadership of national parties.

It is difficult to be born and live in "Gomorra", and deal with the Mafia without the support of the community.

The ineligibility and expulsion of administrators

The laws on ineligibility and the expulsion of local administrators corrupted by the Mafia were conceived as an aid against the Mafia's attempts to gain control, also at a territorial level, and were not intended to be punitive. The parliamentary debate on these measures was extremely interesting and included a speech by a consummate jurist, Giuliano Amato, who called everyone's attention to the need for rigor, but at the same time, respect for the freedom of each citizen to participate in political life, especially when, in accordance with the constitution, he should be considered innocent until proven guilty.

The regulations on ineligibility, suspension, and expulsion from office were also conceived as tools to support party efforts to intervene positively on transparency and the choice of the ruling class. Without firm determination on the part of parties, it would be difficult to reinforce a ruling class capable of resisting Mafia pressure, without having to carry out heroic deeds. Today as yesterday, we are faced with an essentially political issue, which calls into play the direct responsibility of national party leadership, that cannot remain oblivious to local political events, closing an eye to reality only out of political interest.

The decline of parties and forms of anti-politics give rise to the formation of local civil lists that often mask opaque and unsavoury interests. No one contests the so-called *'thousand flowers'* manifestations of autonomy. In areas where there is strong pressure from the Mafia, however, it is impossible to shirk responsibility for a phenomenon which is often the result of the absence or lack of politics, or its detachment from society, creating those voids of power which are exploited by the Mafia. Thus, no one is exempt from respecting freedoms, but neither is it possible to close an eye to situations of criminal sovereignty.

Whatever electoral laws are adopted, in the end, it all comes back to the political question of the selection, training, and transparency of the ruling class.

Chapter 15

15.1 The alarm of 1992

The Mafia's reaction to the initiatives we adopted was not long in coming: it became immediately apparent during some Mafia trial preliminary hearings that there were internal disagreements between clans. The majority were pushing for a terrorist-massacre reaction with sensational attacks capable of blackmailing the State and intimidating the public while at the same time reassuring criminal organization members that the strength of "cosa nostra" was immutable. The Mafia high command did, in fact, commission the murder of some important figures as a signal to various quarters. Firstly, to those sectors of the Sicilian political sphere that had shown new and strong determination to fight organized crime, beginning with the regional administrations of Piersanti Mattarella and of Rino Nicolosi, to the "spring of

Palermo", and the new Sicilian Christian Democrat faction, except for Vito Ciancimino.

In the last months of 1991, Prefect Parisi submitted several confidential reports to my attention regarding the "cosa nostra's" plans to carry out sensational attacks, including an imminent Mafia counterattack, and even a plan to destabilize the entire political system.

After a few months, also in light of corroborative information from the secret service, the Head of Police proposed putting security forces on alert through prefects and police chiefs. Parisi would take charge of keeping the heads of security forces constantly informed. We agreed for the time being, not to inform any other government authorities, not even the President of the Republic, of the specific preventive measures adopted. Thus, in a series of confidential meetings with party leaders, I limited myself to expressing serious concern about the disturbing signs of possible destabilization. Our caution was dictated by the national political situation which was at an extremely delicate stage. It was the eve of the general elections held following the referendum on single preferential voting, which had met with strong opposition from citizens and, as a result, had widened the gap between people and politics even further.

15.2 The institutional political crisis worsens

The beginning of the '90's was, therefore, characterized by increasing political turmoil and a growing crisis in the credibility of the ruling class. In particular, the second half of 1991 was extremely turbulent, with growing tensions in the alliance between the Christian Democrats (DC), the Socialist Party (PSI), and the so-called minor parties. The nature and origin of these contrasts were not clear given that during the DC convention in 1989, resulting in Forlani's election as party secretary, the DC and Craxi had reached an agreement, referred to in the press as the *CAF pact* (Craxi, Andreotti, Forlani).

This agreement had rapidly given rise to the De Mita government crisis in July, leading to Andreotti's return as head of the executive, under the illusion that this would eliminate one of the most important causes of tension between the DC and the PSI. However, the agreement was strong enough to overcome the difficulties of the 1991 government crisis, when Craxi, Andreotti and Forlani opposed Cossiga's proposal for early elections and when, as a result of Berlusconi's pressure on Craxi, they had no hesitation in breaking off the traditional alliance with the Republican Party. The consequences of this, on the eve of elections, turned out to be disastrous for the center-left.

Notwithstanding the tactical agreement between the DC and the PSI, the strategic policies of the two parties continued to diverge and there were reciprocal signs of mistrust. During a lull, the two parties seemed to be more intent on consolidating their respective positions of power by gaining control over a vast network of public bodies and companies built up over the past decade, than in dealing with the storm that was gathering.

In the eyes of citizens, the parties were no longer fulfilling their traditional role of mediating between institutions and society, not to mention, of defending public interests. This was a moment when the public was demanding institutional innovation and strategic policies unfettered by the ideological prejudices of the past, which had become the main obstacle to the country's modernization. Meanwhile, the parties concerned themselves with reproducing, within each party, costly government bodies with departments, commissions, and offices, thus leading to the degenerative practice of illicit party funding.

Italian society had matured a need for autonomy and participation. At that point, the public rejected the parties' tendency to occupy increasingly vast areas of influence which affected the free functioning of civic and financial bodies. Many short-sighted politicians were astonished by the high voter turnout for the electoral referendum and the landslide victory of "yes" votes. What was obvious was, that at the first possible opportunity, citizens had voted in favor of a referendum considered to be a picklock into the system and a means of overriding political parties, which had shown themselves to be incapable of self-reform after the collapse of the Berlin wall.

I am not writing these pages in hindsight. Even back in 1984, after the Christian Democrats resounding electoral defeat in 1983, which was misinterpreted and judged to be just something that happens, I decided to submit my candidature for party secretary. My aim was to call the delegates' attention to the need for a thorough reform of political conduct and of its rapport with civil society. In my speech at the XVI Christian Democratic convention, I said: *"We are facing a transformation, a revolution, in which society is claiming its autonomy from the State, is formulating and creating its own system. It is progressing towards, and has almost achieved, that process which began at an economic level, at the dawn of industrialization, and has now extended to all fields of civil and social life ... The political fact that we cannot ignore is that a society of this type is not raw material for our manipulation. Politics must engage in dialog with this society, look for and find points of convergence, organize new channels of communication to create political loyalty and unity of a new kind. A new social pact must once again blossom between the political and social orders, after a period in which, for too long, politics has looked for its security in a pact of subjugation and dominion....We must engage in a great act of freedom, allowing all citizens access to all public offices. Most public offices, and the most important ones, have now been denied public guarantees of access in their assignment, and are instead allocated through the detrimental and biased system which we euphemistically call "lottizzazione". This system of divvying up public offices between parties brings to mind those pre-modern forms of State which were founded on the private use of public assets and public positions. Here is an area in which we can give clear proof of our modernity and our sense of a State ruled by law. Let's give back all public offices to all citizens – let's not subject Italians to discrimination based on party loyalties, or worse, personal ones. Let's value actual professional qualities and skills, merit and experience, spirit of dedication and loyalty of service, and we will have freed Italian society from one of its plagues. We will have made the most decisive and productive State reform which it is in our power to make[34]".*

Instead, what we have actually done in Italy is codify the private use of institutions through a party "spoil system".

Eight years had passed since the convention and the situation had gotten even worse after the fall of the Berlin wall, which had

---

[34] 10 *Superare la sconfitta e riannodare i fili della nostra iniziativa nella società.* Vincenzo Scotti's speech at the XVI Christian Democratic Convention, 1984. From: *Nuove frontiere per la politica,* by Vincenzo Scotti, Franco Angeli, 1989.

misled many majority party leaders into believing that their electoral positions had been bolstered, given that history had judged Communism to be a failure. In November 1989, after the fall of the Berlin wall, the parties making up the government thought all they had to do was tip their hats to gain consensus.

Their attitude was one of arrogance. Everyone assumed wrongly that the post-communists were the only ones who needed to change. No one realized that we had come out of the "cold war" and so had lost one of the requisites for the forced political stability of our country and, with it, the continuity of electors' consensus to democratic parties. That stability, that is, which Indro Montanelli believed was assured with his famous exhortation to *"hold your nose, and vote DC"*.

The weak and unstable political context, of which I was fully aware, made the prospect of danger seem even more credible, forcing me to declare, without further delay, a State of alert.

15.3 The period of the alert

Therefore, in the first few months of 1992, I linked my assessment of the general political situation, which I knew to be fragile, to all the corroborative information that foretold, on the one hand, a violent response from the Mafia, and on the other, direct legal action against the most important government party leaders on grounds of illegal funding practices.

Despite the fact that the election campaign was in full swing, I felt it was my duty to adopt urgent measures. On the other hand, Parisi was urging me not to waste any more time, while my closest colleagues, starting with Prefect Lauro, advised me not to inform anyone of the measures we would adopt. In that period, I limited myself to providing institutional and political leadership and the public, with a realistic, and therefore, alarming picture of the situation. The general reception was one of great indifference, bordering on disbelief, under the illusion of political stability created by the election of a Christian Democrat as President of the Republic and Craxi's return as Prime Minister. I was even accused of being overly emotional and having a tendency to exaggerate the situation due to who knows what personal ambition, as proven by news stories of the time. For these reasons, I decided to assume full responsibility for the decision and this was the only time, in my longstanding service in government, that I failed to keep my colleague at the Justice Ministry, Martelli, informed. Indeed, when the news of the alert went public, Martelli openly disassociated himself from it. It was the only disagreement I had with him, in the almost two years we worked together.

Despite this climate of diffidence, disbelief, and to a certain extent, discredit, I stated in Parliament that I had no intention of changing my mind. Even today, at a distance of twenty years, I am still firmly convinced of the appropriateness and timeliness of that decision and the need for the subsequent implementation of urgent provisions which the dramatic events, occurring immediately after, have confirmed.

Therefore, I assumed responsibility for and defended my position openly in parliament, notwithstanding the fact that a Bolognese judge, who had sent me the text of "corroborating" anonymous statements beforehand (keeping its author's name secret from me) had leaked the name of its author to the press on the eve of my speech. It was a certain Ciolini, well-known in the Italian court system for dropping red herrings.

This triggered a campaign to discredit me, with accusations of unjustifiable alarmism in the midst of a troublesome election campaign. Even in the face of these accusations of imprudence, starting from Andreotti's disconcerting talk of a "fake alarm", I held firm in my determination. I stated that my decision was legitimate and based on other sources of institutional information than just Elio Ciolini's document. On the other hand, I was convinced that even that misleading document contained some reliable information, as is normally the case with works of counter-information intended to lead people down the wrong track.

Despite the Mafia murders of several eminent figures in the previous weeks, confirming the gravity of the situation, everyone in parliament, from both the majority and the opposition, practically abandoned me to face an organized campaign to discredit me all on my own. But I did not give up defending, together with the Head of Police, the reasons for the measures we adopted. Only the President of the Republic, Cossiga, after some initial and uneasy scepticism, followed by the urgent request for further clarification, gave me his full support in light of all the information in my possession.

Notwithstanding the electoral battle under way, the President of the Anti-Mafia Commission, Chiaromonte, and, to a certain extent, Violante, head of the PDS justice commission, as well as a group of better informed Christian Democrat parliamentarians, did not take part in the crossfire of accusations. In that period, and also later, they did not deny me their personal and political support, going beyond the logic of party alliances[35].

The current judiciary investigations into alleged bargaining and the Anti-Mafia Commission investigations oblige us to examine that episode in a new light, even though many still continue to underestimate it and reiterate the same opinions as before, just as if nothing later happened.

15.4 Called to respond in Parliament

On 20 March 1992, I clarified the chronological chain and logic of events before a joint meeting of the Constitutional Affairs and House and Senate Internal Commissions, from which I had requested an urgent hearing after the publication of the circulars.

The judges investigating the alleged bargaining with the Mafia have decided, opportunely, to have the entire "Radio Radicale" recording of my commission hearing transcribed. Indeed, to my

---

[35] "Fifty-nine Christian Democrat parliamentarians have so far signed Romano Baccarini's and Carlo Giovanardi's call to lend «the personal solidarity of DC parliamentarians to those who are exposed on the front lines of the fight against Mafia crime and may have the unpleasant feeling that their actions are taking place in a void, as has unfortunately happened in the past». The parliamentarians' signatures will be submitted to the Minister of Internal Affairs, Vincenzo Scotti. «We feel it is our duty – says the letter which the two promoters sent to their colleagues – to acknowledge that Scotti is fighting with great courage on the front lines of the fight against Mafia organized crime: on this occasion, together with Claudio Martelli, he has introduced and had approved a decree which is the first concrete response to the expectations of the public». Among the fifty-nine signatories were Francesco D'Onofrio, Pier Ferdinando Casini, Alberto Michelini, Gianfranco Aliveri, and Marco Ravaglioli" from: "Il Popolo" dated 27 June 1992.

knowledge, there is only a summarized report of that session in the acts of parliament. The details, as can be ascertained from the stenographic summary, are decisive in a case such as this one.

For now, therefore, I can only refer to the summarized report. The secretaries of the commissions summarized my statements as follows: *"In the last few months, several events took place which, even considered separately, gave rise to concerns and which, examined later in chronological order, created reasons for alarm. These were a series of threatening messages to various members of the state apparatus ... These events were occurring in the midst of an election campaign, in light of which, moreover, there had already been alarming signs of improper pressure, above all in the southern regions. To this were added signs of possible terrorist activities highlighted, among others, in Genoa by national political representatives. The seriousness of these events was mentioned, moreover, in the presented report, in accordance with article 11 of Law n. 801 dated 1977, by the Prime Minister to the parliamentary committee on information and security services and for State secrecy. Indeed, in this report, clearly on the basis of accurate objective information, what is highlighted is the destabilizing nature of the criminal attack, to the point where it endangered peaceful co-existence and respect for legality in our country. These threats arise in a context of intense socio-political dialectics, not devoid of harsh tones, considering that criminal organizations appear today to be particularly strong, notwithstanding the substantial efforts of security forces, also due to their deeply-rooted international ties ... Even the chairman of the parliamentary investigating commission on the Mafia phenomenon had stressed in his report the existence of a link between the fresh outbreak of Mafia attacks and the imminent elections. And finally, the offices of the SISDE issued a communiqué in which they expressed hopes for appropriate countermeasures which did not under-estimate the complicity between subversive fringes and crime, whose aim is to destabilize the country .... For these reasons, it attests to have convened, since February, meetings with prefects from regional seats* (to whom ministerial powers for public order and security were conferred, N/A) *and the national committee on public order and security, during which a careful examination of the situation was undertaken and the necessary measures were defined to ensure the adequate control of the territory, increasing police forces .... While these preventive measures were put into effect, the judiciary in Bologna, investigating the Bologna massacre, according to the procedure established by the repealed code of penal procedure, in virtue of the temporary regulations of the new code, submitted to the Ministry of Internal Affairs a document written in compliance with article 165ter. This initiative was based on the letter of a witness whose identity was withheld for investigative reasons, which contained information believed to be of a disturbing nature and, in any case, which deserved further investigation in order to establish its credibility. These statements referred to events aimed at destabilizing public order in Italy, some time between March and July* (a strange temporal coincidence, from the Lima crime to the Capaci and via D'Amelio massacres, A/N) *in a general framework which would have been determined at a meeting between members of the European right in Zagabria in September 1991. In light of such information, and on the basis of concerns raised by it on the part of the Head of Police, also in reference to events which took place in the first few months of that year, the minister felt it was his duty to notify once again the prefects, police commissioners, and general command of the Carabinieri and Finance Police to increase vigilance, with the aim of perceiving in a timely manner any further signs of danger. To this aim, the Head of Police informed the prefects of the contents of the document received by the Bolognese judiciary".*

A few days later, and after the alert: *"the same judge,* writes the compiler of the summarized account, *sent a further document, to which was attached another letter sent by the same witness, in which he confirmed the risk of destabilizing acts against individuals and state institutions. In this instance, the judge also made reference to the precedents of the witness himself, revealing at this point his name".*

Even though the report is summarized, the accuracy of the facts seem clear, and at a distance of twenty years!

"Just last Wednesday, wrote Calabrò in the "Corriere della Sera" on 21 March 1992, *when the first two circulars (one signed by Parisi, the other by Scotti himself) had already been sent out, the Viminale was informed by the Bolognese judge Leonardo Grassi (who in the preceding days had refused to reveal the informer's name on grounds of investigative secrecy) that the witness in question was a disreputable person: Elio Ciolini".*

15.5 Beyond the "fake" alarm

At the mere mention of his name, and ignoring the fact that people who send misleading messages often mix fragments of truth in with the false information, (which must always be read and verified scrupulously, using other information in one's possession to corroborate it), a controversy was sparked aimed at, as I mentioned previously, discrediting the initiative and dismissing the declared alert as overly alarmist. The object of the confrontation became, therefore, the unreliability of Ciolini's letter and my levity in making important decisions on the basis of a "fake". The parliamentary debate on my statements, unfortunately, continued until it was threadbare, and the newspapers referred to it as the minister's longest and bitterest day.

Despite my bitterness, I didn't give up, knowing the contents of all the documents and the thoroughness of the Department of Public Security's analysis, which had brought the Mafia's massacre strategy to my attention. I had already commented along these lines before the Anti-Mafia Commission on 17 March 1992, immediately after Lima's assassination. *"If there is anyone that thinks that what I'm saying is false,* I said in those hours, *I'm willing to resign, but I will not yield one step to intimidations"* ... *"I am a minister who has sworn loyalty to the Constitution and I have not given in to urgings to act differently, which have come from people near to me".*

While the joint House and Senate commissions, in practice, exaggerated the scope of my alarm and substantially maintained the line of a "fake" alarm or "dirty trick", (Giulio Maceratini), the parliamentary supervisory commission on secret services, to the contrary, appeared to be more cautious and concerned. At the end of the hearing, its chairman, Tarcisio Gitti, a distinguished parliamentarian from Brescia, stated jointly with the directors of SISDE and SISMI that: *"the events that have taken place are serious, the alarm of organized crime against public order is more than justified. Preventive measures, therefore, must be adequately strong".*

In parliament, Prefect Parisi stressed that there was a close relationship of cause and effect in the war against the Mafia: *"the arrests of members of the Madonia clan, later defeated, were followed by Libero Grassi's murder: then it was the turn of Judge Antonino Scopelliti. The dissolution of the Lamezia Terme town council was followed by the murder of Field Marshall Aversa, the author of the report submitted to the ministry which led to the decision to dissolve it".* And then: *"a similar initiative against another town council was followed by an explosion at the Tortorici police headquarters and the murders of Sebastiano Corrado, Salvo Lima, and Salvatore Gaglio".* To corroborate his analysis, Parisi submitted a lengthy dossier with information from an incredible number of dubious texts and anonymous letters, which however, all demonstrated an uncanny knowledge of the profiles of those to whom they were addressed.

15.6 My denouncement is disregarded: due to the "fake" alarm?

A further two months went by with other Mafia-type assassinations, but none of them triggered a public reaction or the media's interest until the dramatic evening of the Capaci massacre. On that night, as recalled foremost by Borsellino, many of Falcone's enemies did a sudden about face. From former enemies, they suddenly became the authors of teary texts filling the pages of all the newspapers. Only a few newspapers recalled the alarm raised two months previously and rapidly dismissed, asking themselves why it had been under-estimated and finding themselves unable to give a plausible answer. Furthermore, many parliamentary colleagues voiced their sincere regret for not having paid attention to my repeated calls for alarm.

Among the vast number of statements made in June 1992, I have chosen those of a young journalist, Pietro Incagliati, from a newspaper from my city, "il Mattino". Incagliati, recalling the very subtle clue of an "infiltrator" in the security system, asked himself: *"Why should we be surprised that the "onorata società" has actually managed to infiltrate where we hoped it never might? Why should we be surprised if we think that not two weeks ago someone, unobserved, even succeeded in planting – during an international conference on drugs – an anonymous message addressed to Falcone near his briefcase?: 'I ask you to consider that the State also pushes drugs'. Just a few words on a sheet of paper folded in four. Just enough to cause chaos in the hall where the conference was being held .... Who knows, but maybe – if only we had paid more attention to the Minister of Internal Affairs Scotti's circular last March to prefects, the turn of events may have been different. 'I am not nurturing secrets, I'm not hiding anything, and I won't accept judgement or censure. It was my duty to inform.... Keeping silent would have been a political ploy'. But what duty was Scotti referring to? The duty to denounce the risk of destabilization, pressure on the State between March and July. This was the alarm everyone disregarded because the person "crying wolf" was none other than Ciolini, an informer who many called a swindler. And yet, we should have paid attention. Scotti's circular on the desks of prefects throughout Italy was more than disturbing. And it came together with a series of warnings which the Minister had launched on more than one occasion. 'Let's be prepared for more deaths", he had said. So the destabilizing plan really existed. There were the murders of Salvo Lima in Palermo, of Sebastiano Corrado (PDS town councillor) in Castellamare di Stabia, and of Salvatore Gaglio (secretary of the PSI Bramante Bruxelles branch). The Public Security department never had any doubts ... Falcone was convinced of it. He had probably spoken about it to his friend Carla del Ponte, the prosecutor from Lugano... The conversation was about money laundering and the links between the Sicilian Mafia and the Turkish one. Once again the matter of the Balkan route, whose subversive plans, according to Ciolini, had been finalized in Zagabria".*

Over the past few years, I have asked myself many times why no one listened to me, why men of great political stature did not grasp the significance of my message. Instead they faced those months between March and July with superficial arrogance, with no notion of the hurricane that would be the culmination of the winds of growing public dissatisfaction with politics, the Mafia massacre attacks, the "clean hands" operation, the referendum, and finally, also the speculative attack, without precedent, on our currency.

The force of that cyclone would destroy the political system and decapitate most of its ruling class.

15.7 The conflict builds up

In March, the "Il Corriere della Sera"'s scoop on declarations of an alert rendered the news of possible Mafia terrorist attacks public. What could have been the aim if not forcing politicians and the public to loosen its grip and concede, in practice, a truce in the war? The level of conflict between the State and the anti-state was high, even if we had not yet introduced 41bis and the other measures in the penal and penal procedural code which the government approved on June 8th.

The Mafia organization had planned a set of counter offensives, among which were a series of massacre that, according to Ciolini's misleading letter, were to take place during a specific timeframe: *"from March to July"*.

When the massacres took place, the effects on the political system and public opinion - national and international - were to be devastating.

15.8 The approaching storm and election for Head of State

In the house, the elections for Cossiga's successor were underway in a climate of growing uncertainty and confusion. On the eve of the vote, when Andreotti's election still seemed possible, a sudden meeting of the DC majority group "Azione Popolare" was called. A brief introduction by Piccoli was followed by an even shorter discussion, at which point, Gava suggested choosing Forlani as the official candidate to be proposed to the other parties in the majority. Contrary to Cossiga's election, a decision had been made to choose a candidate from the majority and to proceed until the fourth round of votes when a qualifying majority was no longer necessary. Some of my friends and I were astonished not only by the speed of the choice, but by the choice itself. Before the meeting, my friend Naccarato had confirmed the information that Andreotti had given me late that morning. Forlani had informed the Prime Minister that he had no intention of running and thus, Andreotti could consider himself the only DC candidate. In lieu of this abrupt change, I called Andreotti at Palazzo Chigi and the Viminale switchboard put me through to Paolo Cirino Pomicino who, after hearing my account of the Azione Popolare meeting, told me that the situation had changed and that he, along with Andreotti, would be organizing the elections. Furthermore, Pomicino, attempted to assign responsibility for the sudden change on me.

The voting started, in this *Kafkian* atmosphere, on the following morning. It was evident from the start that Forlani did not have the necessary votes for even a simple majority. In a climate of suspicion and mutual accusations between Christian Democrats and Socialists, and within each party itself, the rounds of votes went on, amid growing tension and in the absence of leadership, given that the secretary of the DC was the candidate.
From the fifth round on, the chaos increased. This was also due to the fact that there had been an explosive attack against party leadership and the government on the part of referendum supporters led by Mario Segni, and supported by group leader Gerardo Bianco, at the Christian Democrat group meetings. Forlani withdrew his candidacy and resigned as party secretary. Strange rumors began to circulate and I was asked to bring Leo Valiani to Rome for his possible candidature. Thus, I made a proposal to my friends in the party to consider either the institutional candidature of the Speaker of the Senate, Spadolini, or that of the Governor of the Bank of Italy, Ciampi. Fourteen years later, when his mandate as president expired after being

elected in 1999, Ciampi wrote me that he still remembered clearly, *"when upon your suggestion, my candidature as Head of State was proposed during a particularly troubled electoral round of voting"*.

When we arrived at a point in the voting where the Christian Democrats kept voting blank ballots, Marco Pannella proposed Scalfaro's candidature, while Spadolini told me that Forlani had assured him of his support.

15.9 The Capaci massacre

Voting was suspended and I was with a group of colleagues at the Giolitti café opposite the seat of parliamentary groups when I received a phone call from the Head of Police informing me that there had been an attempt on Falcone's life. There was still no definitive news on the fate of Falcone, his wife, and his police escort. I had just enough presence of mind to notify Ciampino airport that I needed to leave immediately. On my way to the airport, I had time to call Martelli and Chiaromonte, inviting them to come with me. I then called Andreotti and Spadolini who, at that moment, was temporary President of the Republic. I assured both of them that I would call back as soon as I reached Palermo, when I had more information on the situation. During the flight, we received news that Falcone's wife was still alive, while the judge's fate was unknown. No one felt like talking!

Even today, twenty years after the fact, it's hard for me to write about it, and I feel the same chill and anger I felt in those hours, but also the determination to respond, time and again, that we should not give in. When you live through times like those, it's impossible to consider letting down the guard!

I have chosen, instead, the account given by Gerardo Chiaromonte in his book of memoirs; an account which is practically an introduction to the chapter dedicated to Falcone: *"I begin my writing of this chapter with a sense of despair, the same sense of despair I felt on the afternoon of May 23rd when Enzo Scotti called me with the first scanty news of the attack on Falcone and asked me to come with him and Martelli to Palermo. I felt a terrible sense of despair when, from up above in the helicopter flying from the airport to the Prefecture in Palermo, we looked down on that horrifying crater that had once been the highway. I felt the same despair when, at the hospital, they wouldn't let us go into the room where the mangled bodies of Falcone and his bodyguards were lying, and we learned of the death of Giovanni Falcone's wife, Francesca Morvillo, a judge in Palermo. I remember clearly the faces of all those present, among them many judges from that city. Those most stricken and unable to speak were Paolo Borsellino and Pietro Grasso: the latter, with tears in his eyes, but also fury, lashed out against the first absurd statements made by Mancuso, who had been elected senator of the networks, and spoke in the name of the so-called Anti-Mafia commission".*

When I got off the plane in Palermo, I regained enough control to face some of the most dramatic hours of my service at the Viminale. When we arrived in Palermo, I asked repeatedly for more details on how the massacre had been carried out in order to understand the "level" of Mafia attack and thus, what enemy we would have to face. There would be terrible days ahead, and, as Falcone often said, we would have to use our heads and not let our emotions get the best of us. It would be neither a brief nor a bloodless battle, due to the terrorist nature and international links which had contributed to the massacre's organization.

With respect to this last aspect, I remember that, together with the FBI, but in disaccord with other international investigative bodies, we felt it was necessary to adequately examine possible international links which had contributed to the massacre. The FBI was convinced of the existence of these links and therefore supposed there was support from outside of Sicily.

My considerations are those based on the scant notes I took at the time and thus do not reflect the findings from further investigations. The dynamics of the attack could not but convince us of the organization's high level of professionalism and the sophistication of the technology used. It's true that there had been similar car bombing attacks in the past: in Lebanon, the attacks on Admiral Luis Carrero Blanco in Spain, and Judge Rocco Chinnici in Italy. In all of these cases, however, the car bombed had been stationary, not a car moving at top speed. In the case of the Capaci massacre, we were dealing with a car that was speeding down a highway. Exploding a car moving at top speed, and at a precise point, indicated a highly well-planned act of terrorist guerrilla warfare. Flying several times by helicopter over the scene of the massacre, I asked the experts a series of questions but they replied that, at that moment, they were puzzled as to what dynamics, methods, and equipment could have been used to pinpoint the exact moment Falcone's car and his escort would be passing. Later on, they explained to us that there had been a delay of a fraction of a second, leading them to believe that the explosion of the escort car was distinct from Falcone's.

In the dead of night, Martelli and I reached the Palace of Justice where the bodies were lying in state. Only the thought of what awaited us in the following days kept Martelli from letting loose his reaction to the protests of some judges.

The funerals of Falcone and of the other victims of the massacre had become an "orchestrated" opportunity for some of his greatest enemies, who now suddenly proclaimed themselves to be his "heirs", to lash out at political leaders, including the temporary Head of State, Giovanni Spadolini.

Twenty years after that terrible 23rd of May, it would be useful to re-read what Chiaromonte wrote, outlining in just a few lines the basic events in Falcone's troubled, but brave life. Indeed, I feel the need and not just a duty, to remember Falcone today, not by depicting him as a myth, but rather restoring him to his great humanity. I was and remain one of his greatest admirers, but I have never dared to call him my friend, because I don't think that Falcone had many "friends". He spoke bitterly of these false friendships before the CSM commission which had been called to judge him. In rare moments of frankness, when he strayed from issues regarding the fight against the Mafia, he spoke to me of the many who declared their friendship and how he distrusted them. I remember well that he spoke of that at the dinner with the members of the CSM appointed by the DC, when they said that they couldn't vote for him as Anti-Mafia National Public Prosecutor substantially because his independence from political influence was in doubt. This had gone straight to his heart because they had not understood who Falcone really was. I prefer once again to refer to Chiaromonte, another man who spoke his mind without bias: *"A tragic life, that of Giovanni Falcone. After the Capaci massacre, everyone said they were his admirers. How many lies I heard in those days! Ilda Boccassini, the judge from Milan, did the right thing at the meeting held the day after at the Palace of Justice in that city, in taking the floor (...), to denounce and call out the names and surnames of those Milanese judges who had acted afflicted and aggrieved by Falcone's death when just until the day before they had said offensive and insulting things about him. Among the names she cited, unfortunately, there were also those who are today conducting the "clean hands" investigation. In those days, there was also an exploitation, which was just as absurd, of the situation by those that wanted to blame Giovanni Falcone's murder on all those who had criticized and opposed his opinions regarding judiciary policies in the fight against the Mafia. This could not be thrown back in anyone's face. The truth is that behind these dialectics, which were totally legitimate, there was more. Let's not beat about the bush: the main accusation aimed at Falcone, by many of his colleagues and also political groups (...) was of having in practice abandoned the fight against the Mafia and of having become, more or less, an instrument of political power, in order to advance his unbridled personal ambition and to seek attention (...). An attack which, even today, I consider despicable".*

If I could have recorded the words Cossiga used to describe Falcone, I would have his "portrait" today: *a man protective of his independence, as only a true Sicilian can be.* I would have cited them in this book, because they were extraordinarily powerful. But I don't remember all of the words and omitting any would diminish the strength of his testimony. He called me when many had attacked Falcone for having accepted Martelli's invitation to come to the ministry and leave Palermo, recalling for future memory, he told me, that his transfer had already been established by the previous minister, Vassalli. He stressed this fact to highlight the superficiality and bias of the press. I informed Cossiga of Falcone's murder while on my way to the airport to catch the plane for Palermo, and I recalled those words.

15.10 Falcone's death shakes the "palace"

The Capaci massacre had an immediate impact on the political situation. While the funerals were still taking place in Palermo, an agreement was reached between the majority and the opposition on the name of the candidate to be elected on the first round of voting after the funerals: Oscar Luigi Scalfaro.

Notwithstanding this institutional event which could be considered positive compared to the electoral chaos which preceded it, the political crisis deteriorated. The idea gained ground that politicians should hand over the country's government to eminent figures who had not been elected, along the lines of a government of honest men. The Christian Democrats decided to break with the popular representation of ministers, sanctioning the incompatibility of the post of minister with that of parliamentarian. In Milan, the "clean hands" preliminary investigation proceedings were speeded up and news of Craxi's involvement made it more implausible that the President of the Republic would in charge him with forming a new government, as he had told Martelli and me explicitly that he would do. In a short period, the political parties that had not yet done so, changed their names to hide their historic identities. Looming on the horizon was the "party" of the non-politician, who would liberate the country from slavery to the party system.

The second electoral referendum, in the wake of the revolution sparked by "clean hands", brought an end to the parties of the democratic coalitions, which were dissolved by simple telegrams without even bothering to convene a convention, as was the case with the DC.

The new instrument of political communication, television, which placed more emphasis on image than substance, became the real demolition ball of the first republic. The young Mediaset journalist, Paolo Brosio, set a tent up in front of the Milan Palace of Justice and became the favored source of information, receiving sneak previews of the prosecutor's proceedings. The destruction of the First Republic could not have been easier, because the parties had already committed suicide, even before anyone else could plant the last nail in their coffins. At my home, Prefect Parisi and the Carabinieri Chief of Staff, in the presence of Prefect Lauro, explicitly warned Martinazzoli that the DC, having begun its retreat without defending itself, would be wiped away, along with its archives, in just a few months.

15.11 In the storm with Martelli

In the past twenty years, the new media liturgy of parties has supplanted political debates at so-called party conventions. Collective decision-making and debating have given way to spectacular shows, rites, and symbolism, which serve as grand and over-the-top exaltations of political leaders. I think how the great enlightened Lombard leaders of modernity must be turning over in their graves at the sight of an end to reason and the explosion of irrational "barbaric" rites, such as the Northern

League Party's Celtic weddings and phials of Po water: a true and proper regression to the "Dark Ages" which preceded the Renaissance.

In a political context such as the one in the first half of 1992, Martelli and I were caught in the fire between the Mafia and the "clean hands" operation which was, as we might say, "throwing the baby out with the bath water". After the collapse of the Berlin wall, the wind of great laissez-faire was sweeping across the globe. The International Monetary Fund imposed rapid privatization on the former Soviet Union, which led to the birth of "magnates", who were not exempt from criminal influence. The total liberalization of financial markets, of universal banks, and new agents opened up enormous possibilities for money laundering in legal markets.

In the midst of this storm, it was not easy to "keep on course" and proceed with the same determination in the war against the Mafia. Doubts had been insinuated not only in the minds of those in charge, but also in the minds of the public, that we were moving too fast and maybe even too naively. I continued to disagree and thought we should not demonstrate the slightest sign of hesitation. Many thought it was indispensable for us to come out of the corner we had been pushed into by the waves of massacres. The international press judged the government's conduct severely, mixing the massacre bombs together with the "clean hands" arrests. Maybe even within the Mafia, there were signs of differing opinions on how to proceed.

The institutional and political crisis no doubt also hindered the operations of security forces and the judiciary, who were the targets of Mafia massacres. The attacks were shifting from institutional targets to terrorist ones, striking at ordinary citizens who were disarmed and defenceless. Tensions were running high: this could be felt at the funeral of the victims, with the understandable reaction of the family members of the bodyguards and colleagues of the murdered judges. Much determination was needed on these occasions to keep from giving in to emotions and to reason with sufficient clarity. Obviously, no one could rule out the idea of attenuating the violence of the conflict. The issue was how this could be done. We felt that the only way possible to force the Mafia into letting up on its fierce violence was to increase repression. Others implied that, perhaps, lightening the repression would force the Mafia to stop the massacres. Differences of opinion on how to achieve the aim of neutralizing the conflict persisted.

We found ourselves, therefore, at a crucial point in the "war" against the Mafia and we had a pretty clear picture of what would happen. I had already gone before the Anti-Mafia Parliamentary Commission after Lima's murder to try to predict the Mafia's reaction to the State's repressive measures. I had tried to explain, even before the Capaci massacre, that I was fully aware that the foreseeable Mafia terrorist reaction would plant doubts about the war strategy in institutions, with the justification of wanting to save human lives. Instead, we should have been better prepared, also on a psychological level, to respond to an even more violent attack against the loyal servants of the State and social targets. *"Unless*, I said at the time, *we want to settle for a sense of false security, which pax mafiosa would make possible through the acquiescence of state bodies to widespread illegality and the submission of weaker classes of society to organized crime".*

15.12 The days of reflection

In the dramatic days that followed the Capaci massacre, my colleagues and I, especially the Cabinet Secretary and Head of Police, and a particularly astute journalist named Maurizio Costanzo, decided to reflect on the steps we had taken since my arrival at the Viminale. We were trying to determine any possible errors which we and other institutions may have committed, omissions or weaknesses, that we had shown.

We began by examining the events concerning, or even interfering, with the activities of the Court of Palermo pool of investigating judges, where the young Falcone had shown great intuition in choosing the path of maxi-trials to convict many acting Mafia bosses. I have already mentioned that a few days before his death, Borsellino had described the hostile climate surrounding the efforts of that young judge, who was believed to be "not in line" with the tradition of complicity based on the code of silence (*omertà*). The events flowed from our memories one after another, in no particular order, of the terrible Mafia crimes against the politicians Mattarella and La Torre, and eminent servants of the State, from Dalla Chiesa to many judges. We recalled the murders of Chinnici and the young Livatino, the work of the investigating office of the Court of Palermo with Caponnetto, and the failed attempt against Falcone in Addaura.

We re-examined the so-called "crow" case, the ROS report on important Palermo municipality public bids and the adverse rapport between politics and the Mafia as Parliamentarian Cattanei had already done back in 1972, the new Sicilian DC policy against the Mafia, and the importance of the role of the first collaborators in justice, even before a specific law had been passed to regulate their treatment.

On the positive side, we observed the growing moral revolt on the part of young people and entire communities, as in the case of Capo d'Orlando, the voices of single priests in the outskirts and that of Cardinal Salvatore Pappalardo and, above all, that of Pope John Paul II in the Valley of Temples.

In particular, we reflected on the declared state of emergency and on the reaction of many political leaders and the media, which was for the most part superficial: on that refusal to reason, due to short-sidedness, on the concrete elements and acknowledge the challenge facing us.

I have never forgiven myself for not having resigned and for not having made a sensational gesture that would have called people's attention to the duty not to relent on repressive action and not to give in to the cowardly reasons for apparent prudence and false realism.
Would this have been a determining gesture that would set in motion a convergence of all public and private institutions in the war against the Mafia, given that my declared state of alarm had not been heeded, not only by politicians, but by representatives of civil society?

Or would this have just precipitated only slightly the events that followed, and which brought about my leaving the Viminale?

Chapter 16

16.1 Towards a new government

After the dramatic days of the attack and the troubled period of the election for Head of State had passed, the consultation stage for the formation of the new government began at the Quirinale. There were daily turns of events with news from the Milan Prosecutor's Office of notice of investigations served on Craxi and other candidates for minister. I tried to distance myself from the climate at the Palace and, with Martelli, focussed on drafting the legislative decree and applying that part of it which was under my jurisdiction. I urged the heads of police forces, therefore, to set up a plan to arrest the many Mafia fugitives.

It was not easy to concentrate on my job because of the rumors circulating about the formation of the government and news on the "Mani Pulite pool" (clean hands - the pool investigating the corruption of the political system) being sent through the prefects and the Milan Police Commissioner to the ministry. When my collaborators asked me for news on the government, I would reply that, as far as I was concerned, there was nothing to worry about, above all since I thought a change at the Viminale, just a few days after the Capaci massacre, would be improbable and unrealistic, unless they intended to blame me in some way for the attacks. Aside from this alternative, there was no reason for my replacement which would have objectively signalled a rejection of the strategic policy to fight the Mafia. To distract me from my work, Martelli invited me to come with him to meet President Scalfaro; this meeting turned out to be highly disadvantageous for the political future of both Martelli and myself! Martelli met with increasing hostility from Craxi, as well as many of his Socialist colleagues, who practically branded him a traitor. As for me, I met with growing distrust from my party secretary.

I have already reconstructed what happened at that meeting with Scalfaro and its consequences in my summarized diary[36] which, however, is not very relevant to this book. I would just like to note that we also spoke of the Mafia. Just after his election, Scalfaro had gone to Palermo to pay homage to the tombs of the victims and pledge his direct support for resolute efforts against the Mafia. There were no differences of opinion on the strategy we were promoting and which we would later develop, availing ourselves of the legislative decree which Scalfaro had signed and sent to the House. We also mentioned the urgency of rapidly implementing the activities of the DNA, by proceeding with the appointments. The President's comments led me to

---

[36] Diario minimo. Un irregolare nel Palazzo, Memoirs, 2004.

believe that, in some way, he thought continued joint action between Martelli and myself in the government was called for, especially after the Capaci massacre. My many years in politics had, however, prepared me never to take anything for granted. Indeed, as I was leaving the Quirinale, I began to feel uneasy about not only the formation of the new government, but also our participation in it. These doubts were reinforced after I saw how our visit to the Quirinale had been used to overcome the Craxi obstacle, and when Giuliano Amato was entrusted with forming the new government.

That was a clever and cunning political move!

16.2 Change at the Viminale?

My perceptions were amply confirmed in the front page headlines of the most important newspapers, which could hardly go unnoticed by the appointed Prime Minister and the leadership of my party. On June 21st, less than a week after the new government had been formed, Giuseppe D'Avanzo wrote in "La Repubblica": *"He should - they say – be reconfirmed as Minister of Internal Affairs. .... So why, in the last few days, has Vincenzo Scotti looked so worried and upset, with the air of one who wants to send the government, his party members, and colleagues in the majority to the devil? It's enough to sound out his collaborators and listen to the confidences of his most trusted friends to discover the truth that many are starting to realize, but that still isn't public knowledge. Vincenzo Scotti still hasn't decided whether he will accept the post offered him* (no offer had been made! N/A). *The minister confessed: "I'm convinced, and I've been saying this for months, that the ordeal has not yet ended, that the Mafia will strike again and even higher, increasingly higher as the State's action becomes more effective. Not everyone wants to understand this. Some turn a blind eye, others give in to the temptation to under-estimate my warning, those who are guilty of whispering that my apprehension is only alarmism masking my hunger for power. Well, I have already told these gentlemen that I will not go back to Palermo to be met with insults and have coins thrown at me in their stead. No one can think that, faced with a war to carry out against the Mafia, they can just wash their hands like Pontius Pilate. Let's make this clear, only a strong executive, legitimized in time and by consensus, can continue to do the work started by Martelli and myself. It is a policy that must be confirmed and the means to legitimizing that policy is the re-confirmation of us both".* ..... D'Avanzo commented: *"the odd couple, differing in culture, style, and personality, Scotti and Martelli see eye-to-eye in promoting and organizing an Anti-Mafia strategy that breaks with the old government tradition of emergency measures and special bodies, in favour of a pure and simple crackdown ... an initiative which has taken on an international dimension, that has succeeded in putting the "Mafia issue" on the agendas of the European Community, the United Nations, and the American government. The odd couple has made good use of the experience and advice of Giovanni Falcone, and has chosen the path of ordinary measures to fight organized crime, modifying the structure and quality as well as quantity of institutional responses".* D'Avanzo goes on to list the initiatives taken and after noting the existence of opposition to the odd couple, concludes that Scotti wasn't mincing his words when he said: *"either the political forces that support this government move in the direction I have indicated or I no longer intend to remain at the Viminale .... And he confessed to his collaborators that: 'on the other hand, in my own party, as in Martelli's, there are those who would be happy to see both of us go home. I have the increasingly distinct impression that the sooner we get out of here, the greater the number of people who will be satisfied ... ".*

D'Avanzo confirmed that the decisive choice had been the shift from special measures and anti-Mafia institutions, to an "ordinary war" with "ordinary" entities and laws: this was the first matter Falcone brought up at our first meeting at the Viminale, and it was the first suggestion that I felt I could embrace.

After the publication of D'Avanzo's article, many other journalists began reporting news about the participation of Martelli and myself in the government that was newly being formed. In general, the news stories took for granted the impossibility of a replacement. Everyone seemed to agree that a different outcome would be unrealistic given we were engaged in a conflict after Capaci and in lieu of the alarm I had raised in March. Prefect Parisi was oddly silent and almost indifferent to what was happening at the Quirinale. This was an uncharacteristic attitude for such an active servant of the State, always reactive to the slightest detail of institutional, political, and party events. His rapport with Scalfaro was particularly close: he had been nominated by him first as head of SISDE and then as head of the Department of Public Security. Parisi fully understood the situation we had had to face, having himself described it to me in the previous month of March and having shared and supported the strategy adopted, except for the establishment of the DIA. During my Anti-Mafia Commission hearing on 28 October 2010, Senator Serra, who had been Milan Police Commissioner at the time, reminded me of Parisi's opposition to the creation of the DIA.

I did not attribute any particular significance, however, to Parisi's silence, given his skill in following all the political events taking place in that period. And even today, I find it hard to attribute any particular significance to it. I did not think it was appropriate to call the Prime Minister in charge, but decided to just send him a brief note on the most sensitive and urgent issues concerning the development of the government's program. Both he and the President of the Republic had all the elements they needed to evaluate what was most opportune for the government and for the country.

Most recently, some distinguished friends have declared before judges that they had been unaware, during the formation of the government, of the existence of an "odd couple" issue. According to them, my being replaced was just a case of ordinary administration in the formation of the government. It is disturbing to note that they had not even been aware of my statements to the Anti-Mafia Commission after Lima's murder, of my communiqué to Parliament on the occasion of the alert of the preceding March, of the many and frequent interviews before and after Falcone's murder, nor of the legislative decree dated 8 March and the reactions it triggered. What hypocrisy!

Today, these documents are being removed from the archives, forgotten over the course of these last twenty years.

16.3 The night of the change

No one should feel indispensable and I had been mentored by

Pastore who kept reminding me, from the day I had decided to propose my candidature for parliament, that a politician should always keep his "suitcase" packed, ready to leave his post at any time. Luckily, I have always cultivated many cultural and social interests, starting from teaching and academic research, to heading the "Nuovo Osservatore", to chairing the musical festivals at Villa Pignatelli, at Sorrento, and for the league of professional cyclists.

Up until the eve of the presentation of the list of ministers to the Head of State, I had not received any phone call from the Prime Minister in charge, nor from my party. That afternoon, I had stayed at home to read the theses of some of my students at LUISS university.

Towards the evening, the president of my party and the House group leader called to remind me that the party leadership had ruled on the incompatibility of a parliamentarian being head of a ministry and, consequently, that if I wanted to remain at the Viminale, I would have to resign from parliament. I confessed that I had not given the news in the papers much consideration, because I had never thought of the Minister of Internal Affairs as being "political" like the other ministers, who did not have representative "weight and influence", and could thus be relegated to the rank of so-called "technicians". For this reason, I replied immediately to my callers that the ruling of incompatibility seemed to me to be a stretch, above all, if this was to be the precursor of a general constitutional reform to adopt a presidential system, for which the conditions were not ripe. Once again, decisions were being made under emotional duress, resulting in damaging consequences. Just consider that today, of that great reform, as Forlani and De Mita called it, there is not the slightest political trace; what it most certainly did, however, was speed up the "clean hands" judicial proceedings, given that the Milanese judges interpreted it as unconditional surrender: exposing the "naked king!"

Depriving the Minister of Internal Affairs of the legitimization of popular vote and of a position in parliament as an elected official meant significantly reducing his influence in conducting the tough war against the Mafia and his ability to hold out against any form of blackmail. At that moment, the Minister of Internal Affairs, as well as the Minister of Justice, had to resist and stand firm in their war strategy, having the support of the broadest possible spectrum of political forces. I had already experienced several times how subtle the broadsides could be from within organizations, whether deflected or not, such as in the case of the photographs confiscated in 1978, which I had learned of only recently. I could not fathom why, right in the thick of the war, they would want to weaken a minister called to perform a duty that was extraordinarily exposed. Perhaps, in hindsight, many of those broadsides and traps should not be considered entirely random!

Since I did not for one moment doubt my friends' competence, I assumed that the decision was the result of an astute move to discourage some aspiring parliamentarian with judicial problems from becoming minister, as this would mean giving up the immunity afforded to parliamentarians. Even this interpretation, however, turned out to be only part of the story, according to the account Pomicino gives of the exchange of phone calls between Andreotti and Scalfaro regarding his participation in the government[37].

After the formation of the government, Forlani sent me a letter in reply to the one written by a group of friends, stressing that the incompatibility issue was a crucial aspect of the bold constitutional reform we should promote and that the DC had begun to consider as a form of self-reform. This reform would have met with the full support of our electors as being the proper reaction to the "clean hands" scandal. Re-reading that letter today, its contents appear discursive and light years removed from what was actually happening, and which would sweep the party from the Italian political scene. It was a superficial attempt to block a towering wave with a bucket of sand, a flight from the burdens of responsibility, or might there have been other reasons? I calmly replied that this request was just one more reason, in addition to those I had already given in the preceding days, for me to declare the impossibility of my serving in the new government.

My feeling was that, if they had decided it was opportune to replace the minister at the Viminale, they needn't have resorted to such complex machinations – they could have just asked me and I would have stepped down, because just the news of it would have delegitimized me as Minister of Internal Affairs, right in the thick of the anti-Mafia war strategy.

16.4 My pairing with Martelli comes to an end

Martelli called me soon after hearing of the DC's decision and told me that it would be difficult for him to remain in the

---

[37] (Geronimo: strettamente riservato, Mondadori May 2000).

government if I decided not to stay. He added that Amato was willing to propose my name to the Head of State for Minister of Internal Affairs, even in the absence of my party's support, by applying his constitutional powers. I replied that, in that case, I would have no qualms in accepting the post, and that even against my party's wishes, I would not resign from parliament. Martelli told me he would inform Amato of my reply.

Some time after midnight, I received another phone call from Gerardo Bianco who told me my name would be proposed by the DC for Minister of Foreign Affairs. I told him immediately that this change would not make me change my mind in the least. I finally went to bed convinced that if the President of the Republic and the Prime Minister, the final decision-makers, wanted me to continue fighting the Mafia together with Martelli, they had the power to do so, regardless of our parties' orientations. Perfect Laura was at my house to support me throughout that long evening.

When, on the following day, Amato read out the list of ministers, I was shocked to hear I had been nominated Minister of Foreign Affairs and attempted, with some difficulty, to say a few words immediately after the protocol visits to the speakers of both chambers of parliament. I announced my resignation as newly appointed Minister of Foreign Affairs while Amato, citing the difficult economic and political situation asked me to stay on at least until the end of the three following summits, the first of which was the most important; the G7 which would be held in Munich in just a few days' time, immediately following the parliamentary vote of confidence. At the other two summits, the OSCE in Helsinki and Central Europe in Vienna, I would have to participate on the Prime Minister's behalf, because the serious speculative attack on the lira prevented him from leaving Rome.

In light of such valid "reasons of State", I agreed to put off my resignation as Minister of Foreign Affairs. In order not to create problems for the government, however, Amato requested that if my party secretary insisted on my resigning from parliament, I should submit my resignation to the House speaker. I could later withdraw this resignation immediately after resigning as Minister of Foreign Affairs. With these assurances, and solely out of a sense of institutional duty, I started preparing for these summits immediately. Amato came to Munich and then quickly returned to Rome in preparation for the approval of measures against speculation. While I was abroad, I received a pressing request from my party, which seemed more interested in my parliamentary resignation than in the serious financial crisis underway. As I had promised Amato, I sent my resignation to the House Speaker, Napolitano.

On the day set for the House session to acknowledge my resignation as a parliamentary Christian Democrat minister, I handed Prime Minister Amato my resignation as Minister of Foreign Affairs and withdrew, simultaneously, my resignation as parliamentarian. Amato told me quite bluntly that he would reject my resignation and that, in any case, we would discuss it only after I had come back from two more urgent engagements, which he asked me to attend; the first was in Jerusalem. I restated my firm intention to leave the government, but reassured him that I would go to Jerusalem and the other important meeting taking place that afternoon with the Iranian Minister of Foreign Affairs.

16.5 As expected, I resign

That evening, there was a dramatic turn of events. While I was having dinner with my Iranian colleague at Villa Madama, I received an urgent call from the Quirinale. Amato informed me that President Scalfaro, upon the insistence of my party secretary, was signing the decree to accept my resignation. I went back to the table and informed my guest that he was no longer talking to the Italian Minister of Foreign Affairs. After hiding his initial surprise, he invited me over for coffee the next day. I stayed on at Villa Madama for an interview with Paolo Galimberti, while the agencies were issuing the first hot declarations on my "irresponsibility".

Almost as if he were unaware of every single detail of the story, and, above all, of the fact that I had expressed my intention to resign as soon as I had been nominated, President Scalfaro, after signing the decree accepting my resignation, treated it almost as an act of high treason. *"If service to the people is replaced by other interests or the taking of sides that override the interests of the State, this is a crime against the State. These are harsh words, but they come at the end of a hard day of events which are intolerable in a democratic regime, in a country which is already suffering from terrible afflictions".*

I left my bodyguards at Villa Madama and set out for home on foot. Walking through the streets on a hot Roman night, I meditated on those words. Had it been a decision based on bias because I had not wanted to accept my party's peculiar imposition, refusing the obligation to resign as a parliamentarian? Or rather, was it of the person who, just one month after the Capaci massacre, had decided to replace me as Minister of Internal Affairs, on grounds which were most definitely not in the public's interest? If they had thought my resignation was so disruptive, why had they accepted it, with such solicitude, under pressure from a party secretary, as the Prime Minister had told me bluntly in that bureaucratic call from the office of the Head of State?

I arrived home without managing to find a logical reason for the reactions which were so harsh and without appeal. The following morning, the headlines of all the newspapers were devastating. Everyone had a go at "pigeon shooting" and "La Repubblica" wrote that the Ministry of Foreign Affairs was in a frenzy and under shock. It didn't seem to me as if anyone had raised a shield in my defence a few weeks previously when I had been replaced at Internal Affairs, even though this had sent a message, which, to some extent, was inopportune given the Capaci massacre. That same morning, at the presentation of the Confesercenti report with the Rome Public Prosecutor Michele Coiro, I spoke at length of the strategy adopted against the Mafia and refused to answer journalists' provocative questions about my resignation from Foreign Affairs, because it seemed utterly useless.

I realized that, in just a few days, my stint at the Ministry of Internal Affairs had all but been forgotten. Scalfaro, however, wrote me a few months later, in October 1992: *""Storms" don't change feelings. Of course, if we had spoken with each other, things would have gone differently"*.

16.6 The silence of friends

Since that day, I have believed my decision to maintain silence on the Internal Affairs Ministry has been for the best.

I only spoke of it at the DC National Council, on a sultry afternoon at the beginning of August, where I went to perform a duty; approve the agreement on the Amato government. I called for reflection and an awareness of what was about to befall us. My words met with indifference, just as when I had informed political leaders in March of that same year of the dangers on the horizon. No one paid any attention to my words on the institutional crisis, the Mafia's attack, and the judiciary proceedings of the "clean hands" pool. *"There is within us, in this phase, an awareness, which is at times expressed, and other times repressed out of fear or interest: we must carry out, here and now, an extraordinary and courageous reform. We absolutely must turn the page, with the subsequent choice of leadership for this period: if this doesn't happen, I think that we will have neither the time nor the political space to face the institutional crisis, which could spell doom for the first republic. There is Mafia aggression which has for some time destabilized our institutions.... But it is not just a question of government, it is a question of general policy and we are giving the impression, once again, of closing a blind eye to a dramatic reality. The Mafia is a political counter-power (there is no third political level) that attempts, day after day, to bend institutions to its criminal affairs. It is not, as we believed for a long time in the '80's, one of many forms of criminal aggression typical of industrialized societies .... Every day, our fellow citizens feel the effects of this profound corruption in political procedures and conduct which is undermining the foundations of the pact which binds citizens to this republic ad thus, gnaws away at the solidity of democratic institutions... The time has come to choose those most qualified".* (Appendice n° 7)

Notwithstanding the hurricane's advance, everyone wanted to just go on vacation and wait until autumn to decide on Forlani's resignation as party secretary and elect his replacement. Not a single colleague moved for debate and the session was rapidly adjourned.

16.7 They keep asking me….. and I keep asking myself

I have asked myself, and others have asked me in judiciary and parliamentary settings, for my opinion of my replacement at Internal Affairs, Nicola Mancino. Most recently, my distinguished friends have testified before Palermo judges that the change at the Viminale was a normal affair in compliance with the application of the Cencelli[38] manual or Gava's request that Nicola Mancino be replaced as president of the group of Christian Democrat senators.
None of these reasons seem plausible. The application of the Cencelli manual would not have led to me being assigned a ministry, which in State protocol, is less important than that of Internal Affairs. As for Gava's request, the newspapers in the days preceding the formation of the government had already hinted that Mancino would head another important ministry. I cannot believe that Mancino would have posed his nomination as Minister of Internal Affairs as a condition for his participation in the government. Mancino is an eminent political figure, who was even been talked about as a possible President of the Republic,

---

[38] DC Massimiliano Cencelli created the so-called "Cencelli manual" to calculate mathematically the number of ministerial posts to which each Christian Democrat faction was entitled on the basis of the faction's strength in the party in percentage terms.

highly esteemed by all, myself included: therefore, I have never disputed, nor can dispute the personal qualities of my successor. To the contrary, I have praised them.

I have already commented on Parisi's uncharacteristic silence during the entire negotiation phase of the Amato government. Some time after I had left the government, I noted in my diary: *"throughout these years, I have tried to understand the personality and role of an extraordinary servant of the State, who remains a mystery to me: Vincenzo Parisi. In the spotlight of Italian politics, he demonstrated great skill and discretion. He was the link between political opposition and the other bodies of the State. Of his encounters with the opposition, he told me almost everything, even though at times after a reasonable delay. I have always favored harmony over discord and he remained, until his premature death, the repository of important secrets, both as head of SISDE and as Head of the Police .... My cabinet head, Lauro once gave him a tape of the excellent film with the fascinating title, "Supping with the Devil", telling him that he had the talents of both Talleyrand and Fouchet. This was my opinion as well"*. His silence in the days preceding the formation of the government have become increasingly incomprehensible to me as the years go by, especially in recent times, and also in light of his close daily dealings with Scalfaro.

For a better understanding of that period of my political life, the interested reader may refer to the official record of the Anti-Mafia Commission hearing dated 28 October 2010. My spontaneous responses may be more useful than any further comments.

Chapter 17

17.1 From Falcone to Borsellino

Only a few days had passed since the Capaci massacre. Before that tragic event, I had been invited to present Pino Arlacchi's book "Gli uomini del disonore" with Vincenzo Parisi, Paolo Borsellino, Claudio Martelli and Leonardo Mondadori. The author had worked with me at the Ministry of Internal Affairs on several occasions. While Borsellino was speaking, I thought to myself that the time had come to pose two questions without further delay: why shouldn't the Magistrates' Internal Board of Supervisors (CSM) reopen the selection process for the new Anti-Mafia Public Prosecutor now that Falcone's death had created a totally different scenario? Why shouldn't Paolo Borsellino submit his candidature?

Falcone's nomination had been no secret. I had suggested it several times in parliament and had written to the CSM Deputy Chairman calling his attention to the appropriateness of placing Falcone and De Gennaro at the head of the two new anti-Mafia institutions. Therefore, it seemed natural to me that many distinguished judges would not have submitted their candidature out of respect for Falcone, knowing that he would do so.

After Falcone's death, who better than Borsellino could succeed him by submitting his candidature? Borsellino had always been in line with Falcone's ideas, and above all, represented an absolute guarantee that the war on the Mafia would continue. His staunch determination was always balanced by total respect for the law. At the end of his speech, I posed those questions and noticed the bewildered looks on the faces of Borsellino and the journalists present: my speech had come as a complete surprise.
A few minutes later, Arlacchi's book presentation came to an end and I approached the Deputy Public Prosecutor to explain the reasons for my suggestion more fully. It was absolutely essential for us to give a strong sign of continuity in the fight against the Mafia and ensure that Falcone's legacy would not be in the least bit lost. There was simply no alternative: we could not let up on the Mafia. I asked him to give it his careful consideration. Even President emeritus Cossiga referred to Borsellino as Falcone's heir, the only person at that moment who could guarantee that the repressive action against the Mafia would continue and that the State would not yield one inch. Borsellino listened to me, but didn't comment; he limited himself to saying that he needed time to think about it and would send me a written reply.

The next day, many journalists wrote a lot of nonsense, and

many vicious ones even accused me of having put Borsellino at risk, that is of having practically placed him in the Mafia's sights, because *"one of the likely aims of the Capaci massacre was preventive, that is the Mafia wanted to block Falcone's appointment as National Anti-Mafia Public Prosecutor and they would have done the same with Borsellino"*.

The reasons for the murders of Falcone and Borsellino, went, perhaps, much beyond their appointment as National Public Prosecutor! From the CSM commission's decision to reject Falcone's candidature, to all the statements read and heard, to Galloni's silence on my letter, Falcone had been completely out of the running for Super Prosecutor. There was not a shadow of a doubt: Falcone had told me so openly after our dinner at Villa Medici. And the Mafia knew that as well: it's not as if they didn't know what was going on – to the contrary!

I received a letter from Borsellino in which he declined, courteously, but firmly, my invitation to submit his candidature after having consulted with his father-in-law, Angelo Piraino Leto, ex- president of the court with a sterling reputation as a jurist.

Therefore, Borsellino was killed even though he was never a candidate for Super Prosecutor!
The Mafia was always well-informed!

As the judiciary proceedings underway are now demonstrating, the reasons for the via D'Amelio massacre must be looked for elsewhere. The contents of the letter Borsellino sent me confirm, if there was any need to do so, which there isn't, his strong commitment as a judge to fighting the Mafia and his intention to hold firm in his determination. *"Dear Mr. Minister, I would like to respond to the unexpected invitation you made during the meeting to present Pino Arlacchi's book. My longstanding feelings of friendship for Giovanni Falcone would make it extremely painful for me to consider assuming an office to which I could never have aspired if he were still alive. Indeed, Giovanni Falcone's death has left me with a sense of grief that prevents me from benefiting from a situation which is in any way linked to this mournful event. The reasons which have induced those who support my candidature as the head of the National Anti-Mafia Division flatter me, but do not lead me to presume that they exceed the qualifications possessed by other candidates aspiring to that office, especially if the selection process is reopened. It is true that many of my valiant colleagues did not submit their names because they believed Giovanni Falcone was the natural choice, or rather, because they did not feel legitimized in proposing their names for reasons which have been circumvented by the Magistrates' Board of Supervisors. As far as I am concerned, the aforementioned considerations, together with the fond insistence of many of my collaborators, have induced me to remain in Palermo and continue the work I have just started, at a Prosecutor's Office of the Republic which is surely the one most directly and strongly committed to carrying out investigations on organized crime".*

Borsellino thus justified the reasons for refusing my invitation, but the CSM had excluded him regardless of what his answer to my request would have been. Ernesto Stajano, Chairman of the Executive Appointment Commission stressed that *"the seriousness of the situation indicates specific choices, but certain rules still have to be respected"*. The possibility of Borsellino's irregular candidature was struck down. Giuseppe Gennaro, Deputy Prosecutor of Catania, added: *"while the qualities of the man are indisputable, I cannot imagine under what juridical rule the selection process could be reopened".*

The only one who supported the validity of Borsellino's invitation was Giovanni Tinebra, who stated that the country demanded a strong response and that he believed the CSM could give one, within the context of their institutional duties.

17.2 Why in Rome?

In June and July, Borsellino became keenly engaged in activism. On many occasions, he recalled his friend Falcone to rally young people to openly fight the Mafia and to urge security forces, his colleagues, and all those working for public institutions not to give up, not to allow themselves to be intimidated, and not to slacken their efforts. In the first hours of Sunday July 19th, he wrote a letter to a teacher at a school in northern Italy to apologize, above all, for not having been able to attend a meeting on the Mafia on January 24th to answer the ten questions the high school students there had prepared. The answers to those questions, read today, can practically be considered his spiritual testament. (See Appendix 2).

On June 29th, Borsellino had planned a trip to Rome to interrogate some collaborators in justice but before leaving, he granted Gianluca Di Feo, a journalist from "Corriere della Sera", an interview. *"There are some collaborators which can become*

*important instruments. If they help us in Rome...... Otherwise..".
It's early in the morning, just a few days ago. Paolo Borsellino is at home in his study, not far from the site of the new massacre. Buildings all the same, the homes of public workers. Outside, the armored car and car of his bodyguards. They don't seem anxious, just surprised to see a visitor so early in the morning. The bodyguard who takes me upstairs in the elevator is very sad ... He has already been given the orders to prepare to move; he will have to protect his judge on the way to the airport, along that highway where three of his colleagues have already met with death. Borsellino greets me at the door to his apartment. It's only 7:30 but it looks like he's been up for hours. He apologizes for having cancelled yesterday's appointment.*

... He leads me to the nice study, the one not cluttered with papers .... We start talking immediately. The topic is a hot one; the Mafia, arms trafficking and possible links to Falcone's murder. ... "Drug and arms trafficking share similar characteristics" – Borsellino stated – "they both require enormous investments and yield huge profits. This is why there can be common financial channels for these activities. But it doesn't seem to me that Mafia members engage firsthand in arms trafficking. It's not their business, they aren't equipped. They prefer to leave that to others. Who often try to cheat them". And, during the interview, he expressed bitterness over Falcone's fate, betrayed and abandoned. "We don't need to look far for the causes of the Capaci massacre. The instigators are right here in Sicily. And the reasons are more technical than people admit. Giovanni had contacted some collaborators who could have been extremely valuable. But he was blocked at every turn. The information from those people could have been very useful. Some were only on the fringes of "cosa nostra". But they were still capable of inflicting a terrible blow. That's why they

killed him". "The duty is now ours, above all, mine. We're doing the best we can. They have promised a law on collaborators: in just a few hours, I will fly to Rome to discuss this. Without it, every attempt will be useless". But who were these collaborators that the clans were so afraid of? Borsellino didn't name names. However, he spoke at length of Giuseppe Lottusi, the treasurer of the Madonia clan and the Colombian narcos. A Milanese financier who had transferred huge quantities of cocaine dollars. Lottusi had been arrested thanks to an American informer during an investigation conducted by the FBI and coordinated by Falcone. "Lottusi" – stressed Borsellino – "was not a member, but outside the Mafia, who managed the most important criminal business activities of the '80's. But, for this reason, he is a weak link in the chain of 'omertà'".

Who did Borsellino meet in Rome? And was his visit in some way related to the alleged bargaining with the Mafia carried out by government officials? Many are working to solve this puzzle, but the facts are not sufficiently clear.
The day after Borsellino's departure from Palermo, on July 1st, I entered Palazzo Viminale as a minister for the last time, to hand everything over to my successor. After a brief ceremony, I stopped in the hallway crowded with high level ministry functionaries and the chiefs of security forces. I quickly said my goodbyes to my Head of Cabinet, the Chief of Police, my closet collaborators and my guardian angels, the assistants who had shared the long hours of every day with me, who had brought me something to drink, and often, to eat, with a simple smile, supporting me during the toughest times. At the end of the dimly lit hallway, I caught a glimpse of Borsellino. I couldn't stay because the functionaries were entering the office of the new minister and I wasn't able

to greet him. It was the last time I saw him. His blurred image remains impressed on my memory!

17.3 The Via D'Amelio massacre

I had been in Brussels for a few hours on that terrible Sunday in July, when the ambassador, our permanent representative at the European Community, told me that a phone call had been put through from the government in Rome to inform me that there had been a horrific attack in Palermo: Borsellino and his entire police escort had been killed. After a short time, the RAI television crew arrived for an interview. We moved outside into the garden. It was the most painful interview I have ever given. I had not had the same familiarity with Borsellino as I had had with Falcone; we had spoken together on only a few occasions. I don't think Borsellino liked dealing with the government apparatus and was not often seen at the capital. Each time I spoke with him, I was struck by his strong personality and hard determination. He was calm and straightforward: the only course was to wage war without quarter and there was not a moment to lose until the Mafia was completely destroyed. My interview that evening was extremely terse. I expressed the hope that calm would be maintained and that the path chosen by Falcone and Borsellino would be adopted, one in which we acted without hesitation, leaving no room for the Mafia to maneuver. The next morning, before going to a meeting at the Minister of Foreign Affairs, I received a call from my former Head of Cabinet, Lauro, who had stayed on with my successor Mancino. With his customary courtesy and kindness, he gave me some advice: not to concern myself with issues not within my jurisdiction. I did not immediately understand what he meant by this.

Shortly after, at the European Council of Foreign Affairs Ministers, I limited myself to thanking all of my colleagues who had sent their heartfelt condolences to Italy and had lent their support to our country at this tragic moment.

17.4 Remembering Giulio Pastore

During the entire European Community meeting, my mind continued to wander: I wanted to be back in Italy to say goodbye for the last time to the victims of that terrible massacre. I was thinking of Palermo and I remembered the day, so many years ago, that I had spent in that city with Giulio Pastore, who was Minister for Mezzogiorno at that time. It was in the middle of 1963 and I was secretary general of the Ministerial Commission for the Mezzogiorno. I was in Palermo with Minister Pastore, who had been chairman of the Commission for seven years. We were in the car with the prefect of Palermo, who put Pastore on his guard about contacts with local political figures. I was shocked by the frankness with which he explained how the Mafia exercised control over the city council. In particular, he named Vito Ciancimino as a figure with strong links to the Mafia.

Pastore paid close attention to the prefect's report. He asked him many questions and expressed his growing concern for the negative impact that all types of organized crime were having on the development of southern Italy. When we got back to Rome, Pastore told me he wanted to take an official position on the issue and write an editorial together for the magazine he directed, the

"Nuovo Osservatore". He dictated an outline of the editorial and asked me to complete it. I prepared a first draft which he read carefully and to which he made many additions. At the end, we wrote a text to present to the press before publication. *"We have had to wait fifteen years for the parliamentary commission to be established.... The country demands to know the truth about things and wants to know why the Mafia continues to prosper and expand, in cities and towns, to whom – small consolation – everyone is rushing to issue unsolicited certifications of nobility. We must most definitely remove the social and economic causes that strengthen the Mafia, but the country wants to assign responsibility, which is objectively due, on the local political class which, until now to a large extent, has denied, if not with its complacence than certainly with its silence, the responsibility of the Mafia and want to know what links there are between the former and the financial, agrarian, industrial, and commercial interests operating in this country".*

The Cattanei report of 1972, which I have mentioned several times, attempted to provide preliminary answers to these questions.

17.5 My last speech as Minister of Internal Affairs

We were close to forming the new government and I had agreed to make a speech at the end of the security inter-force course at Santa Costanza in Rome. I thought it would be useful to evaluate the work that had been done and provide some suggestions to submit to the nascent government. I had absolutely no idea *that this would be my last speech as Minister of Internal Affairs.*

"The State is not on its knees; it has the means, the will, and the determination to win the battle against the anti-state, against organized crime which has become a very dangerous influence on institutions and the democratic life of the whole country. I call for all information agencies, to which the new legislation has just granted powers regarding the capture of fugitives, to collaborate with dedication and commitment, in addition to their specific professional skills. I appeal to everyone's sense of responsibility not to aid, directly or indirectly, the strategy of organized crime to weaken, or create disunity in institutions or among the servants of those institutions. I believe that anyone who accepts a government position must stand firm against the barbaric assault of organized crime which has become such a dangerous power, an anti-state yielding great political influence in policy-making, corrupting, and poisoning. The problem affects all of us personally, because the flow of wealth from organized crime has already penetrated and corrupted the economic, social, political, and institutional life of many countries around the world".

In that speech, my considerations and hopes were that the extraordinary efforts, costing the lives of so many servants of the State, should not have been in vain.

Chapter 18

18.1 The judiciary takes another look

With the passing of the years, the judiciary investigations into the Capaci and via D'Amelio massacres have not only broken new ground, but have also improved our knowledge of the blurred lines, the gray area, between legality and illegality. Many questions remain without convincing answers and many new questions have arisen. In the meantime, the search goes on for further elements to verify if the alleged contacts with the Mafia to conduct supposed bargaining took place; some judges even believe that the specific aim of the via D'Amelio massacre was to prevent Borsellino from having the time to block the idea of bargaining.

Regardless of the judiciary findings on these matters, a fact cannot be denied: the existence of a cause and effect relationship between the Mafia massacres and the specific government, judiciary, and security force initiatives which were adopted against the Mafia in those years.

It is quite obvious that the Mafia would have done everything in its power to stop or restrict the application of the harsher measures adopted in those years. All of the issues regarding the failed renewal of the application of 41bis for a certain number of Mafiosi are linked to the Mafia's massacre strategy and its main objective.

Up until now, the news stories and press have focused on the judiciary proceedings, but have not considered the political aspect which constitutes the key question, at least for Italy's unity, which should be posed to politics and which politics should pose itself. Will we have to accept coexisting with this type of organized crime forever, without succeeding in destroying the anti-State's power, with its strong capacity to control the territory and corrupt institutions? The decision is political: we cannot be satisfied with the results unless we succeed in giving back to citizens, institutions, and the economy, a State ruled by law. We may not be able to imagine a society without crime, but we can certainly imagine a society without the Mafia!

18.2 *"Sit finis libri non finis quaerendi"* - This may be the end of the book but not the end of the matter

What conclusions can we draw from the reflections in this book? Above all, I think the time has come for a more truthful analysis of the Falcone and Borsellino years. Twenty years after the facts, we cannot enact just a ritual commemoration of their extraordinary commitment as servants of the State. We cannot repeat, at every anniversary, the same speech without asking ourselves what has happened since and what their legacy has been.

Having played a key role in those two brief years, I ask myself what the best way would be to remember the hours spent together and the road we shared. I believe the best way would be to renew a discussion, without bias, on the fight against the Mafia in order to provide an answer to that question Falcone was asked when he was abroad: Will you Italians live with the Mafia forever?

The answer must derive from a critical analysis of the massacre period and the years following it. I repeat that this means shedding light on the difficulties, the obstacles, and the traps overcome by the initiatives created in Palermo that were at the core of the national fight. This also means clarifying the conflict, at times explicit and other times concealed, between the two lines of conduct which were and are still present in Italian society.

To raise civil awareness in our country, it would be useful to re-examine the documents, putting aside all the prejudices that have nurtured the classic and Manichean political distinction between the party that is "different" and the party of sinners. That is not the way it was and it is in everyone's interest to re-establish the country's unity based on a shared decision to put an end to the anti-state's power once and for all.

Achieving an understanding would not just be useful for the past, but even more so for the future, if we want to ensure the prospect of total liberty and legality for our country. I think it is right that we should understand events, aside from any personal implications, which have had an objective impact on the strategy of the fight against the Mafia.

On a personal level, however, the initiatives on various fronts to discredit me remain inexplicable. I feel that it would be opportune to clarify them at some later point.

18.3 And today?...

What are the terms of the Mafia's challenge today? The impression conveyed by the heaps of investigations and books published in the past few years is that the Mafia organization has changed some of its traits with respect to those we discussed with Falcone. Various investigative and judiciary activities have made progress in the fight against the Mafia since the '80's, when the Palermo pool began its preliminary investigations for the maxi-trial. But the criminal organization, the anti-state (in its various forms: Mafia in general, "'ndrangheta", "camorra" and "sacra corona unita", "Chinese Mafia", narco-traffickers, narco-guerriglia, etc.) has expanded its control over vast territories and perhaps even extended its penetration and control over local institutions.

Some important changes can be noted. The first is the expansion, at a global level, of the so-called gray area: the area created by the intermingling of legal and criminal activities. Dirty money can be laundered quickly and channelled back into legal activities, using the cover of de-regulated financial markets and then invested in legal activities which, given the origin of this money, alters the proper functioning of the market of goods and services. Shedding light on this gray area, in which there are vast zones of apparently legal activities, is extremely difficult. This is due both to the lack of cooperation between nations and to the speed with which criminal revenues are turned into legal and revered wealth.

When we created the DIA, as Francesco Cossiga has recalled on several occasions, we were imagining a large-scale intelligence agency against crime, capable of identifying and analyzing the links between various subversive and criminal entities (terrorists and different types of Mafia), between diverse criminal activities linked to each other (terrorism, narco–trafficking, arms trafficking, gambling and prostitution), between Mafia organizations on different continents, and between these activities and criminal organizations with formally legal corporate structures that make them difficult to identify. That is to say, an intelligence agency that could carry out 360° analyses and provide investigative and judiciary bodies with reliable information and scenarios that could lead to legal action aimed at striking at the heart of the Mafia, its financial and economic interests. Essentially, the DIA would have taken over the duties of the Anti-Mafia High Commission, an important agency for the analysis of the gray area of crime and its infiltration, not only into private financial activities, but also into public institutions.

It was absolutely not our intention to create a fourth police force, of which we felt there was no need. Our aim was to build an organization with people of extraordinary professional skill that could be rapidly trained, selected also from outside existing police corps in order to be able to adopt the most sophisticated technology.
Just as with the preliminary investigations for the Sicilian Mafia

maxi-trial, when Falcone opened the way and introduced new investigative methods, we must today take further steps to improve organizations and laws, to provide investigative and judiciary institutions with a full understanding of the complexity of national and international Mafia organizations, their myriad affairs, their links, and their global scope.

The above-cited evolution risks to widen the gap between the Mafia's "dynamism" and the "static" nature of the State bodies which must crush them, as Falcone said back in 1990 when the DNA and anti-Mafia district public prosecutor's offices were first established.

This is why, notwithstanding the results achieved, the Mafia organizations have continued to extend their tentacles at a national and international level, and above all, have succeeded in expanding the gray area of legality and illegality, with growing white zones where legal activities are linked to illegal ones, making them more difficult to identify. To carry out an effective analysis of the networks at a local and global level, we should continue along the path we have chosen, improving legislation, and judicial and investigative systems.

If the Mafia has reinforced its ties with different forms of terrorism, if it has expanded its international networks, if it has branched out into legal activities, and if it has increased its corruption of institutions, we should ask ourselves some questions which need urgent answers. It appears evident that there is a need not only for traditional forms of international cooperation, but also for the harmonization of legislation and systems in order to enable us to carry out more joint investigations. In this way, perhaps, we will also be able to establish an international court to deal with important anti-state criminal networks.

There have been recent Italian investigations, for example the one recalled by the Anti-Mafia National Prosecutor Grasso, carried out by the Naples Prosecutor's office, which has unmasked the links between terrorism, arms trafficking, narco-trafficking, and money laundering which involves international criminal organizations based in large areas in crisis, from the Balkans, to Italy, to Spain and to Colombia. These important initiatives give rise to questions similar to those we asked ourselves in those years regarding the problem of various self-contained units, that is those investigating terrorism and those investigating organized crime, or large-scale financial networks.

Wouldn't it perhaps be useful for the DNA to widen the horizon of its responsibilities? Every innovation always triggers a wave of diffidence and obstruction. But the barriers arise precisely due to the incomplete understanding of a phenomenon and its dangers, such as the Mafia which today continues to corrode from within the foundations of liberty and democracy in many weak States. We need to understand the anti-state which we have before us!

Regarding its global dimension, the planetary penetration of crime is increasingly widespread and is so embedded as to force President Barack Obama, for example, to declare a sort of war against European, Central American, and Far Eastern organized crime. These criminal organizations have constant contact with American ones, resulting in the increased contamination of the legal financial and economic activities of the most industrialized nations.

The gray area has expanded and is increasingly linked to corruption and financial crime, which is also growing. The objective responsibility of financial players must be called to account. The presence of an anti-state criminal organization remains, therefore, the sword of Damocles of a world that yearns to expand freedom and democracy. With a particularly attentive eye to forms of international crime, the United Nations has launched an alarm which has stimulated reflection and attempts to enact change. But these attempts must go beyond the traditional forms of cooperation between nations in matters of crime and go beyond traditional forms of collaboration between States.

It is obvious that we need to take decisive steps towards the adoption of common programs, beginning with the harmonization of legislation and systems, to increase our effectiveness against the Mafia. The fragility of State institutions with fragmentary jurisdictions is evident, as well as the instability of the functioning of representative democracies in many countries on various continents. There is something which we still haven't completely grasped in our understanding of the fight against the Mafia. There is a difficult choice which we have not fully come to terms with, because it carries a very high price.
We have to choose definitively between resoluteness and acquiescence!

Between *pax mafiosa* and war!

What we tried to do in Italy in the '90's was only the beginning and is looked upon as a model to follow by other countries facing the same problems.

Post scriptum

I would like to acknowledge the contribution of many people very dear to me in the conceptualization and writing of this book, starting from my wife Stefania, Raffaele Lauro and Marco Emanuele. I first discussed and then read this book with them, page by page. I am grateful to them, above all, for the final editing of the text, which required hours of painstaking work.

During the writing stage, I spoke with many friends who were by my side in those years, in particular Sergio Zoppi and Paolo Naccarato, but also many of the people involved in investigative and judicial activities.
I sorely missed the advice of Francesco Cossiga.

These pages represent an inadequate, but heartfelt, tribute to the memory of the many patriots and the many defenceless victims who gave their lives for my and our liberty, some of whom I had the honor to work with, including Piersanti Mattarella, Pio La Torre, Paolo Borsellino and Giovanni Falcone.

In the name of these patriots, the families continue to expect, as their young wives have repeatedly requested, a strong response from the State.

When writing this book, my thoughts were always on young people, who yearn to be "free to live", to those I see every day, my daughters Chiara, Giulia, and Lucrezia and the students at Link Campus University. They also want to understand and expect answers.

Appendices

Appendix 1

FOCUS – Transnational organizations and the globalization of crime - updated to 2014

<u>Latest developments in the world of transnational criminal organizations: a comparison between old and new activities</u>

In recent years, transnational criminal organization activities in Europe have increasingly become focused on the use of new technologies as well as on criminal cooperation. The Europol report, "Serious and organized crime threat assessment", clearly explains how the approximately 3,600 criminal groups spread across Europe have raised their level of interconnection and the division of routes by exploiting the economic crisis in order to expand old and new criminal business activities.

Indeed, from the economic point of view, the "euro" crisis, together with the traditional but lucrative drug markets and illegal immigration, has favored the growing high-standard product (luxury goods) counterfeiting business as well as food adulteration and other types of goods counterfeiting. The crisis in the corporate sector has led to the development of illegal waste disposal and the illicit proceeds are increasingly being recycled into the real estate sector. A further evolution highlighted in the report is the trafficking of animals in danger of extinction, a criminal market which until quite recently has been underestimated by the authorities.

At an organizational level, digital communication is changing criminal organizations from a technical and ontological standpoint: it has not only allowed big transnational organizations to raise their internal communication standards, but has also allowed them to exploit it for criminal purposes. The globalization of crime favors ethnic heterogeneity (favored at the operational level) and has opened up the recruitment process by making it less restrictive.

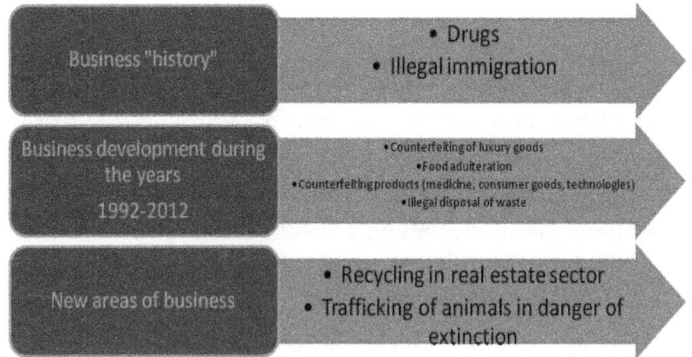

(Based on EUROPOL Data)

"Follow the money"

Taking the "Falcone method" as a timeless model, the cash flow of illegal revenues deriving from various criminal activities must be studied in order to understand the phenomenon of transnational crime in all its complexity.

According to the UNODC[39] report on the study of illicit financial dealings from the sale of narcotics and other transnational criminal activities, it is estimated that approximately 2.7% of global GDP is the product of money laundering. On the contrary, the International Monetary Fund sets the estimate at 3.5%. Therefore, considering the global importance of the phenomenon, the main negative economic impact of this activity is its economic-financial capability to continue to operate and expand criminal activities through self-financing.

Summary of estimates of criminal proceeds and amounts laundered at the global level						
	Reference year / period	Criminal proceeds		Amounts laundered		
		Best estimate	Range	Best estimate	Range	
As % of GDP		3.6%	(2.3%-5.5%)	2.7%	(2.1%-4.0%)	
In trillion US$	2009	2.1	(1.4-3.2)	1.6	(1.2-2.3)	
Memo: IMF 'consensus range' (as % of GDP)	1998			3.5%	2.0%	5.0%

The $2 trillion of annual illicit profits, of which 1.6 recycled, create serious consequences in socio-economic terms both if they are not considered part of the economic and financial system of a

---

[39] http://www.unodc.org/documents/data-and-analysis/Studies/Illicit_financial_flows_2011_web.pdf.

country, and if they are "legally" considered:

- increase of public health costs:
    - between $400-700 billion (treatments, care, prevention, research)
    - 200.000 deaths per year caused by drug abuse (World Health Organization)
    - lack of manpower and productivity

- cost of crime and violence related to drug trade:
    - arms dealing
    - murders

- cost of corruption

More specifically, even though estimates differ, it must be emphasized that the drug trade generates - economically - the highest profits: $75-100 billion, of which $85 billion is derived exclusively from the cocaine trade. Out of this total, $53 billion is recycled annually, while $27bn remains in the areas where it is generated (North America, Central and Western Europe, and South America).

The business of human trafficking is estimated to total approximately $32 billion and has a negative impact on both the country of origin, in that it reduces economic prospects and human resources (the so-called "brain drain"), and on the countries of destination where it creates illegal labor practices, increases prostitution and inter-ethnic violence, reduces the competitiveness of enterprises, and increases unemployment.

The market of counterfeit medicine, worth about $75 billion, is characteristic of developing countries, which explains why it is concentrated in Asia and Latin America. This market has a direct impact on public health costs (with negligible or no effects on traditional medicine) and on the financial results of pharmaceutical companies.

SUMMARY OF CRIMINAL ACTIVITY COSTS (DIRECT AND INDIRECT)

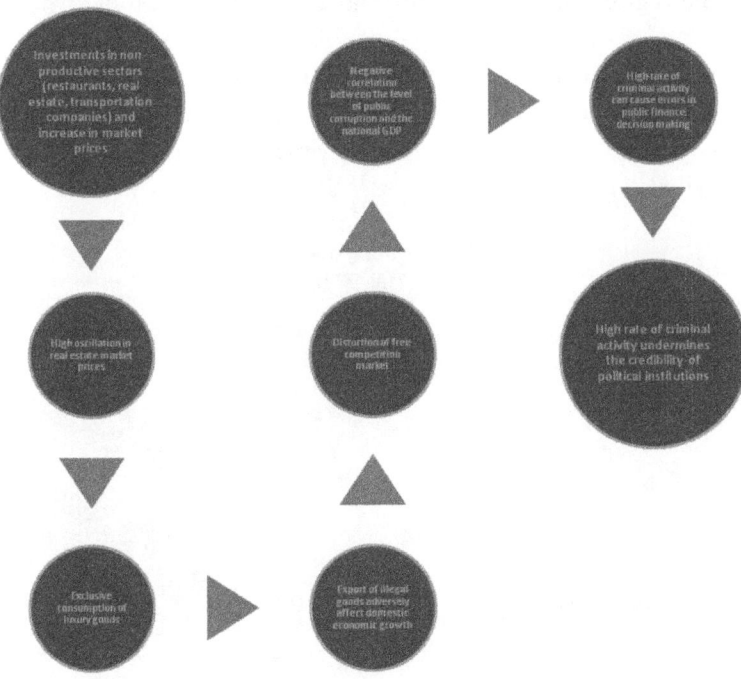

(Based on UNODC data)

What's happening in Italy?

The activities of transnational crime in Italy are well documented and actively opposed.

The Ministry of Internal Affairs reports that in 2013, goods were seized amounting to over €3 billion linked to Italian organized crime, and over €2 billion worth of goods were confiscated mainly in the regions of Sicily, Campania, Calabria and Lombardy.

Foreign criminal organizations in Italy, which often operate in close collaboration with local domestic criminal organizations, have a lesser incidence (in terms of crime) than national organized criminal organizations.

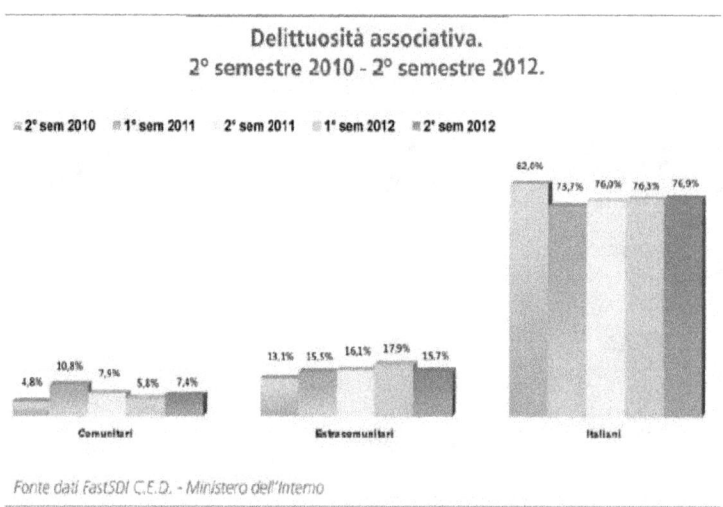

Co-operation between the various Mafia-type organizations is now considered routine and useful for the recruitment of criminal manpower as well as essential for drug trafficking.

Ministry of Internal Affairs data show that, in general terms, Albanian and Romanian organizations are the most active and are capable of managing the entire criminal supply chain, especially in the drug market and human trafficking. Another unique feature of Romanian crime is its specialization in the field of debit and credit card cloning and counterfeiting. Although they are less active, South American organizations also deal in the same activities.

With regards to the exploitation of prostitution, Nigerian and Eastern European organizations stand out above others. In addition, Nigerian criminal organizations also deal in counterfeiting, drug trafficking and illegal labor as do the Chinese groups who are also involved in illegal gambling, extortion, usury, money laundering, tax fraud, illegal immigration and prostitution.
On the contrary, criminal groups from the former Soviet Union countries, favor activities related to petty crime (theft and robbery) and smuggling.

The potential of North African criminal organizations is currently underestimated; even though they are split up into groups by ethnicity, the greatest danger does not come from illegal activities related to drug trafficking or illegal immigration. The greatest risk is that the North African groups could act as a strategic hub between Europe and Africa, which could then be exploited by other criminal organizations.

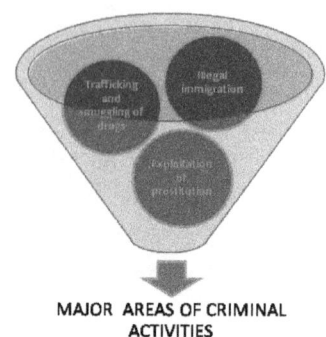

MAJOR AREAS OF CRIMINAL ACTIVITIES

It should be noted, however, that confronted by the growing challenge posed by transnational crime, the Mafia continues to be fought energetically by police forces as evidenced by the number of seizures and confiscations carried out over the years by the Anti-Mafia Investigative Agency (DIA[40]).

VALUATION OF SEIZURES AND CONFISCATIONS FROM 1992 TO 2011
(all values are espresse in euros)

ORGANIZATIONS	Seizures (art. 321 cpp)	Seizures (lex 575/65)	Confiscations (lex 575/65)
Cosa nostra	1.855.481.080	4.646.913.599	917.686.114
Camorra	1.901.142.500	2.261.042.220	637.162.000
'Ndrangheta	270.965.813	694.312.254	216.381.444
Crim.Org.Pugl.	68.797.795	98.562.000	73.978.698
Others	584.769.000	176.653.000	102.906.102
Total	4.679.906.438	7.706.360.367	1.902.145.373

[40] http://www.interno.gov.it/dip_ps/dia/page/rilevazioni_statistiche.html.

Appendix 2

This is Paolo Borsellino's last letter, written at 5 o'clock in the morning on 19 July 1992, twelve hours before a car bomb exploded at 5 o'clock on the same day in front of n. 9 Via D'Amelio, killing him and all of his bodyguards.

LETTER TO THE PRINCIPAL OF THE HIGH SCHOOL IN PADUA WHERE HE WAS SUPPOSED TO ATTEND A MEETING WITH STUDENTS IN JANUARY. HE WAS UABLE TO ATTEND DUE TO A SERIES OF PRESSING ENGAGEMENTS THAT GAVE HIM NOT A MOMENT'S PEACE.

"Dear" Teacher,
I use quotation marks because you used them when you wrote me, I don't know whether to highlight something, but "repentant", I apologize profusely for the disappointment which I caused the students at your high school by not attending the meeting on

Friday 24th January.

First of all, I would like to assure you that I did not, in the least, hide behind an obliging switchboard (I suppose you mean the Prosecutor's office in Marsala) if for no other reason than because in that period I was busy for almost the entire week at the Palermo Court Prosecutor's Office, where just a few days ago, I finally took on my duties as Deputy Prosecutor. If you were phoning me in Marsala, I'm not surprised that no one was able to locate me.

If I remember well, in that period I also had to go to Rome twice in the same week and, in between, I stayed in Agrigento for investigations regarding the Mafia feud in Palma di Montechiaro. I certainly remember that last January the editor of the Pungolo in Trapani, Vento, spoke to me of your planned event in order to confirm my availability, which I consented to in general, while explaining to him that I am subjected to tragic work conditions. He explained that I would be contacted by a principal, giving me also a name which I don't remember, and then I no longer heard from anyone.

Then on 24th January when I got back to Agrigento, someone here told me that they had heard on the radio that I was in Padua that day and asked me what means of transportation I had used to get back to Sicily so fast. I understood that "in any case" my attendance at your meeting had been announced but believe me, I didn't have time to feel bad about it because I have so many engagements and they are so pressing that I rarely have time for anything else.

I hope that next time, you will be so kind as to contact me personally and not to trust in intermediaries or telephone calls to the wrong number.

Today is certainly not the most suitable day for me to reply to you because, in the meanwhile, my city has once again been barbarously stained with blood and I don't even have time to spend with my children, who I see rarely because they are still sleeping when I leave the house and when I get home, very late almost every night, they are sleeping again.

But today is the first Sunday after almost three months that I have compelled myself not to work and have no difficulty in answering, if only concisely, your questions.

1. I became a judge because I had a great passion for civil law and joined the judiciary with the idea of becoming a litigator, devoted to judicial investigations and freed from the need to depend on clients' fees. The judiciary seemed the most suitable career to fulfill my desire to carry out investigations, which could not be satisfied with a university career which required more time and connections in "high places" than I had. I was lucky and became a judge nine months after I graduated (1964) and until 1980 I dealt mostly with civil cases, which I dedicated myself to whole-heartedly. It's true that in 1975 to come back to Palermo, where my family continued to live, I landed in the Penal Trial Investigative Office, but I obtained occasional appointments to a civil division where I continued to deal with problems related to rights in rem, legal disputes and inheritance rights, etc.

On 4 May 1980, Captain Emanuele Basile was killed and Judge Chinnici asked me to carry out the investigation for the proceedings. At the same time, my childhood friend Giovanni Falcone had also landed in the same office and from then on I understood what my job should be.

I had decided to stay in Sicily and this choice had to have a reason. Our problems were the ones I had started dealing with almost by chance, but if I loved this land, I would have to deal with them exclusively.

I never stopped doing this work and from that day on I have dealt almost exclusively with Mafia crime. And I'm optimistic because I see that young people today, both Sicilians and non-Sicilians, have a very different attitude from the guilty indifference that I clung to until I was in my forties. When these young people become adults, they will have much more power to react than my generation and I ever had.

2. The DIA is an investigative body composed of members of the Carabinieri, Police, and Financial Police forces and its establishment is aimed at achieving coordination between these three investigative bodies which, until now, with praiseworthy but rare exceptions, have acted without ensuring the mutual exchange of information and a desirable, rational division of institutional duties which have been assigned randomly and not codified.

The DNA instead is a new juridical body which aims to ensure, above all, the circulation of information between various organs of the Public Prosecutor's offices located in numerous districts nationwide.

Until now, these organs have acted in total autonomy and independently from one another (independence and autonomy which remain despite the new position of Super-Prosecutor), but also under conditions of total isolation, unaware in most cases of the investigative and trial work of the other organs even in bordering districts, and without a supervisory body in charged with ensuring the necessary coordination, capable of quickly intervening with its own resources and legal staff in cases where the necessity arose.

3. The Mafia (cosa nostra) is a criminal organization, united and vertically organized which distinguishes itself from any

other due to its "territorial" characteristics. It is subdivided into "families", linked among each other by a mutual dependence on a common high command (Cupola), which tends to exercise on the territory the same sovereignty which the State should legitimately exercise on it.

This means that "cosa nostra" tends to appropriate for itself all the wealth produced and flowing into a territory, mainly through kickbacks (comparable to the State's tax collecting) and by hoarding public bids, also providing a series of services that apparently seem to mete out justice, public order, jobs, etc. which should be exclusively provided by the State.

It is obviously only an apparent provider because its sum is mathematically zero given that every case of justice administered by the Mafia comes at the expense of an equivalent injustice. In the sense that protection from other forms of crime (historically, above all, terrorism) is provided by imposing other and more serious forms of crime. In the sense that jobs are assigned to some (few) taking them away from others (many).

The production and sale of drugs, which although they have provided "cosa nostra" with financial means which were unfathomable, are coincidental to this criminal system and not necessary for its perpetuation.

The inevitable conflict with the State, with which "cosa nostra" is substantially a competitor (they operate in the same territory and assume the same roles) is resolved by conditioning the State from within, that is by infiltrating public bodies so as to manipulate their decisions in such a way as to orient them towards satisfying Mafia interests and not those of the whole community.

The other criminal Mafia-type organizations (camorra, "'ndrangheta", Sacra Corona Unita, etc.) lack these characteristics of unity and exclusiveness. They are criminal organizations that act with the same characteristics of oppression and violence as "cosa nostra" but they don't have the same vertical and unified structure. Furthermore, they take less advantage of the "consensus" which "cosa nostra" uses to accredit itself as an alternative to the State, which nonetheless it tends to infiltrate.

Appendix 3

PATRONAGE AND ORGANIZED CRIME

23 July 1991 - page 12 section: COMMENTS - *by VINCENZO SCOTTI*

TAKING the recent SVIMEZ Report on the Mezzogiorno as a point of departure, I would like to examine one of its most important points in more detail. Indeed, southern Italians should pay close attention to the new role which it claims public entities should play in the economy of the Mezzogiorno, especially those belonging to the State. I feel particularly engaged in this debate, since as Minister of Internal Affairs I was able to ascertain just how essential it is, also in order to fight organized crime effectively, that the roles of each entity (State, businesses, citizens) be clearly defined. Indeed, the time has come to put an end to the perverse relationship between the economy, the "Camorra", society, and institutions by establishing clear rules that separate legal activities from illegal ones, defining the lines between the legal economy and the criminal one. Organized crime has indeed found fertile ground in a State which, over the years, has replaced a non-existent, or better, a very weak market, taking on an improper role not only with respect to the quantity of interventions, but also with respect to the way they are carried out. This has led to what has been referred to as the "hypertrophy" of the State, creating a widespread, molecular system resulting in the erosion of the gap between the State and society and therefore, between political, administrative, managerial, and supervisory roles. Thus, institutions have often transformed themselves into extensions of the patronage system, incorporating the values of the welfare model instead of the values of the market model. An important study conducted by the Anti-Mafia High Commission and the Palermo Carabinieri has demonstrated a well-known fact: public works have become increasingly motivated not so much by the final outcome, but by reasons linked to the assignment of planners and businesses; a situation which is aggravated by a lack of monitoring during the project and by the frequent use of chain sub-contracting making it possible to avoid any envisioned inspections. These instances of true corruption also have a devastating impact on the market, which can be put into motion only by transparent bidding procedures that stimulate market competition. It is precisely this aspect of free competition, within the context of established rules, that can ensure the vitality of the market, without hindering, but rather bolstering, the economic system. The State must therefore increasingly withdraw to its basic function, which is not one of forcibly creating companies and entrepreneurs, but that of establishing valid rules for all, without interfering and arbitrarily attributing privileges or imposing obligations. In defining these rules, the State can, on the one hand, safeguard the "weaker" parties, and on the other, allow the free market to reward the entrepreneurial skills of players. The recovery of a culture of legality which safeguards its citizens, legitimizing in full the role of the State, cannot ignore these considerations. Otherwise, what prevails is "friendship", mutual interests, a disregard for rules, and votes in exchange for favors. A "Mezzogiorno" which has progressed immensely, in which we see significant signs of modernity and great potential for growth, needs today a State which stands by its side, not to create a market, but to create the conditions for a market to flourish. And this means infrastructure, efficient services, streamlined procedures, and workers' safety. But it also means transparency in public administrations and responsible investments which must have specific objectives which are economically justifiable and technically sound. On these points, it would be useful to carry out an intense debate, at all levels, so that each individual, within their specific role, can do his duty to build a culture of profound renewal. This is what I have tried to do, also by imagining a conference on legality of a permanent nature; because, by discussing the issue at all levels involved, we can change people's convictions and consequently their conduct, in all institutional and social bodies, from the center outwards, and vice-versa.

Appendix 4

"La Repubblica" newspaper
AND NOW LET'S PUT AN END TO EARLY RELEASES
18 March 1992 — *by VINCENZO SCOTTI*

Yesterday, the Anti-Mafia Commission felt it was its duty to reiterate that in the savage acts of violence committed by the Mafia, it is not difficult to perceive the clear signs of a sinister but intentional plan to destabilize democratic institutions and the social and private life of every citizen. There are those who claim that certain Mafia crimes are a sign of the Mafia's invincibility. Others agree with my "theory" according to which these crimes against important figures must be considered within the logic of Mafia conduct, even when they use terrorist techniques, and as being related to the acts and conduct of those who oppose-especially in performing their institutional duties – their criminal designs or alter the balance of interests.

Regarding this affirmation, there is no doubt that in Palermo, a legislative decree dated February 1991 brought about the incarceration of Mafia bosses; and that in November, there was an appellate court ruling that did the same to another seventy bosses. And again in '91, investigative and monitoring tools were being set up to carry out a 360° battle against the Mafia as an "organization", starting from money collecting to laundering. Indeed, any hypothesis put forth must stand up, in terms of credibility, to two undeniable facts: the Mafia apparatus always reacts in a savage and targeted manner when action against it is intensified; following this line of reasoning, important investigative tools and new legislation are being implemented to disrupt the Mafia's plans. My opinion on this has not been and is not optimistic, nor does it aspire to tranquilize. Instead, it is a strong warning of what awaits us. Let us not forget the concrete acts of moral revolt which, from all quarters, are now being carried out by common people who are pressing charges to free themselves from this intolerable burden, for the survival of democratic freedom itself. It's no longer enough to kill Libero Grassi. The Mafia is trying to send threatening messages of increasing cruelty to people in increasingly higher places. And the "camorra" and the "'ndrangheta" are imitating them in Taranto, Lecce, Castellammare, and Lamezia.

In sounding this alarm, I would like to invoke the dutiful wholehearted commitment of all democratic, social, and institutional forces of the Republic, without however, pleading for useless and ambiguous forms of unanimity. In this legislature, the Parliament (and, above all, the Anti-Mafia Commission) and the Government have worked to draft and approve a first significant package of legislative proposals to effect a strategic change in the fight against the Mafia, coherent, furthermore, with the outcomes of the maxi-trial. Let us not forget as well, the measures aimed at cutting off the links between organized crime and the world of politics, by dissolving town councils and establishing strict rules for eligibility for office, expulsion, and the suspension of local and regional administrators and functionaries.

Also during this election campaign, upon the Anti-Mafia commission's request, I have ordered that prefects check the position of candidates, which should allow us to get a picture of the situation of pending charges and court records; a picture which will be made available to the Commission itself. But the war on the Mafia, if we want to truly strike at its heart both within and outside our country, will be long and hard.

The price for achieving this aim is certainly high and we will experience moments of increased grave tension as we open the "can" and discover what is really inside and that which is often under-evaluated. Keeping quiet would be dishonest: criminal organizations have grown to the point where they have become dangerous enough to subvert the democratic State and this is exactly why we have asked information and security agencies to collaborate in this battle. There has fortunately been growing awareness, also in other democratic countries, of the increasing gravity of the Mafia phenomenon fed by the enormous profits from drug trafficking and money laundering, which was not spoken of until recently.

If, as President Bush has claimed, Italy and other modern democratic States, really intend to free themselves from international Mafia influence, they need to have the courage to understand that this may mean accepting some restrictions on sovereignty, not to mention undergoing the painful ordeal of criminal attacks which may trigger special measures and thus favor authoritarian tendencies. This is, thus, the reason why it is necessary at this time, as it has been at other crucial moments in our country's history, to rediscover increased unity of intention among political parties with the aim of contributing, all together, to the defeat of an enemy which is strong, instilling in people a sense of courage and trust in the future.

The Mafia is different from terrorism: the latter wishes to destroy the State; the former wishes to "dominate" the State and manipulate it in order to make profits. This legislature, which has come to an end, and the government which will step down after the elections, leave to the new parliament and its future executive a precious and difficult legacy: the balance of what has been done up to now and a resolute and constant determination to fight the Mafia. It will be up to the new parliament and the new government, within their respective roles, to develop an operative plan coherent with the legislative plan already established, as well as to implement further laws and tools, especially in the area of penitentiary measures regarding the actual serving out of sentences. This need is too strongly felt by the national community to under-estimate or ignore it. The reaction of the public is not against the government, but against those laws which by allowing early releases, as in the case of Verona, seems to have produced by the same killer's hands, new cases of mourning for security forces and for the community. The "Gozzini" law must be further modified for specific cases. We must not allow ourselves to be influenced by the irresponsible vision of the blind protection of civil liberties. We should re-consider a series of propositive elements which were set aside during the parliamentary debate, in order to prevent penitentiary privileges from being granted to those who have not yet served their entire minimum sentence as established by law: we have to disallow any shortening of sentences to criminals. But we should also reflect on the way we determine the dangerousness of a criminal, avoiding arbitrary distinctions based on the seriousness of a crime, requiring that in each case, a thorough examination be carried out to exclude any possibility of ties between the person and criminal or terrorist organizations. And we can also no longer avoid reflecting on the need to consider the recommendations of public security officials to probation officers, when granting privileges on parole, to be binding – in all cases.

It cannot be excluded that in the following legislature, it will be necessary to reinstate laws that enhance the tools available to the police, above all with regards to investigations and the validity of evidence. Indeed, if we want proof of Mafia crimes, we need to change the laws governing the new penal procedure code which, as it stands today, makes that impossible. Only in this way, and by severing all forms of Mafia conditioning and co-existence with politics, can we continue to ask citizens to have faith in democratic institutions.

Appendix 5

Victims of the Mafia from the 1940's to the present

- Antonio Mancino (02-09-1943).
- Santi Milisenna (27-05-1944).
- Andrea Raia (06-08-1944).
- Calogero Comajanni (28-03-1945).
- Filippo Scimone (1945).
- Calcedonio Catalano (1945).
- Nunzio Passafiume (07-06-1945).
- Agostino D'Alessandro (11-09-1945).
- Calogero Cicero (18-09-1945).
- Fedele De Francisca (18-09-1945).
- Michele Di Miceli (1945).
- Mario Paoletti (1945).
- Rosario Pagano (1945).

- Giuseppe Scalia (25-11-1945).
- Giuseppe Puntarello (04 -12-1945).
- Gaetano Guarino (16-05-1946).
- Marina Spinelli, (16-05-1946).
- Pino Camilleri (28-06-1946).
- Nicolò Azoti, (23-12-1946).
- Accursio Miraglia (04-01-1947).
- Massacre of Portella della Ginestra (01-05-1947).
- Massacre of Partinico (22-06-1947): Giuseppe Casarrubea, Vincenzo Lo Iacono, Epifanio Li Puma.
- Placido Rizzotto (10-03-1948).
- Calogero Cangelosi (02-04-1948).
- Giuseppe Biondo (22-10-1948).
- Salvatore Carnevale (16-05-1955).
- Giuseppe Spagnolo (13-08-1955).
- Pasquale Almerico (25-03-1957).
- Cataldo Tandoy (30-03-1960).
- Cosimo Cristina (05-05-1960).
- Paolo Bongiorno (20-07-1960).
- Massacre of Ciaculli (30-06-1963).
- Carmelo Battaglia (24-03-1966).
- Mauro De Mauro (16-09-1970).
- Pietro Scaglione (05-05-1971).
- Antonino Lo Russo (05-05-1971).
- Giovanni Spampinato (27-10-1972).
- Gaetano Cappiello (02-07-1975).
- Giuseppe Russo (20-08-1977).
- Carlo Napolitano (21-11-1977).
- Giuseppe di Fede (21-11-1977).
- Peppino Impastato (09-05-1978).
- Antonio Esposito Ferraioli (30-08-1978),

- Salvatore Castelbuono (26-09-1978).
- Carmelo Di Giorgio (05-01-1979).
- Calogero Di Bona (28-08-1979).
- Filadelfio Aparo (11-01-1979).
- Mario Francese (26-01-1979).
- Michele Reina (09-03-1979).
- Carmine Pecorelli (20-03-1979).
- Giorgio Ambrosoli (12-07-1979).
- Boris Giuliano (21-07-1979).
- Cesare Terranova (25-09-1979).
- Lenin Mancuso (25-09-1979).
- Piersanti Mattarella (06-01-1980).
- Emanuele Basile (04-05-1980).
- Giovanni Losardo, (21-06-1980).
- Gaetano Costa (06-08-1980).
- Vito Lipari (13-08-1980).
- Marcello Torre (11-12-1980).
- Vito Jevolella (10-10-1981).
- Sebastiano Bosio (06-11-1981).
- Alfredo Agosta (18-03-1982).
- Pio La Torre (30-04-1982).
- Rosario Di Salvo (30-04-1982).
- Gennaro Musella (03-05-1982).
- Massacre of circonvallazione (16-06-1982): Salvatore Raiti, Silvano Franzolin, Luigi Di Barca, Giuseppe Di Lavore, Alfio Ferlito.
- Paolo Giaccone (11-08-1982).
- Massacre of via Carini (03-09-1982): Carlo Alberto Dalla Chiesa, Emanuela Setti Carraro, Domenico Russo.
- Calogero Zucchetto (14-11-1982).
- Giangiacomo Ciaccio Montalto (26-01-1983).

- Mario D'Aleo (13-06-1983).
- Pietro Morici (13-06-1983).
- Giuseppe Bommarito (13-06-1983).
- Bruno Caccia (26-06-1983).
- Massacre of via Pipitone Federico (29-07-1983): Rocco Chinnici, Mario Trapassi, Salvatore Barlotta, Stefano Li Sacchi.
- Salvatore Zangara (08-10-1983).
- Giuseppe Fava, (05-01-1984).
- Mario Coniglio, (14-11-1984).
- Roberto Parisi (23-02-1985).
- Piero Patti (28-02-1985).
- Giuseppe Spada (14-06-1985).
- Strage di Pizzolungo (02-04-1985).
- Giuseppe Montana (28-07-1985).
- Ninni Cassarà (06-08-1985).
- Graziella Campagna (12-12-1985).
- Claudio Domino (07-10-1986).
- Alberto Giacomelli (14-09-1988).
- Antonino Saetta (25-09-1988).
- Mauro Rostagno (26-06-1988).
- Antonino Agostino (05-08-1989).
- Giovanni Trecroci (07-02-1990).
- Emanuele Piazza (16-03-1990).
- Giuseppe Miano (18-03-1990).
- Gioitta Nicola (21-03-1990).
- Giovanni Bonsignore, (9-05-1990).
- Rosario Livatino (21-09-1990).
- Nicolò Di Marco (21-02-1991).
- Sergio Compagnini (05-03-1991).
- Antonino Scopelliti (09-08-1991).
- Libero Grassi (29-08-1991).

- Tobia Andreozzi (30-08-1990).
- Paolo Arena (27-09-1991).
- Serafino Ogliastro (12-10-1991).
- Salvo Lima (12-03-1992).
- Giuliano Guazzelli (14-04-1992).
- Paolo Borsellino (21-04-1992).
- Massacre of Capaci (23-05-1992): Giovanni Falcone, Francesca Morvillo, Antonio Montinaro, Rocco Dicillo, Vito Schifani.
- Vincenzo Napolitano (23-05-1992).
- Massacre of di via D'Amelio (19-07-1992): Paolo Borsellino, Emanuela Loi, Walter Cosina, Vincenzo Li Muli, Claudio Traina, Agostino Catalano,
- Rita Atria (27-07-1992).
- Giovanni Lizzio (27-07-1992).
- Ignazio Salvo (17-09-1992).
- Paolo Ficalora (28-09-1992).
- Gaetano Giordano (10-12-1992).
- Giuseppe Borsellino (17-12-1992).
- Beppe Alfano (08-01-1993).
- Massacre of via dei Georgofili (27-05-1993): Nadia Nencioni, Angela Fiume, Fabrizio Nencioni, Dario Capolicchio.
- Pino Puglisi (15-09-1993).
- Cosimo Fabio Mazzola (05-1994).
- Liliana Caruso (10-07-1994).
- Agata Zucchero (10-07-1994).
- Domenico Buscetta (6-03-1995).
- Carmela Minniti (01-09-1995).
- Pierantonio Sandri (03-09-1995).
- Serafino Famà (09-11-1995).
- Giuseppe Montalto (23-12-1995).
- Giuseppe Di Matteo (11-01-1996).

- Antonio Barbera (07-09-1996)
- Antonino Polifroni (30-09-1996).
- Giuseppe La Franca (4-01-1997).
- Gaspare Stellino (12-09-1997).
- Domenico Geraci (08-10-1998).
- Filippo Basile (05-07-1999).
- Vincenzo Vaccaro Notte (03-12-1999).
- Giueseppe Montalbano (18-11-1998).
- Stefano Pompeo (22 -04-1999).
- Salvatore Vaccaro Notte (05-02-2000).
- Giuseppe D'Angelo (22-08-2006).
- Vincenzo Fragalà (26-02-2010).

Appendix 6

From the Information to the Collective Intelligence age: ideas and tools to prevent and fight Organized Crime and Terrorism.

Twenty years after the massacres of Falcone and Borsellino, the arrests first of Riina and then of Provenzano, ten years after the attack on the Twin Towers and several years after the maxi-arrests of the most dangerous fugitives from justice, the scenario of organized crime and Mafia organizations, as well as national and international security, has significantly changed.
In today's scenario, the gap between the actual physical world and cyberspace has been bridged.
The obvious demonstration of this fact is that actions initiated in cyberspace have a direct impact on the physical world and vice-versa. This means that asymmetric threats and, for example, international and national criminal and terrorist acts start online

and take place in the real world, or are even guided directly via the internet with devastating effects on the real physical world.

The phenomenon is more common than one might think, if we consider the STUXNET worm attack on the turbines of the Iranian nuclear plant, or the case of wikileaks. Even the North African revolutions, as well as the drop in the value of Italian bonds last August, and finally the latest national events linked to protests against the government and, in a more general sense, against the distance between Italian politics and the concrete issues of citizens, as well as the events that have taken place in Rome over the last months, originated online and relied on Information Technology. This same information technology, used improperly, becomes an instrument for criminal activities that go hand in hand with the digitization of the Public Administration and the increased virtualization of public and private services for consumers, clients, businesses, and private citizens.

In reality, in the last ten years there has also been a change in nomenclature, since we have gone from using the term hacking, to cracking, and now use the term cyber war, that is we have gone from actions aimed at paralyzing software and applicative solutions (with the advent of hacking) to actions aimed at paralyzing systems (with the spread of cracking) and have arrived at the destruction of crucial infrastructure (with the onset of cyber war). The terrorists, insurgents, and, more generally, organized crime and revolutionaries of the future will operate on the internet, while on the streets, on the ground, and in the field, only their expendable operatives will remain. Therefore, our defences and reactions must also be transferred to the web and crucial infrastructure, because otherwise, we will only act on and treat the effects and never the primary causes of the various phenomena. The current scenario demonstrates, therefore, the growing use of ICT technology, to the point where many believe that the new millennium should be referred to as the Information Age. If, on the one hand, it is true that the international community has continued to develop technologies to increase connectivity, on the other hand, there has been little, or perhaps not enough attention paid to the implications this technology has on security measures and protecting information privacy. Indeed, up until now, Information infrastructure has been treated along the same lines as infrastructures for Energy, Logistics, Transportation, Health, etc, including CNI (Critical Network Infrastructure) to be protected from asymmetric threats, for example, cyber-terrorism, that is to say actions aimed at acquiring data of specific interest for an individual or the citizenry through fraudulent means, by manipulating or deleting information, and thus paralyzing any possible activity. The bulk of computer sabotage/attacks/ incidents on classified and non-classified Defence networks and those of other governmental and non-governmental bodies is continually on the rise. The same is true with the situation of credit institutions, banks, industrial and business concerns. If we had a figure on illegal revenues gained on the web by various means, we should not be surprised if the figure was followed by nine or ten zeros.

Until the last decade, each one of these infrastructures could consider itself to be a substantially independent, autonomous system, managed by a vertically organized structure. For a series of reasons, this structure as been profoundly modified so that the various infrastructures are increasingly interdependent, above all due to their shared presence in so-called cyberspace, that is to say the virtual space created by the interconnection between computers, telecommunications systems, applications, and data. This means that a breakdown - whether accidental or induced - in one of these infrastructures can easily spread, with a domino effect, to other infrastructures, amplifying its effects and causing dysfunctions and malfunctions also to remote users, both in a geographic and functional sense with respect to where the original breakdown occurs. In other words, the web nullifies the Galilean and Newtonian concepts of space, not to mention Einstein's relativity, substituting the limits of the speed of light with instantaneous communication. We are therefore living in small and super-fast worlds: each one can be reached instantaneously wherever there are electricity and optic fibers.

Thus, while the majority of the population is aware that we are living in the Information Age, the savviest among us have already incorporated the concept of interdependence and are living and preparing for the challenges of the new era, the one that will most likely be called the age of Collective Intelligence. This will be the age in which every action will be instantaneously shared at a global level, travelling on virtual networks, which no longer require material support.

It is exactly for this reason that in the last five years, the international community is placing emphasis on "cyber" or online/telecommunications type asymmetric threats. Indeed, thanks to these communication technologies, it is easy to create new identities, realities and even truths, since with the internet, what is happening is that who you are is not as important as what others see about you on Google. So even a perfect gentlemen, if targeted by a social hub group (that is, individuals with many social network contacts), can become a criminal, a killer, or a swindler in the eyes of the world, without ever having been charged with a crime. At the same time, criminal organizations can enhance their credibility and reputation on the web, committing fraud and crimes of every sort before they are prosecuted for the crimes they have committed against a State or organization.

The current scenario, therefore, is characterized by both growing and diversified threats to CNI and a modified infrastructural framework due to existing interdependencies, and new forms of systemic and state vulnerabilities. This requires us to heighten and diversify our attention to all aspects of protection, security, and strength, and the fight against organized crime, focussing on the factors leading to criminal activities specific to each CNI, as well as those in general for the whole of national CNI taken together.

Therefore, in the Information Age, and the current post-industrial structure, our society is highly interconnected and interdependent: a growing number of its components cannot lower their operative levels without creating an impact on the whole system. These points of conjunction, real hubs of our global society, are the so-called "critical infrastructure", that is to say, the infrastructure pertaining to connections that are fundamental to the functioning of the entire National System and the Global System.

The majority of these infrastructures which control fundamental sectors of modern society, Economics, Energy, Transport, Telecommunications, and Defence are dependent and interconnected via network systems that ensure the proper functioning of a society and their various communities, whether civil or military, economic or social. This is precisely why they are of interest to organizations linked to crime or terrorism.

Telecommunications and Information Technology are necessary for the transfer of messages, data, and information, that is, they allow the proper coordination of local and remote resources (human and technological). At the same time, these technologies can also act as weapon systems and solutions for crime or afford ways to carry out criminal activities. The focus of politics, the social and industrial spheres, scientific and research communities, not to mention police forces will have to be increasingly effective in the future in order to create empowering synergies capable of preventing crime, while protecting the principles of legality and democracy, which are essential to a society which aspires to being called civil.

Index of the names

A
Abbate, Giovanni 124
Alfano, Sonia 184
Almerighi, Mario 179
Amato, Giuliano 46, 202, 237, 244, 245, 246, 248, 250
Amato, Nicolò 165
Amatucci, Alfonso 181
Andreotti, Giulio 48, 87, 99, 101, 104, 112, 117, 143, 173, 174, 175, 178, 180, 193, 194, 207, 219, 221, 228, 223, 242
Arlacchi, Pino 121, 251, 252, 254

B
Basile, Emanuele 287
Bellu, Giovanni Maria 106
Beria D'Argentine, Adolfo 159

Berlinguer, Enrico 84, 88, 89
Berlusconi, Silvio 99, 135, 207
Bertoni, Raffaele 170, 176
Bianco, Gerardo 229, 244
Binetti, Enzo 108, 182
Boccassini, Ilda 179, 180, 227
Borsellino, Paolo 13, 25, 32, 38, 39, 46, 51, 77, 142, 163, 170, 171, 176, 196, 218, 224, 232, 251, 252, 253, 254, 255, 256, 257, 258, 263, 264, 273, 285, 309, 310, 311, 315
Brosio, Paolo 229
Bruti Liberati, Edmondo 183
Buscetta, Tommaso 125, 172
Bush, George 19, 297

C
Calabrò, Maria Antonietta 129, 216
Calderone, Antonino 125
Caponnetto, Antonino 24, 38, 79, 123, 171, 232
Carli, Guido 102, 189
Carnevale, Corrado 130
Carrero Blanco, Luis 225
Caruso, Aldo 155
Casalinuovo, Mario 195
Caselli, Gian Carlo 113
Cattanei, Francesco 23, 28, 29, 30, 55, 56, 57, 59, 61, 63, 64, 71, 94, 178, 232, 260
Ceracchi, Cinzia 118
Chiaromonte, Gerardo 24, 49, 50, 72, 73, 95, 104, 105, 114, 179, 180, 196, 212, 223, 224, 226
Chiesa, Mario 46, 90
Chinnici, Rocco 124, 225, 232, 287, 306

Ciampi, Carlo Azeglio 189, 222, 223
Ciancimino, Vito 131, 206, 259
Cicala, Mario 183
Ciolini, Elio 212, 216, 217, 219, 220, 221
Cipriani, Gianni 101
Cirillo, Ciro 102
Ciuni, Candido 61
Coccia, Franco 181
Coiro, Michele 247
Collidà, Ada 187
Colombo, Gherardo 179
Conso, Giovanni 43, 161
Contorno, Salvatore 125, 172
Cordova, Agostino 180
Corrado, Sebastiano 218, 220
Cossiga, Francesco 82, 101, 109, 111, 112, 113, 153, 169, 175, 207, 212, 221, 227, 228, 252, 267, 273
Costanzo, Maurizio 232
Craxi, Benedetto detto Bettino 82, 85, 88, 89, 91, 92, 99, 112, 207, 211, 228, 235, 236, 237
Cristofori, Nino 153
Cutolo, Raffaele 102

D
Dalla Chiesa, Carlo Alberto 22, 30, 66, 123, 124, 232, 306
da Rotterdam, Erasmo 83
D'Avanzo, Giuseppe 237, 238, 239
De Felice, Renzo 13
De Gasperi, Alcide 23, 24, 85
De Gennaro, Giovanni detto Gianni 113, 134, 169, 252
De Martino, Francesco 85, 88

De Mauro, Mauro 61, 304
De Mita, Ciriaco 82, 88, 89, 99, 207, 242
Di Cillo, Rocco 123
Di Fazio, Maria 118
Di Feo, Gianluca 255
Donat Cattin, Carlo 87

F
Falcone, Giovanni 13, 17, 18, 19, 25, 27, 32, 33, 34, 35, 37, 38, 39, 40, 46, 47, 49, 51, 52, 59, 63, 65, 67, 71, 72, 77, 78, 97, 113, 114, 115, 116, 117, 122, 124, 130, 131, 134, 135, 137, 142, 143, 163, 164, 167, 168, 169, 170, 171, 173, 174, 175, 176, 177, 178, 179, 181, 183, 191, 192, 196, 218, 219, 220, 223, 224, 225, 226, 227, 228, 232, 238, 239, 240, 251, 252, 253, 254, 255, 256, 257, 258, 264, 265, 266, 268, 273
Forlani, Arnaldo 91, 99, 100, 207, 221, 222, 223, 242, 243, 249
Fortunato, Giustino 66
Franchetti, Leopoldo 19, 20
Frattini, Franco 134

G
Gaglio, Salvatore 218, 220
Galimberti, Paolo 246
Galloni, Giovanni 181, 182, 253
Gargani, Giuseppe 194
Gargiulo, Nino 118
Gava, Antonio 100, 101, 104, 106, 107, 221, 249
Gennaro, Giuseppe 255
Geraci, Vincenzo 173
Giammanco, Pietro 177
Giolitti, Giovanni 24

Giovanni Paolo II, Papa 115, 140, 147, 148, 233
Gitti, Tarcisio 217
Giuliani, Rudolph 116, 134, 168, 169
Giuliano, Boris 124, 304
Giuliano, Salvatore detto "Il Bandito Giuliano" 22, 302
Gorbaciov, Michail 19
Gozzini, Mario 80, 159, 160, 165, 191, 192, 298
Grassi, Leonardo 216
Grassi, Libero 115, 147, 218, 296, 309
Grasso, Pietro 224, 269
Grasso, Tano 147
Greco, Salvatore 155
Guercio, Vincenzo 61

I
Incagliati, Pietro 219

J
Januzzi, Lino 169
Jotti Nilde, 112

L
La Licata, Francesco 59
Lama, Luciano 105
La Torre, Pio 30, 232, 273, 305
Lauro, Raffaele 66, 116, 118, 184, 210, 229, 250, 258, 273
Leone, Giovanni 85
Liggio, Luciano 61, 301
Lima, Salvo 121, 126, 128, 131, 215, 217, 218, 220, 231, 240, 309
Livatino, Rosario 80, 232, 309
Lo Bello, Ivan 147

Longo, Pietro 105
Luciano, Charles detto "Lucky" 21
Lutero, Martin 83

M
Macaluso, Emanuele 72, 112
Maceratini, Giulio 217
Maddalena, Marcello 113, 176, 177
Malinconico, Sabato 116, 118
Mancino, Nicola 249, 258
Manente Comunale, Peppino 103
Mannoia, Marino 125, 307
Manzini, Vincenzo 97
Martelli, Claudio 32, 49, 50, 51, 52, 75, 76, 78, 103, 116, 117, 124, 143, 152, 157, 160, 167, 168, 176, 178, 180, 181, 191, 192, 193, 196, 211, 213, 223, 224, 226, 227, 228, 229, 230, 235, 236, 237, 238, 239, 243, 244, 251
Martinazzoli, Mino 100, 229
Mattarella, Piersanti 30, 205, 232, 273, 305
Mazzocchi, Silvana 153
Meli, Antonino 171, 173
Mitterand, François 88
Mondadori, Leonardo 251
Montanari, Antonio 123
Montanelli, Indro 210
Monti, Mario 109
Moro, Aldo 16, 23, 84, 85, 86, 87, 90, 166
Morvillo, Francesca 46, 123, 224, 309
Mosca, Carlo 116, 118
Mosino, Enzo 169
Mussolini, Benito 13

N
Naccarato, Paolo 118, 169, 222, 273
Napolitano, Giorgio 102, 105, 245
Nicolosi, Rino 205

O
Obama, Barack 269
Occhetto, Achille 19
Orlando, Leoluca 38, 73, 173, 174, 175

P
Padovani, Marcelle 27, 65, 68
Palombelli, Barbara 89
Pandolfi, Filippo Maria 105
Pannella, Marco 223
Pansa, Giampaolo 172
Pappalardo, Salvatore (Cardinale) 115, 233
Parisi, Vincenzo 175, 184, 185, 206, 210, 216, 218, 229, 239, 240, 250, 251
Pastore, Giulio 18, 105, 241, 259
Patrono, Mario 180
Pecchioli, Ugo 104
Pellegritti, Giuseppe 173, 174, 178
Pendinelli, Mario 189
Piraino Leto, Angelo 253
Pirani, Mario 183
Pisanu, Beppe 15, 128, 131, 162, 196
Pizzorusso, Alessandro 181
Pomicino, Paolo Cirino 104, 222, 242
Priore, Rosario 102
Pullarà, Giovambattista 154, 155

R
Ramponi, Luigi 118, 187
Rey, Luigi 187
Rimi, Vincenzo 61
Rognoni, Virginio 79
Ruffino, Giancarlo 167
Ruggiero, Giuseppe 182

S
Salvi, Cesare 195
Saviano, Roberto 40
Scaglione, Pietro 61, 304
Scalfaro, Oscar Luigi 82, 104, 194, 223, 228, 236, 239, 242, 246, 247, 250
Schifani, Vito 123, 309
Sciacchitano, Giusto 135
Sciascia, Leonardo 34, 38, 163, 164
Scopelliti, Antonino 218, 309
Segni, Mario 222
Serra, Achille 184, 239
Setti Carraro, Emanuela 123, 306
Sica, Domenico 41
Sinisi, Giannicola 33
Spadolini, Giovanni 16, 90, 112, 222, 223, 226

T
Tajani, Diego Antonio 20, 28
Talleyrand, Charles Maurice 250
Tanzi, Calisto 92
Taviani, Paolo Emilio 23
Terzi di Sant'Agata Giulio 33

Tinebra, Giovanni 255

V
Valiani, Leo 222
Vassalli, Giuliano 79, 115, 117, 178, 228
Viesti, Antonio 185
Viglietta, Gianfranco 181
Violante, Luciano 73, 104, 105, 112, 113, 212

W
Weber, Max 18
Wieser, Famiglia 169

Z
Zemin, Jang 101
Zolla, Michele 194

Eurilink Edizioni (created in 2006) became the "Link Campus" University and Foundation Press in 2011.

Its vision is to meet the requirements of all those, researchers and students, scholars and non-scholars alike, who feel the need for an open and international interpretation of society and the world and are eager to draw on the new frontiers of knowledge.

Its mission is to create a cultural bridge between the university and society at large by offering highly scientific publications with the engagement of top opinion leaders, professors, and women and men of culture and learning. It also offers its students and readers innovative texts on current issues and debates.

Through its editorial offering, made up of 14 different series, Eurilink:
- provides up-to-date teaching materials at an international level in several languages
- promotes the values, research, and knowledge of the University and Foundation
- takes on strategic issues that are not commonly discussed, stimulating the interest of scholars and the general public
- supports the integration of different fields of study
- consolidates a clear editorial strategy, reinforcing the synergy between various types of publications: series, scientific and specialized journals and the Foundation's annals
- creates a nationwide and web distribution network.

Series:
1. Modern times: current political, economic and social issues - Italian and international
2. Essays: monographic studies in various fields
3. Historia: historical and intercultural studies
4. The Criticism: analysis and interpretation of the cultural and social phenomena of our times
5. Campus: manuals and university essays
6. Legal studies and dialogues: current laws and regulations
7. Political Studies, International and Diplomats: analysis of the globalization processes of political phenomena and international relations
8. Research: results of the University's research activities
9. Alumnia: university theses worthy of publication
10. EurInstant: emerging issues represented by updated data and information
11. Traces: life paths
12. Arts and Traditions: the arts and traditions of Italian regions
13. Link: publications of various topics of interest for Link Campus University
14. Codes: collection of regulations for various legal sectors

www. eurilink.it

SAGGISTICA

Taking its name from the Italian—which means essays, essay writing, or nonfiction—*Saggisitca* is a referred book series dedicated to the study of all topics and cultural productions that fall under what we might consider that larger umbrella of all things Italian and Italian/American.

Vito Zagarrio
  The "Un-Happy Ending": Re-viewing The Cinema of Frank Capra. 2011. ISBN 978-1-59954-005-4. Volume 1.
Paolo A. Giordano, Editor
  The Hyphenate Writer and The Legacy of Exile. 2010. ISBN 978-1-59954-007-8. Volume 2.
Dennis Barone
  America / Trattabili. 2011. ISBN 978-1-59954-018-4. Volume 3.
Fred L. Gardaphè
  The Art of Reading Italian Americana. 2011. ISBN 978-1-59954-019-1. Volume 4.
Anthony Julian Tamburri
  Re-viewing Italian Americana: Generalities and Specificities on Cinema. 2011. ISBN 978-1-59954-020-7. Volume 5.
Sheryl Lynn Postman
  An Italian Writer's Journey through American Realities: Giose Rimanelli's English Novels. "The most tormented decade of America: the 60s" ISBN 978-1-59954-034-4. Volume 6.
Luigi Fontanella
  Migrating Words: Italian Writers in the United States. 2012. ISBN 978-1-59954-041-2. Volume 7.
Peter Covino & Dennis Barone, Editors
  Essays on Italian American Literature and Culture. 2012. ISBN 978-1-59954-035-1. Volume 8.
Gianfranco Viesti
  Italy at the Crossroads. 2012. ISBN 978-1-59954-071-9. Volume 9.
Peter Carravetta, Editor
  Discourse Boundary Creation (LOGOS TOPOS POIESIS): A Festschrift in Honor of Paolo Valesio. ISBN 978-1-59954-036-8. Volume 10.
Antonio C. Vitti & Anthony Julian Tamburri, Editors
  Europe, Italy, and the Meditteranean. ISBN 978-1-59954-073-3. Volume 11.

www.ingramcontent.com/pod-product-compliance
Lightning Source LLC
Chambersburg PA
CBHW031428160426
43195CB00010BB/656